First World War
and Army of Occupation
War Diary
France, Belgium and Germany

14 DIVISION
43 Infantry Brigade
Duke of Cornwall's Light Infantry
6th Battalion
7 February 1915 - 20 February 1918

WO95/1908/2

The Naval & Military Press Ltd
www.nmarchive.com
Published in association with The National Archives

Published by

The Naval & Military Press Ltd

Unit 10 Ridgewood Industrial Park,
Uckfield, East Sussex,
TN22 5QE England
Tel: +44 (0) 1825 749494

www.naval-military-press.com

www.nmarchive.com

This diary has been reprinted in facsimile from the original. Any imperfections are inevitably reproduced and the quality may fall short of modern type and cartographic standards.

© **Crown Copyright**
Images reproduced by permission of The National Archives, London, England, 2015.

Contents

Document type	Place/Title	Date From	Date To
Heading	WO95/1908/2		
Heading	14th Division 43rd Infy Bde 6th Bn D.C.L.I. May 1915-Feb 1918		
Heading	14th Division. 6th D.C.L.I. Vol I 22-30.5.15 Feb 18		
Miscellaneous	14th Division 6th D.C.L.I. Vol II 22.5-30.6.15.		
War Diary	Bologne	22/05/1915	24/05/1915
War Diary	Volkerinckhove	25/05/1915	27/05/1915
War Diary	Zuytpeene	28/05/1915	28/05/1915
War Diary	Caestre	29/05/1915	30/05/1915
War Diary	Ypres	25/06/1915	29/06/1915
War Diary	Vlamertinghe	30/06/1915	30/06/1915
War Diary	La. Clytte	06/06/1915	12/06/1915
War Diary	Near Ypres	13/06/1915	18/06/1915
War Diary	Zevecoten	19/06/1915	20/06/1915
War Diary	Poperinghe	21/06/1915	23/06/1915
War Diary	Ypres	24/06/1915	25/06/1915
Heading	14th Division 6th D.C.L.I. Vol. III 1-31.7.15.		
War Diary	Vlamertinghe	01/07/1915	17/07/1915
War Diary	Trenches E. Of Ypres (D6 To D9)	18/07/1915	26/07/1915
War Diary	Vlamertinghe	27/07/1915	30/07/1915
War Diary	Zouave Wood	30/07/1915	31/07/1915
Heading	14th Division 6th D.C.L.I. Vol IV August 15.		
War Diary	Zouave Wood	30/07/1915	31/07/1915
War Diary	Ypres	01/08/1915	05/08/1915
War Diary	Dug Outs	06/08/1915	09/08/1915
War Diary	Ypres	10/08/1915	13/08/1915
War Diary	Bivouacs	14/08/1915	29/08/1915
War Diary	H.1.C.88	29/09/1915	29/09/1915
War Diary	Trenches	30/08/1915	31/08/1915
Heading	14th Division 6th D.C.L.I. Vol 5 Sept. 15.		
War Diary	Trenches	01/09/1915	02/09/1915
War Diary	G.H.Q & F.13.	03/09/1915	04/09/1915
War Diary	G.H.Q.	05/09/1915	08/09/1915
War Diary	San Jan Ter Biezen	08/09/1915	15/09/1915
War Diary	Trenches	16/09/1915	23/09/1915
War Diary	Bivouacs	24/09/1915	24/09/1915
War Diary	Ramparts Ypres	25/09/1915	25/09/1915
War Diary	GHQ	26/09/1915	29/09/1915
War Diary	Bivouacs	30/09/1915	30/09/1915
Heading	14th Division 6th D.C.L.I. Vol. 6 Oct. 15		
War Diary	Vlamertinghe	01/10/1915	04/10/1915
War Diary	Trenches	05/10/1915	14/10/1915
War Diary	Watou	15/10/1915	31/10/1915
Heading	14th Division 6th D.C.L.I. Vol 7. Nov. 15		
War Diary	Near Watou L.3.c.10.4 (Sheet 27)	01/11/1915	11/11/1915
War Diary	Canal Bank	12/11/1915	17/11/1915
War Diary	Poperinghe	18/11/1915	21/11/1915
War Diary	Trenches	22/11/1915	29/11/1915
War Diary	Billets	30/11/1915	30/11/1915
Heading	14th Div. 6th D.C.L.I. Vol: 8.		

Heading	War Diary 6th Batt D.C.L.I. December 1915.		
Miscellaneous			
War Diary	Support Trenches	01/12/1915	01/12/1915
War Diary	Trenches	02/12/1915	11/12/1915
War Diary	B. Camp	12/12/1915	15/12/1915
War Diary	C. Camp Rest Area	16/12/1915	27/12/1915
War Diary	A Camp	28/12/1915	28/12/1915
War Diary	Trenches	29/12/1915	31/12/1915
Heading	6th Bn DCLI		
War Diary	6th. (Service) Battalion Duke Of Cornwall's Light Infantry.	20/12/1915	20/12/1915
Miscellaneous	6th D.C.L.I. Vol. 9 43 Bde		
War Diary	Trenches in C 14 D Sheet 28 1:10,000.	01/01/1916	04/01/1916
War Diary	Rest Camp	05/01/1916	08/01/1916
War Diary	Trenches In C.15.c Etc.	09/01/1916	14/01/1916
War Diary	Camp 4.	15/01/1916	19/01/1916
War Diary	Trenches C.15.c.	20/01/1916	24/01/1916
War Diary	Trenches	24/01/1916	26/01/1916
War Diary	Camp 4	27/01/1916	31/01/1916
Heading	6th D.C.L.I. 14th Div. Vol 10		
War Diary	No. 4 Rest Camp A.8.B.10.4. Sheet 28.	31/01/1916	01/02/1916
War Diary	Trenches	02/02/1916	07/02/1916
War Diary	Trenches No.4 Rest Camp	07/02/1915	10/02/1915
War Diary	A Huts	11/02/1916	12/02/1916
War Diary	Billets in Houtkerque Sheet 27.	13/02/1916	22/02/1916
War Diary	Vignacourt	23/02/1916	23/02/1916
War Diary	Beauval	24/02/1916	24/02/1916
War Diary	Coullemont	25/02/1916	27/02/1916
War Diary	Simencourt	28/02/1916	29/02/1916
War Diary	Agny	01/03/1916	11/03/1916
War Diary	Trenches	12/03/1916	17/03/1916
War Diary	Berneville	18/03/1916	23/03/1916
War Diary	Trenches	24/03/1916	29/03/1916
War Diary	Agny	30/03/1916	31/03/1916
Miscellaneous	To A.G. Office Base	05/05/1916	05/05/1916
War Diary	Agny	01/04/1916	04/04/1916
War Diary	In Trenches	05/04/1916	10/04/1916
War Diary	Bernaville	11/04/1916	24/04/1916
War Diary	Agny	25/04/1916	01/05/1916
War Diary	Trenches	02/05/1916	06/05/1916
War Diary	Dainville	07/05/1916	12/05/1916
War Diary	Trenches	13/05/1916	18/05/1916
War Diary	Agny	19/05/1916	24/05/1916
War Diary	Trenches	25/05/1916	30/05/1916
War Diary	Dainville	31/05/1916	07/06/1916
War Diary	Trenches	08/06/1916	12/06/1916
War Diary	Agny	13/06/1916	18/06/1916
War Diary	Trenches	19/06/1916	19/06/1916
War Diary	Arras	20/06/1916	20/06/1916
War Diary	Trenches	21/06/1916	30/06/1916
Heading	War Diary For July 1916. 6th Bn. Duke Of Cornwall's Light Infantry. Vol 15.		
War Diary	Trenches	01/07/1916	31/07/1916
Heading	43rd Brigade. 14th Division. 1/6th Battalion Duke Of Cornwall's Light Infantry August 1916.		

Heading	War Diary. August 1916. 6th Bn. Duke Of Cornwall's Light Infantry. Vol 16.		
War Diary	Bonnieres	01/08/1916	01/08/1916
War Diary	Lemeillard	02/08/1916	07/08/1916
War Diary	Near Albert	08/08/1916	12/08/1916
War Diary	Montauban	13/08/1916	14/08/1916
War Diary	Delville Wood	15/08/1916	19/08/1916
War Diary	Near Fricourt	20/08/1916	25/08/1916
War Diary	Montauban Defences	26/08/1916	30/08/1916
War Diary	Near Dermancourt	31/08/1916	31/08/1916
Heading	War Diary. For The Month Of September 1916. 6th Bn. Duke Of Cornwall's Light Infantry. Vol 17.		
War Diary	Aumont	01/09/1916	11/09/1916
War Diary	Laleu	12/09/1916	12/09/1916
War Diary	Near Albert	13/09/1916	14/09/1916
War Diary	Near Bercordel	15/09/1916	15/09/1916
War Diary	Montauban Defences	15/09/1916	15/09/1916
War Diary	York Alley	15/09/1916	15/09/1916
War Diary	Gap Trench	15/09/1916	16/09/1916
War Diary	Bull Trench	16/09/1916	16/09/1916
War Diary	Bulls Road	16/09/1916	17/09/1916
War Diary	Near Bercordel	17/09/1916	18/09/1916
War Diary	Ribemont	19/09/1916	22/09/1916
War Diary	Sus St Leger	23/09/1916	27/09/1916
War Diary	Arras	28/09/1916	30/09/1916
Miscellaneous	A Form. Messages And Signals. Appendix I		
Miscellaneous	A Form. Messages And Signals. Appendix II		
Miscellaneous	A Form. Messages And Signals. Appendix III		
Operation(al) Order(s)	43rd L/I Bde. O.O. No. 67. Appendix IV.		
Operation(al) Order(s)	43rd Bde. Operation Order No. 68. Appendix V	16/09/1916	16/09/1916
Miscellaneous	A Form. Messages And Signals. Appendix VI		
Miscellaneous	A Form. Messages And Signals. Appendix VII		
Miscellaneous	A Form. Messages And Signals. Appendix VIII		
Miscellaneous	A Form. Messages And Signals. Appendix IX		
Miscellaneous	A Form. Messages And Signals. Appendix X		
Miscellaneous	Copy Of Orders Appendix XI		
Miscellaneous	List of Code Calls. Of The 14th (Light) Division Appendix XII		
Heading	War Diary of 6th Bn Duke Of Cornwall's Light Infantry. October 1st 1916-October 31st 1916.		
War Diary	Arras	01/10/1916	03/10/1916
War Diary	In Trenches	04/10/1916	09/10/1916
War Diary	Arras	10/10/1916	15/10/1916
War Diary	In Trenches	16/10/1916	21/10/1916
War Diary	Arras	22/10/1916	27/10/1916
War Diary	Izel Lez Hameau	28/10/1916	31/10/1916
Heading	War Diary of 6th D.C.L.I. From 1st November To 30th November 1916 Volume 19.		
War Diary	Izel-Lez-Hemeau.	01/11/1916	08/11/1916
War Diary	Mincheaux & Monts. Ent Srnois	09/11/1916	27/11/1916
War Diary	Moncheaux	28/11/1916	30/11/1916
Heading	Vol 20 War Diary 6th D.C.L.I. December 1916.		
War Diary	Moncheaux	01/12/1916	15/12/1916
War Diary	Grand Rullecourt	16/12/1916	16/12/1916
War Diary	Wanquetin	17/12/1916	17/12/1916
War Diary	Cavalry Bks Arras & Trenches.	18/12/1916	18/12/1916

Type	Location	From	To
War Diary	Trenches	19/12/1916	23/12/1916
War Diary	Trenches & Cavalry Bks Arras	24/12/1916	24/12/1916
War Diary	Cavalry Bks Arras	25/12/1916	30/12/1916
War Diary	Cavalry Bks Arras & Vicinity.	31/12/1916	31/12/1916
Heading	War Diary 6th D.C.L.I. January 1917. Vol 21		
War Diary	Arras & Trenches "H".2. Sub-Sec.	01/01/1917	01/01/1917
War Diary	H.2. Subsector	02/01/1917	06/01/1917
War Diary	Trenches & Brigade Reserve. Arras And Vicinity.	07/01/1917	07/01/1917
War Diary	Arras & Vicinity	08/01/1917	12/01/1917
War Diary	Arras & Vicinity And Trenches	13/01/1917	13/01/1917
War Diary	H.2. Sub-Sector.	14/01/1917	19/01/1917
War Diary	Trenches H.2. Sub-Sector	20/01/1917	20/01/1917
War Diary	Trenches H.2. Sub-Sector & Arras	21/01/1917	21/01/1917
War Diary	Cavalry Bks Arras	22/01/1917	24/01/1917
War Diary	H.2. Sub-Sector	25/01/1917	27/01/1917
War Diary	Trenches H.2. Sub-Sector	28/01/1917	30/01/1917
War Diary	H.2. Sub-Sector. Arras & Vicinity.	31/01/1917	31/01/1917
Operation(al) Order(s)	6th. (Service) Battalion Duke Of Cornwall's L.I. Operation Order No. 46.	05/01/1917	05/01/1917
Heading	War Diary 6th D.C.L.I. February 1917. Vol 22.		
War Diary	Arras & Vicinity.	01/02/1917	02/02/1917
War Diary	Arras & Vicinity & Cavalry Barracks	03/02/1917	03/02/1917
War Diary	Cavalry Bks & Berneville	04/02/1917	04/02/1917
War Diary	Berneville	05/02/1917	10/02/1917
War Diary	Bernville & Arras	11/02/1917	11/02/1917
War Diary	Arras	12/02/1917	23/02/1917
War Diary	Arras And H.1. Sub-Sector Trenches.	24/02/1917	24/02/1917
War Diary	Trenches H.1. Sub Sec.	25/02/1917	28/02/1917
Heading	Confidential. War Diary of 6th Service Battalion Duke Of Cornwall's Light Infantry. From 1st March 1917 To 31st March 1917. Volume 23.		
War Diary	Trenches H.1. Sub-Sector	01/03/1917	01/03/1917
War Diary	H.1. Sub-Sector And Dainville	02/03/1917	02/03/1917
War Diary	Dainville And Arras.	03/03/1917	03/03/1917
War Diary	Arras	04/03/1917	07/03/1917
War Diary	Arras And H.1. Sub-Sector.	08/03/1917	08/03/1917
War Diary	Trenches H2. Sub-Sector	09/03/1917	14/03/1917
War Diary	Arras	15/03/1917	17/03/1917
War Diary	Ronville And H.2. Sub Sector.	18/03/1917	18/03/1917
War Diary	Arras-Ronville & H2 Sub Sector	18/03/1917	18/03/1917
War Diary	H2. Sub-Sector. Ronville & Old German Trenches.	19/03/1917	21/03/1917
War Diary	H2. Sub Sector. Ronville & Caves	22/03/1917	23/03/1917
War Diary	Arras	24/03/1917	31/03/1917
Heading	War Diary 6th D.C.L.I. Volume 24 April 1917.		
War Diary	Arras	01/04/1917	02/04/1917
War Diary	Arras & Trenches	03/04/1917	03/04/1917
War Diary	Trenches	04/04/1917	09/04/1917
War Diary	Trenches & The Caves Ronville	10/04/1917	11/04/1917
War Diary	Montenescourt	12/04/1917	12/04/1917
War Diary	Beaufort	13/04/1917	14/04/1917
War Diary	Warlozel	14/04/1917	22/04/1917
War Diary	Warluzel & Saulty	23/04/1917	23/04/1917
War Diary	Saulty & Bailleuval	24/04/1917	24/04/1917
War Diary	Bailleuval	25/04/1917	26/04/1917
War Diary	Bailleuval And "W" Camp M.12.c.	27/04/1917	27/04/1917
War Diary	W. Camp.	28/04/1917	30/04/1917

Miscellaneous	Narrative Of Operations Of The 6th. Batt. D.C.L.I. On 9th And 10th April, 1917.	09/04/1917	09/04/1917
Map	Beaurains.		
Heading	War Diary. For Month Of May 1917. 6th (S) Battalion Duke Of Cornwall's Light Infantry. Vol 25.		
War Diary	W. Camp Telegraph Hill M.12.C.	01/05/1917	01/05/1917
War Diary	W. Camp Telegraph Hill M.12.C. And Bivouac Area N.15.C.	02/05/1917	02/05/1917
War Diary	W. Camp Telegraph Hill M.12.C. And Bivouac Area N.15.C. And Nepeal Trench.	03/05/1917	03/05/1917
War Diary	Nepeal Trench.	04/05/1917	04/05/1917
War Diary	Trenches	05/05/1917	14/05/1917
War Diary	Support Area	15/05/1917	15/05/1917
War Diary	Reserve Camp	15/05/1917	24/05/1917
War Diary	Support Area	25/05/1917	31/05/1917
Operation(al) Order(s)	6th. (Service) Battalion Duke Of Cornwall's Light Infantry. Operation Order No. 64.		
Operation(al) Order(s)	6th. (S). Battalion Duke Of Cornwall's L.I. Operation Order No. 65.	04/05/1916	04/05/1916
Operation(al) Order(s)	6th. (S). Battalion Duke Of Cornwall's L.I. Operation Order No. 66.	10/05/1917	10/05/1917
Heading	War Diary 6th D.C.L.I. June 1917 Volume 26.		
War Diary	Support Area	01/06/1917	03/06/1917
War Diary	In Trenches Front Line	04/06/1917	06/06/1917
War Diary	Support Line	07/06/1917	08/06/1917
War Diary	In Trenches Support	09/06/1917	11/06/1917
War Diary	Neuville Vitasse	12/06/1917	12/06/1917
War Diary	Beaumetz	13/06/1917	13/06/1917
War Diary	Laherliere	14/06/1917	14/06/1917
War Diary	Bus-Les-Artois	15/06/1917	15/06/1917
War Diary	Bus-Les Artois Authie Rest Camp	16/06/1917	30/06/1917
Operation(al) Order(s)	Dun Operation Order No. 68.	02/06/1917	02/06/1917
Heading	W.D.		
Operation(al) Order(s)	Operation Orders No. 69.		
Operation(al) Order(s)	Operation Order No 70.	10/06/1917	10/06/1917
Operation(al) Order(s)	6th. (Service) Battalion Duke Of Cornwall's L.I. Operation Order No. 71.	12/06/1917	12/06/1917
Operation(al) Order(s)	6th. (Service) Battalion Duke Of Cornwall's L.I. Operation Order No. 72.	13/06/1917	13/06/1917
Operation(al) Order(s)	6th. (Service) Battalion Duke Of Cornwall's L.I. Operation Order No. 73.	14/06/1917	14/06/1917
Heading	War Diary of 6th Duke Of Cornwalls Light Infantry From July 1st 1917 To July 31st 1917. Vol 27.		
War Diary	Bus-Les-Artois	01/07/1917	09/07/1917
War Diary	Bus Les Artois And Gezaincourt	10/07/1917	10/07/1917
War Diary	Gozaincourt	11/07/1917	11/07/1917
War Diary	Bailleul & Corunna Camp	12/07/1917	12/07/1917
War Diary	Corunna Camp.	13/07/1917	31/07/1917
Operation(al) Order(s)	6th. (Ser.) Battn. Duke Of Cornwall's L.I. Operation Order No. 74.	09/07/1917	09/07/1917
Heading	O.O. File		
Operation(al) Order(s)	6th. (Service) Battalion Duke Of Cornwall's L.I. Operation Order No. 75.	11/07/1917	11/07/1917
Heading	War Diary 6th D.C.L.I. August 1917 Volume No. 28.		
War Diary	Corunna Camp	01/08/1917	05/08/1917
War Diary	Corunna Camp And Castre Area.	06/08/1917	06/08/1917

War Diary	Hazewinde	07/08/1917	15/08/1917
War Diary	Wippen Houck	16/08/1917	17/08/1917
War Diary	Camp Dickebush	18/08/1917	21/08/1917
War Diary	Trenches	21/08/1917	24/08/1917
War Diary	Zillebeke Bund	24/08/1917	25/08/1917
War Diary	Dominion Camp	26/08/1917	28/08/1917
War Diary	Le Roukloshille	29/08/1917	31/08/1917
Operation(al) Order(s)	6th. (Service) Battalion Duke Of Cornwall's Light Infantry Regiment. Operation Order No. 76.	05/08/1917	05/08/1917
Map	Trenches and British Front Line Corrected to 13-8-17		
Operation(al) Order(s)	6th. (Ser:) Battalion Duke Of Cornwall's L.I. Operation Order No. 77.	14/08/1917	14/08/1917
Operation(al) Order(s)	6th. (Service) Battalion Duke Of Cornwall's L.I. Operation Order No. 78.	20/08/1917	20/08/1917
Operation(al) Order(s)	6th. (Service) Battalion Duke Of Cornwall's Light Infantry. Operation Order No. 80.	29/08/1917	29/08/1917
Map	Trench Operation Map		
Miscellaneous	Narrative Of The Operation On 22nd. And 24th. August.	22/08/1917	22/08/1917
Heading	War Diary. September 1917. 6th Bn. Duke Of Cornwall's Light Infantry. Volume 29.		
War Diary	Le Roukloshille	01/09/1917	03/09/1917
War Diary	Le Roukloshille And Camp At B.20.d.9.7.	04/09/1917	04/09/1917
War Diary	Camp At B.20.d.9.7.	05/09/1917	08/09/1917
War Diary	Camp. B.20.d.9.7. Sheet 36 Near Nieppe	08/09/1917	15/09/1917
War Diary	Neuve Eglise	16/09/1917	20/09/1917
War Diary	Messines	21/09/1917	24/09/1917
War Diary	Front Line Trenches Near Messines	25/09/1917	28/09/1917
War Diary	Front Line Near Messines.	28/09/1917	28/09/1917
War Diary	Camp Canteen Corner	29/09/1917	30/09/1917
Operation(al) Order(s)	6th. (Ser:) Battalion, Duke Of Cornwall's Lt. Inf. Operation Order No. 81.	03/08/1917	03/08/1917
Operation(al) Order(s)	6th. (Service) Battalion Duke Of Cornwall's Light Infantry. Operation Order No. 82.	14/09/1917	14/09/1917
Operation(al) Order(s)	6th. (Service) Battalion Duke Of Cornwall's Light Infantry. Operation Order No. 83.	20/09/1917	20/09/1917
Operation(al) Order(s)	6th. (Service) Battalion Duke Of Cornwall's Light Infantry. Operation Order No. 84.	24/09/1917	24/09/1917
Operation(al) Order(s)	6th. (Service) Battalion Duke Of Cornwall's Light Infantry. Operation Order No. 85.	28/09/1917	28/09/1917
Heading	War Diary. October 1917. 6th Bn. Duke Of Cornwall's Light Infantry. Volume 30.		
War Diary	Canteen Corner Camp T.26.c.5.0	01/10/1917	06/10/1917
War Diary	Camp At M.7.d.5.5.	07/10/1917	08/10/1917
War Diary	Camp At M.7.c.5.5.	09/10/1917	09/10/1917
War Diary	Chippewa Camp	10/10/1917	11/10/1917
War Diary	Bedford House	12/10/1917	15/10/1917
War Diary	Sanctuary Wood	16/10/1917	17/10/1917
War Diary	Sanctuary Wood And Front Line Trenches About J.15.b And J.16.a. Sheet 28 France Belgium.	18/10/1917	18/10/1917
War Diary	Front Line Trenches About J.15.b. And J.16.a. Sheet. 28 Belgium And Part Of France.	19/10/1917	21/10/1917
War Diary	Ridgewood Camp	22/10/1917	22/10/1917
War Diary	Bivouacs At H.36 b.3.5. Sheet 28	23/10/1917	30/10/1917
War Diary	No 10 Area Berthen	30/10/1917	31/10/1917

Type	Description	Start	End
Operation(al) Order(s)	6th. (Service) Battalion Duke Of Cornwall's Light Infantry. Operation Order No. 86.	05/10/1917	05/10/1917
Operation(al) Order(s)	6th. (Service) Battalion Duke Of Cornwall's Light Infantry. Operation Order No. 87.	08/10/1917	08/10/1917
Heading	O.C. A. Coy.		
Operation(al) Order(s)	6th. (Service) Battalion Duke Of Cornwall's Light Infantry. Operation Order No. 88.a.	16/10/1917	16/10/1917
Operation(al) Order(s)	6th. (Service) Battalion Duke Of Cornwall's Light Infantry. Operation Order No. 89.	22/10/1917	22/10/1917
Operation(al) Order(s)	6th. (Service) Battalion Duke Of Cornwall's Light Infantry. Operation Order No. 90.	29/10/1917	29/10/1917
Heading	War Diary. 6th Bn Duke Of Cornwalls Light Infantry. November 1917. Volume 31.		
War Diary	Billets	01/11/1917	05/11/1917
War Diary	Billets No 10 Area Near Berthen	06/11/1917	13/11/1917
War Diary	Acquin	13/11/1917	30/11/1917
Operation(al) Order(s)	6th. (Service) Battalion Duke Of Cornwall's Light Infantry. Operation Order No. 91.	11/11/1917	11/11/1917
Operation(al) Order(s)	Amendments To Operation Order No. 91.	12/11/1917	12/11/1917
Heading	War Diary. 6th D.C.L.I. December 1917. Volume 32.		
War Diary	Acquin	01/12/1917	03/12/1917
War Diary	Junction Camp.	04/12/1917	08/12/1917
War Diary	In The Line	09/12/1917	12/12/1917
War Diary	Junction & Calafornia Camps.	13/12/1917	15/12/1917
War Diary	In The Line	15/12/1917	19/12/1917
War Diary	Red Rose Camp	20/12/1917	26/12/1917
War Diary	Boisinghem	27/12/1917	31/12/1917
Heading	War Diary of 6th D.C.L.I. January 1918 Volume 33		
War Diary	Boisdinghem	01/01/1918	02/01/1918
War Diary	Bray-Sur-Somme	03/01/1918	22/01/1918
War Diary	Wiencourt L'Equire	23/01/1918	23/01/1918
War Diary	Carrepuits	24/01/1918	24/01/1918
War Diary	Quesmy	25/01/1918	25/01/1918
War Diary	Remigny	26/01/1918	26/01/1918
War Diary	In the Line	27/01/1918	31/01/1918
Operation(al) Order(s)	6th. (Service) Battalion Duke Of Cornwall's Light Infantry. Operation Order No. 96.	01/01/1918	01/01/1918
Miscellaneous	Battalion Orders By Lieut-Col R.J. Hewitt, D.S.O., Commanding 6th (Service) Battalion, D.C.L.I.	24/01/1918	24/01/1918
Miscellaneous	Operation Orders.	26/01/1918	26/01/1918
War Diary	In the Field	01/02/1918	01/02/1918
War Diary	Ly Fontaine	02/02/1918	02/02/1918
War Diary	Jussy	03/02/1918	12/02/1918
War Diary	Crissoles	13/02/1918	20/02/1918

w995/508(2)

w997/808(2)

14TH DIVISION
43RD INFY BDE

6TH BN D.C.L.I.
MAY 1915 - FEB 1918

DISBANDED

12/5484

43/14th Division.

8th D.C.L.I.

Vol I 22 – 30.5.15

Feb. 18

2.

181/5991

14th Division

6th DCLI.

Vol II 22.5 — 30.6.15

Army Form C. 2118.

WAR DIARY
or
INTELLIGENCE SUMMARY
(Erase heading not required.)

Instructions regarding War Diaries and Intelligence Summaries are contained in F. S. Regs., Part II. and the Staff Manual respectively. Title pages will be prepared in manuscript.

Place	Date	Hour	Summary of Events and Information	Remarks and references to Appendices
BOLOGNE	22/5/15	1 a.m.	Disembarked at BOLOGNE and marched to LARGE REST CAMP.	
" "	23/5/15	—	REST CAMP	
" "	24/5/15	5 p.m.	Marched to PONT DE BRIQUE STN. & entrained to CASSEL.	
VOLKERINCKHOVE			Billets	

Signed,
Lt Col
Comdr 6/D.C.L.I.
30/5/15.

Army Form C. 2118.

WAR DIARY
or
INTELLIGENCE SUMMARY.
(Erase heading not required.)

6th W. C. L. I.

Place	Date	Hour	Summary of Events and Information	Remarks and references to Appendices
YPRES	25/6/15	9 p.m.	Carrying parties to Somerset in fire trenches. Two casualties – wounded	
"	26/6/15	6 a.m. 6.6 P.m.	Work on dugouts and obtaining & filling all available petrol cans for Somerset in trenches.	
"	27/6/15	9 p.m.	Carrying parties to fire trenches. Rations, Water, R.E. Stores. Lt Carter & 2 men wounded During day time filling water tins for Somerset. Improving dugouts.	
"		9 p.m.	Carrying Parties. Two men wounded much shelling on Menin Road and on Battery near sally Port. None of our men hit.	
"	28/6/15		Shelling on Battery in Ypres town. Shells all over our heads. No damage. One large Gas shell exploded near Sally Port. All ranks put on smoke helmets Btn H.Q. shelled & burnt to Ground. Some of our men on carrying duty hit by bricks &c but no serious casualties. 3 wounded while carrying to Somerset.	
"	29/6/15		All quiet during day. Lieut Noughton wounded when on carrying party at 11 P.m.	Reconnoitred Ypres
VLAMERTINGHE	30/6/15		Marched back to rest near VLAMERTINGHE	

Army Form C. 2118.

WAR DIARY
or
INTELLIGENCE SUMMARY

6ᵗʰ D.C.L.I.

(Erase heading not required).

Instructions regarding War Diaries and Intelligence Summaries are contained in F. S. Regs. Part II. and the Staff Manual respectively. Title pages will be prepared in manuscript.

Place	Date	Hour	Summary of Events and Information	Remarks and references to Appendices
LA Clytte	6/6/15	9–1am	Digging G.H.Q. Switch near Yser Canal. 1 mile S.E. of Ypres.	
"	7/6/15	"	Do. Do. (Detailed A Coy 6 dig near trenches held by 1ˢᵗ D.6.C.S. E of Ypres.)	
"	8/6/15	"	Do. Do. (A Coy reported 1 man killed)	
"	9/6/15	"	Do. Do. (A Coy relieved. B Coy relieved them there)	
"	10/6/15	"	Rest. B Coy continued digging.	
"	11/6/15	—	— — — — — —	
"	13/6/15	7am.	A & D Coys moved to huts at ZEVECOTEN.	
		7pm.	C Coy & Hd Q. joined B Coy in trenches in 14ᵗʰ Inf Bde. The 2 coys were distributed throughout the 1ˢᵗ & 4ᵗʰ Bde for 48 hours instruction.	
Near Ypres	13/6/15		C & B Coys still in trenches. Casualties 1 killed & 1 wounded.	
"	14/6/15		C & B Coys relieved by A & D Coys at 10.30 p.m. Casualties 1 killed & 2 wounded	
"	15/6/15		A & D in trenches. No Casualties	
"	16/6/15		A & D Coys relieved by B & C Coys at 10.30 pm & H.Q. 1 accidentally wounded & wounded. 1 killed	
"	17/6/15		B & C in trenches	
"	18/6/15		B & C relieved by A & D 2 wounded.	
Zevecoten	19/6/15		A & D in trenches B & C in hut at ZEVECOTEN	
"	20/6/15		A & D returned to ZEVECOTEN and at 11pm. the Batt. moved to Poperinghe.	
Poperinghe	21/6/15		Entrained getting Bomb Throwing Squad together and also Batt. Sappers	
"	22/6/15		Do	
"	23/6/15		Do	
Ypres.	24/6/15		Bomb throwing classes. Marched to Dugouts in ramparts in Ypres between the MENIN Gate and the SALLY PORT Sent 1 Coy to work all day on dugouts and went in at 9.30 p.m. and occupied them	
"	25/6/15	6am. 6pm.	Work on improving dugouts Ypres, was shelled during day but on ramparts there was no damage	

3N.

43/14 15 Division

121/6300

6th D.C.L.I.

Vol: III 1 — 31.7.15

Army Form C. 2118.

WAR DIARY
or
INTELLIGENCE SUMMARY. 6th Duke of Cornwall L I

(Erase heading not required.)

Place	Date	Hour	Summary of Events and Information	Remarks and references to Appendices
VLAMERTINGHE	1/7/15	—	Rest in bivouac in field between VLAMERTINGHE and POPERINGHE	
—	2/7/15	—	—	
—	3/7/15	—	—	
—	4/7/15	—	—	
—	5/7/15	—	—	
—	6/7/15	—	POPERINGHE rather badly shelled. All shells over our heads	
—	7/7/15	—	—	
—	8/7/15	—	—	
—	9/7/15	—	—	
—	10/7/15	—	Battalion employed in digging making a redoubt nr G.H.Q 2nd line about mile S.E. of VLAMERTINGHE	
—	11/7/15	—	do.	
—	12/7/15	—	do.	
—	13/7/15	—	do.	
—	14/7/15	—	do.	
—	15/7/15	—	do.	
—	16/7/15	—	do.	
—	17/7/15	—	do.	

WAR DIARY
or
INTELLIGENCE SUMMARY.
(Erase heading not required.)

Army Form C. 2118.

C.1 Duke of Cornwall L.I.

Instructions regarding War Diaries and Intelligence Summaries are contained in F. S. Regs., Part II. and the Staff Manual respectively. Title pages will be prepared in manuscript.

Place	Date	Hour	Summary of Events and Information	Remarks and references to Appendices
Trenches E.H YPRES (D6 & D9)	18/7/15	10pm	5th Battalion took over trenches D6 & D9 from 42nd Bde. Relief accomplished successfully. 4 casualties on the way up from Wolf Camp over the Communication Trench. We took over D6 from 9th KRRC and D7 to D9 from the 6th K.S.L.I. The other 2 were in G.H.Q. line.	
"	19/7/15	7pm	The 3rd Division exploded a large mine under the German trenches at HOOGE. We were ordered to support their accompanying infantry attack with our rifle & machine gun fire. This we did satisfactorily, as the 3rd Division suffered much day to that effect. We lost some 20 casualties that night from German shell fire	
"	20/7/15	7pm	The German Artillery bombarded our trenches somewhat heavily but we lost about half what we had lost the night before.	
"	21/7/15	-	A quiet day except for the fact that the enemy shelled our trenches morning & evening with "whizz-bangs"	
"	"	10pm	Our half Battalion holding D6 &D9 were relieved by the 2nd Batt in G.H.Q line	
"	22/7/15	-	Exactly the same as the 21st	
"	23/7/15	-	A quiet day beyond intermittent shelling & trench mortaring which latter we silenced by our trench howitzers	
"	24/7/15	noon	The C.O. was wounded by a trench mortar & the second in command took over. Otherwise nothing to report.	
"	25/7/15	2pm	Heavy shelling of our trenches by enemy whizz-bangs. This was silenced by our batteries in YPRES. Our parapets knocked about a good deal.	
"	26/7/15	2pm	2/Lt Scoler and 2/Lt Harrison wounded, also a large shell transports from the Battalion on our left that the enemy were preparing for an attack in our line. Our 2 Batts in G.H.Q. wanted to support if required. These rumours turned out to be nothing. At 10pm the Battalion was relieved by 42nd Bde. and marched back to bivouacs west VIAMERTINGHE. Our tour in trenches resulted in 4 officers & 60 men casualties	

1577 Wt. W10791/1773 500,000 1/15 D. D. & L. A.D.S.S./Forms/C. 2118.

WAR DIARY (2nd Batt. of Connaught.) Army Form C. 2118.

INTELLIGENCE SUMMARY.

(Erase heading not required.)

Instructions regarding War Diaries and Intelligence Summaries are contained in F. S. Regs., Part II. and the Staff Manual respectively. Title pages will be prepared in manuscript.

Place	Date	Hour	Summary of Events and Information	Remarks and references to Appendices
VLAMERTINGHE	27/7/15	—	Reo' re equip in billets	
—	28/7/15	—	— do —	
—	29/7/15	—	— do —	
—	30/7/15	4 am	The Battalion ordered to stand to owing to 41st Bde. being driven in & opposn. trenches by liquid fire	
		6 am	Battalion ordered to march to dug outs W. of YPRES and to render themselves in reserve for 41st Bde counter attack	
		11 am	Battalion ordered to march to support Counter attack on the two trenches	
		2:00 pm	Battalion arrived was dropped to an area of Sanctuary Wood & in rear of Zouave Wood. We suffered from enemy's bombardment while moving away. at which Major Jones-Parry killed. Some 30 other ranks killed & wounded.	
		3:00 pm	Battalion moved to advance through ZOUAVE WOOD though. The remnants of the 41 & 81 Bde (which had failed in their counter-attack) and to hold the 2 edge of Zouave Wood known as S.3 & S.4. We suffered very heavily in going through the wood but got into position alright & held on.	
ZOUAVE WOOD	30/7/15	7 pm	The Germans delivered an attack on our position. They reinforced our left on S.3. The enemy had liquid fire jets but our artillery "on the barrage" our own rifle machine gun fire drove them back. By day break we were still in the same position but had lost 6 officers, 20 others, our M.O. Lt Callum R.A.M.C. killed & 2 officers wounded other ranks killed wounded & missing about 100.	

WAR DIARY
or
INTELLIGENCE SUMMARY.

(Erase heading not required.)

Army Form C. 2118.

6th Duke of Cornwall L.I.

Place	Date	Hour	Summary of Events and Information	Remarks and references to Appendices
ZOUAVE WOOD	31/7/15		until midnight and at 3.0 we suffered from heavy shelling from Saulting the loss heavily and at midnight the Germans delivered another attack. Result scattered the same as previous night. Losses Capt. Hahn + O.C. Bros. + Hullon Sams killed. 2 officers wounded and some 80 other ranks killed & wounded	

W Sugar?
Capt

121/6753

4.

14th Division

6th S.C.J.
Vol: IV
August 15

6th (Sv) Bn. Duke of Cornwall's Light Infantry

WAR DIARY
or
INTELLIGENCE SUMMARY.
Army Form C. 2118.

Place	Date	Hour	Summary of Events and Information	Remarks and references to Appendices
ZOUAVE WOOD	30/7/15	7 p.m.	The Germans delivered an attack on our front. The Durham L.I. had at this been reinforced our left in S.3. The enemy was behind the and bombs but our artillery "Tir de Barage" and our own rifle & machine gun fire drove them back. By day break we were still in the same position but had lost Lt Paddison, 2Lt Challoner and our M.O. Lt McCallum R.A.M.C. killed and 2 officers wounded. Other ranks killed & wounded about 100	
"	31/7/15		Until midnight on the 31st we suffered from heavy shelling from 3 directions. We lost heavily and at midnight the Germans delivered another counter attack. Rev'd Scoath the same as previous night. Capt Aston & Lts Birch and Hulton Sams killed, 2 officers wounded and some 80 other ranks killed & wounded	
Ypres	1/8/15	1 a.m.	Relieved by 4 KRRC. And marched back into reserve at Ramparts in Ypres. We had had no food or water since marching from VLAMERTINGHE and relief was imperative.	
Ypres	2/8/15	-	All quiet in ramparts	
"	3/8/15	-	" "	
"	4/8/15		" "	
"	5/8/15	9 p.m.	Battalion employed in carrying parties to trenches	

J.P.W. Carr
Lt Col
6/D.C.L.I.

WAR DIARY
or
INTELLIGENCE SUMMARY.

1st (Se) Bn. Duke of Cornwall's Light Infantry.

Army Form C. 2118.

Place	Date	Hour	Summary of Events and Information	Remarks and references to Appendices
Ypres	5/8/15	11 pm	Relieved 1st Queens Westminster Rifles (6th Division) and marched to Dug outs 1 mile N. of Ypres on the Vlamertinghe Road.	
enroute	6/8/15	11 am	Shelled by enemy but no casualties	
		12 non	marched to field ½ mile N.W. of Vlamertinghe and bivouacked	
	7/8/15	—	Resting	
	8/8/15	—	"	
	9/8/15	3 am	Stood to while 6th Division attacked HOOGE. We were allowed to fall out at 9 am.	
YPRES	10/8/15	—	Bn marched to Cellars in Ypres. 4/3 Bde. relieving 4/2 Bde. Bn H.Q., H.Q. Coy & 100 men were put into cellars of Ecole Moyenne opposite to Infantry Barracks. 150 men in cellars of Convent to Left near Ly in same street. The rest of the Battalion - C & D Coys were put in St Martin's Cloisters, the southern wing of the Cathedral. These cloisters were on abroad inclusion.Coy D. Ofmen together with two Chaplains, R.C. Jaffé (CofE) & Mr Harris (Nonconf) were in cellars of Notre Dame Hospital between the Place & the MENIN GATE.	This is the list below of Officers who were killed on the 12th in attempt movement to put men of the 1st in St Martin's Cloisters, the YPRES being in whose disembarked bombardment & Belgian.
	11/8/15		E. j. & Officers from the Bn. — 2/Lt Mills, Brookes, Sec. Lt. Yarnold, Andrew, Allen, Orchard, Gillett & Pilgrim. Enemy aircraft very active.	

1st (6th) Bn. Duke of Cornwall's Light Infantry.

Army Form C. 2118.

WAR DIARY
or
INTELLIGENCE SUMMARY.
(Erase heading not required.)

Place	Date	Hour	Summary of Events and Information	Remarks and references to Appendices
YPRES	12/8/15	6.30am	Enemy commenced to shell Cloisters & Place at 6.15. The heavy to Cloister thinking they were safe did not move. Enemy fires open fire every smaller hour or after a few shells. On hour a after a few shells. The first direct hit brought down most of the ceiling of cloisters & buried several men. The enemy continued to fire for five hours, putting in 17 inch shell every minute & lots, every half hour, with smaller shells & shrapnel in between. Many of the men who went to rescue their comrades were then also buried. The wounded men first managed to Bn. HQ. Winnipeg. Major Barnett and the Adjutant Capt. Blayne ran over to the Cloisters to endeavour to get the men out. Both were instantly killed by the explosion of a very large shell which apparently fell in open space just in front of the Cloisters. The morning had meantime been brought to the B.S.C. Coys Officers	
		8am		

Captain Andrew D.C. Coy and was frozen at once was not in that

J.M. Williams
2/Lt 6th April (15)

6th (Service) Bn. Duke of Cornwall's Light Infantry

Army Form C. 2118.

WAR DIARY or INTELLIGENCE SUMMARY.

(Erase heading not required.)

Instructions regarding War Diaries and Intelligence Summaries are contained in F.S. Regs., Part II. and the Staff Manual respectively. Title pages will be prepared in manuscript.

Place	Date	Hour	Summary of Events and Information	Remarks and references to Appendices
Ypres	10/8/15	8.15	Part of C. Coy. out let ton himself hit Mr Harris the Scoutmaster Chaplain who died on the scene church at once & emphatic against the men going out. The order was then given to B. Coy Officers for everyone to keep well away from the shelled area. Lieut. Mr Harris into lines in sorry to hush with four platoons of the D.C.L.I. (including Cpl Bishop Coy 3. who behaved most gallantly), in the search for Harris was severely wounded. As they developed (Pioneers) his members came upon the scene & continued shelling. Mr Holley moving despite heavy & continuous shelling. Mr Holley most an airplane returned & help on him. The men Mr T.P. D.C.L.I. Casualties were 2 officers killed, 2 wounded (including Mr Harris attached) 18 O.R. killed & 17 O.R. wounded. Some for him in all were recovered. To was Barrett Thompson were buried in the Rev. Parson near the Charge hutte Jones Trevernie Rd 17 — from shelter in HOUTHULST WOOD.	

HOUTHULST WOOD

6th (Sv) Bn. Duke of Cornwall's Light Infantry.

Army Form C. 2118.

WAR DIARY
or
INTELLIGENCE SUMMARY.
(Erase heading not required.)

Instructions regarding War Diaries and Intelligence Summaries are contained in F. S. Regs., Part II. and the Staff Manual respectively. Title pages will be prepared in manuscript.

Place	Date	Hour	Summary of Events and Information	Remarks and references to Appendices
Ypres	12/8/15		Nearly 10 miles away. It is not known whether the Germans had discovered our new [?] aeroplane or whether they were after an O.P. (Secret to be R.M.A.) which was then in the Tower of the Ypres Cathedral.	
		noon	The battalion left temporary refuge in the dugouts in the ramparts N.S.D. the MENIN GATE but during the afternoon took over the dug-outs S.D the MENIN GATE near the 43rd Bde H.Q.	
		2.30		
		5pm	from Some units of the VI Division. Camp sector: 16 officers & 16 trenches, 15 to Somersets & D.L.I. H	
	13/8/15		- " - The battalion with travers at G.I.A.7.6. Sect 28 troops	
Ramparts	14/8/15	Between	Digging & carrying fatigues to & trenches.	
	15/8/15	-		
	16/8/15	-	Ops repeated.	
	17/8/15	-	2/Lt Izard + taking parties & patrol to H.P.C. About 10 men slightly gassed by shell C, Sgt Phills [?] & G.G.C., 2/Lt Bennett joined & posted to B. Coy.	
			Men at on YPRES road near H.11. 2/Lt Bennett joined & posted to D.Coy.	
	18/7/15	-	Lt. J.A Carless reporting sick. G.S. C.6.6. 2 N.C.O.s gassed.	
	19/8/15	-		
	20/8/15	-	trans into Red Blue X retain. 5 prt gassed + command spy of A Coy.	
	21/8/15	-	& 4 [?] & evacuated to Dr. Hon. Caro &	
	-"-		not killed.	
	29			

6th (Ser) Bn. Duke of Cornwall's Light Infantry

Army Form C. 2118.

WAR DIARY
or
INTELLIGENCE SUMMARY.
(Erase heading not required.)

Place	Date	Hour	Summary of Events and Information	Remarks and references to Appendices
H.I.C.88	29.9.45		The Battalion marched from the rest billets and relieved the 5 K.S.L.I. in the trenches. We took over trenches H13 to H18ª. The front line was held by C & D Coys. Also two platoons A & B Coys (each less one platoon) were in support in F13 & F.H.P. between EAST LANE and railway. Bn. H.Q. at log dug-out at 210 6.7.6. Was F.O.O. also stayed.	
Trenches	30 Aug. 1.10am		Relief successfully completed at 1.0 am.	
	30	—	Enemy quiet. Some strays & trumps a trench mortaring by the enemy led to us quickly silenced by our retaliatory fire. During night 30 to 31st wire improved in front of H13-920. Work in support H16-H17.	
	31	—	Situation normal. Y. Wood shelled. M. Sun emplacement at H.15 damaged. 9 Cpl Bright (Lewis corporal) wounded. Both in trenches held up for want of sandbags and did not arrive at the place stated. The Coys in support and 2 Platoons & work in front line.	
	1 Sept.			

P. Barran Lt Col
2/1st Sept. 07

43/14

6k se l.2.
rot: 5

14th Kurunn

12/7693

Sept. 15

5-N

WAR DIARY
or
INTELLIGENCE SUMMARY.
(Erase heading not required.)

Army Form C. 2118.

Place	Date	Hour	Summary of Events and Information	Remarks and references to Appendices
Trenches	1 Sept	—	The day was quiet. During the evening A. Coy was moved out of S.H.Q. up to support trench F.2 on S. side of MENIN RD. Also Battalion H.Q. Bro Germain aeroplane	
—	2nd	4.70 am	Third Division on our right (i.e. S) commenced a heavy bombardment at 4 am, the enemy replied and did considerable damage to our trenches especially MUDDY LANE. F.2 was also heavily shelled but beyond leaving in a trench the damage was small. The telephone comm. holes guns wires thereby to the front. On the evening of the 2nd the Somersets relieved us. Rain was just delay confusion partly owing to the rain & new approved (i.e. MUDDY LANE being used as advanced instead of WEST & EAST LANES), parts now of	
S.H.Q. Q F.13	3rd	1.30 am	the presence of the guides. The relief was completed at 1.30 am & the Bn. went back to S.H.Q. at L.FARM — C. & D. Coys halfs battns 16 L. FARM (I. 15 c.8.8.), A.T.S. Coys 6 S.H.Q. & Bn. H.Q. as before 16 Coys dug in at I.10.a.6.55. The day was quiet.	
—	4th	—	Day quiet, working parties on S.19. & S.16 & comm. tr. from S.19 to F.A. wood. Enemy (?) the French right flung new enemy bombardment at 9.90 pm on night of 3/4th. No enemy crafts to show between P.20 and H.13	Roshamouth Wright MAJ & DCLI

Army Form C. 2118.

WAR DIARY
or
INTELLIGENCE SUMMARY.
(Erase heading not required.)

Place	Date	Hour	Summary of Events and Information	Remarks and references to Appendices
S/H Q.	5 Sept.		Very quiet. An new Rifle Battery was placed at night on S. end of F.13 near railway & trained to fire upon the S. End of NO MANS WOOD (I. 12, 6, 4, 5). [From lates information (Sept 1st '5 14) it was quiet N. of this point that the Germans had a large work in progress.] S.H.Q. had improved relaimed wiring from H.14 to Q.20 completed S.15 house into a fire house.	
	6 Sept		Situation quiet. F.13 dummies went unclaimed on S.H.Q. telephone cable from Bosn X. Rds to Y. Wood buried. Dug-outs prepared N.P.S. & section of a new Comm. Tr. to R.4 begun. S1.9 repaired	
	7 Sept		Day quiet. Bn. relieved on evening 7 – 8:15 by 5 K.R.L.I. Relief completed at 11.0 pm. Bn. returned to POPERINGHE by train leaving YPRES at midnight; & then marched to Rest camp at L.3.C near SAN JAN TER BIEZEN (Sheet 27)	
SAN JAN TER BIEZEN	8/5		Rest camp. Bn. inspected at 5pm by General Plumer. Lt Barraclough trans. by regiment from hospital. Captain Houghton joined from 1WR Coy. 2/Lt Cock joined from 1WR Coy.	
	9/5		[final entry, partly illegible] to YPRES.	

Signed [illegible] D 3 Officers & 266 O.R. by train night R by train [illegible]
A.D.S.S./Forms/C. 2118.

Army Form C. 2118.

WAR DIARY
or
INTELLIGENCE SUMMARY.
(Erase heading not required.)

Instructions regarding War Diaries and Intelligence Summaries are contained in F. S. Regs., Part II. and the Staff Manual respectively. Title pages will be prepared in manuscript.

Place	Date	Hour	Summary of Events and Information	Remarks and references to Appendices
SAN JAN TER BIEZEN	10 Sept	11⁵⁄₁₂	In rest billets, working parties as on 9th.	
	11		"	
	12		"	
	13		" Major Mercher returned from leave	
	14		"	
	15		Batt. relieved the 9th K.R.R.C. in trenches, RAILWAY WOOD sector	
			E. of YPRES.	
Trenches	16		Fairly quiet day. Work was begun on tonk and SAA stores and cut into SUNKEN ROAD preparation for later attack by 42nd L.I.Bde.	
	17		Our artillery bombarded enemy in the morning about 4 a.m. Enemy's reply feeble. Day otherwise quiet and work on stores. Lieut. J.A. Cate wounded.	
	18		Bombardment continued. Enemy's reply was vigorous and some damage done to trenches and casualties caused. Work on stores and also on repair of trenches.	
	19		Bombardment continued. Our trenches slightly damaged. 2/Lt J.S.F. Mann A.A.D.C wounded.	
	20		Bombardment about entrances all day. German reply effective in places and own injuries than before. Much damage to trenches. 2/Lt S.G.P. Cuddon-Kites and 2/Lt S.E. Gillette wounded.	for Mackay ? Galliard

1577 Wt. W10791/1773 500,000 1/15 D. D. & L. A.D.S.S./Forms/C. 2118.

WAR DIARY
or
INTELLIGENCE SUMMARY.
(Erase heading not required.)

Army Form C. 2118.

Place	Date	Hour	Summary of Events and Information	Remarks and references to Appendices
Trenches	21		Hostile artillery action to which enemy's reply became increasingly vigorous. Continued on special digging and construction, and a spasmodic damage to trenches. We kept up vigorous rifle and m.g. fire to prevent repair of enemy trenches.	
"	22		Artillery fire died down. He commenced a very quiet day. No marked advantage was taken from work as shown above.	
"	23		Artillery bombardments still predominates the situation. Withdrew above. Enemy's aeroplane active. Relieved at night by 9th R.B. Marched back to bivouacs near VLAMERTINGHE.	
Bivouacs	24		After 13 hrs out of trenches Batt. marched back to rampart YPRES, being in Divisional Reserve to the attack by 42nd Bde on German trenches N. of HOOGE.	
Ramparts YPRES.	25		In Ramparts. After success and failure of attack moved up from RAMPARTS to L.FARM dugouts about 10 a.m. Thence about 6.30 p.m. to G.H.Q. N. of YPRES - ROULERS railway.	
GHQ	26		Situation quiet. Work [illegible] begun on improving F.13 and improving communication and strengthening GHQ.	
—	27		Quiet day. Work as above.	

[signature]

Army Form C. 2118.

WAR DIARY
or
INTELLIGENCE SUMMARY.
(Erase heading not required.)

Place	Date	Hour	Summary of Events and Information	Remarks and references to Appendices
G.H.Q	28		Quiet day. Some heavy shrapnel on our left. Work 9 p.m. at night sharp. M.G. and rifle fire broke out beginning from the line just S. of HOOGE. A heavy exchange of artillery fire followed. Eventually all died down & situation was again quiet. Work continued as above.	
G.H.Q	29		Quiet day. Work continues as above. Relieved at night by – in part – by 7th R.B. Marched back to bivouacs nr VLAMERTINGHE. some	
Bivouacs	30		Refitting proceeded with. 2nd Lieut. en/Adjt. Roxburgh was went on leave.	Roxburgh Lieut

1577 Wt.W10791/1773 500,000 7/15 D.D.&L. A.D.S.S./Forms/C. 2118.

43/14

121/7431

6N.

14th Kuzun

6th scale.
vol: 6
Oct 15

Army Form C. 2118.

WAR DIARY
or
INTELLIGENCE SUMMARY.
(Erase heading not required.)

Place	Date	Hour	Summary of Events and Information	Remarks and references to Appendices
Bivouac VLAMERTINGHE	Oct. 1		Bivouacs	
"	2		"	
"	3		"	
"	4		"	
			Batt. relieved 7th E. Yorks in trenches W.N.W. of ST. ELOI, into sector where while Brigade was in trenches. 2/Lt. G.H. Faith went on leave. C & D Coys in fire trenches, A & B in reserve.	
Trenches	5		Quiet day. Began work on strengthening parapet in many places not bullet proof, on wiring and trench boarding of main C.T., and which dugouts for reserve companies, no history of parados - practically non existent	
"	6		Quiet day. Lieut. of Adj. RM Bannington-Ward returned from leave. Relieved above.	
"	7		Quiet day. Work as above continues.	
"	8		Some shelling without much damage to our trenches. Most shells burst behind. A & B Coys relieved C & D Coys in the fire trenches. C & D to reserve.	
"	9		Fairly quiet day.	
"	10		" " Some rapid fire taken up from our right as result of bombing incident. 2/Lt Faith rejoined from leave.	RM Bannington-Ward Lt. & Adjt. 6 Dec 15

1577 Wt.W10791/1773 500,000 1/15 D.D.&L. A.D.S.S./Forms/C.2118.

Army Form C. 2118.

WAR DIARY
or
INTELLIGENCE SUMMARY.
(Erase heading not required.)

Instructions regarding War Diaries and Intelligence Summaries are contained in F. S. Regs., Part II. and the Staff Manual respectively. Title pages will be prepared in manuscript.

Place	Date	Hour	Summary of Events and Information	Remarks and references to Appendices
Trenches	Oct. 11		Usual reciprocal trench mortar & bomb exchanges as on previous days. MG emplacements constructed.	
	12		Quiet day	
	13		We cooperated with rifle & m.g. fire in demonstration which took place along 2nd Army Front about 3.30 p.m. Our trenches slightly damaged by hostile fire which was slow in retaliation.	
	14		Quiet day. 9th R. Suss. Regt. relieved the Batt. which marched back (2 Cos. by train from VLAMERTINGHE) to rest bivouacs near WATOU, L.3.c.10.4 Sheet 27.	
WATOU	15		Bivouacs. Training in very muddy ground. Spit. etc. for physical recreation. Agmen started.	
	16		—	
	17		—	
	18		—	
	19		—	
	20		— 14th. (Light) Division passed into Corps Reserve.	
	21		—	

Resubmit W.D.
Lt. 1/Adjt
6/DCLI.

Army Form C. 2118.

WAR DIARY
or
INTELLIGENCE SUMMARY.
(Erase heading not required.)

Remounts W
Lt-/Adjt
6/DCLI.

Place	Date	Hour	Summary of Events and Information	Remarks and references to Appendices
WATOU	Oct. 22		In out billets. Training as shown above, together with work in camp construction, building of huts, drains? etc.	
	23			
	24			
	25			
	26			
	27			
	28			
	29			
	30			
	31.			

1577 Wt.W10791/1773 500,000 1/15 D.D.&L. A.D.S.S./Forms/C. 2118.

14 M/S Braun

6th sess.
vol: 7

D/
7708

Nov. 15

7n.

Army Form C. 2118.

WAR DIARY
INTELLIGENCE SUMMARY.
(Erase heading not required.)

6th Duke of Cornwall's L.I.

Place	Date	Hour	Summary of Events and Information	Remarks and references to Appendices
near WATOU L.3.c.10.4. (Sheet 27)	Nov. 1		Standing Camp. In huts and tents near WATOU. A Map reference in transfers Division to corps reserve. Batt. occupies with training (especially in grenades), route marches and building of huts. Several of the latter were taken into occupation. Camp very wet and muddy. Brick paths constructed.	
"	2.			
"	3.		Organization of Grenadiers into 2 Platoons, and Coy. grenadiers. the latter team no. platoons. Training as above.	
"	4.			
"	5.			
"	6.			
"	7.			
"	8.			
"	9.			
"	10.			
"	11.		The Batt. (less 3 platoons B Coy, A Coy and No.2 Platoon (grenadiers) moved to dugouts in CANAL BANK near YPRES C.25.d and I.1.a (Sheet 28). Here we relieved 7th KRRC and were attached to them, to 18th Infy. Bde., 6th Div. for purpose of digging and carrying. Dispositions: HQ, D Coy and 1 Platoon B Coy in dugouts on CANAL BANK EAST. No.1 Grenade Platoon in dugouts in SWITCH CANAL (I.1.6 and d.). C Coy garrisoned the KAAIE SALIENT defences (I.2.c) and was not available for working parties. 2 Machine Guns were in position just N. and S. of ST JEAN RD. and 2 in reserve in CANAL BANK dugouts. A Coy. 3 platoons B Coy. and No.2 Platoon Grenadiers were in Standing Camp D. Rest area (next to our late camp) under Maj STERICKER, with 6/KOYLI.	Ref. Sheet 28
CANAL BANK	12		Carrying parties and digging parties provided for 2nd Durh.L.I. and Essex Regt. 1st Leicesters occupied dugouts in CANAL BANK.	

J. Stevens Lt.Col.
cmdg 6/DCLI

Army Form C. 2118.

WAR DIARY
or
INTELLIGENCE SUMMARY.
(Erase heading not required.)

6th Duke of Cornwall's L.I.

Place	Date	Hour	Summary of Events and Information	Remarks and references to Appendices
CANAL BANK etc.	Nov. 13		C Coy worked on KAAIE SALIENT defences. Party of 60 men of D worked on dugouts in CANAL BANK. Working parties provided overnight for 2nd D.L.I. and Essex R.	Ref- Sheet 28
"	14		In anticipation of expected German attack, extra SAA issued. Working parties returned early, having been provided as above. All precautions taken.	
"	15		Passed off quietly. Working parties as above. Few shrapnel shells burst near our end of CANAL. No damage.	
"	16		Working and digging parties as above.	
"	17			
POPERINGHE	18		Moved back a day earlier than expected. Joined the others at Batt. in billets at large Hop Warehouse by POPERINGHE railway station - south of the line.	
"	19		In billets. Resting and refitting.	
"	20		Moved into Divl. reserve at hut camp, A 30. Considerable trouble and confusion caused by being ordered to CAMP A and countermanded by 6th Div. to camp B. In huts. A 30.	
"	21			
Trenches	22		Moved to trenches Bg. B 10 Sub A, Sqa and ST JEAN and ST JEAN around WIELTJE, relieving 6/KOYLI. HQ at HASLER HO, ST JEAN. Dispositions:- Bg. B 10. A Coy, B Coy, ½ C Coy, No.1 Plat. Grenadiers. Sub A. ½ C Coy. Sq A. D Coy. Trenches in a bad condition. Communication trenches impassable. Front line visited seven times after by night. Front line trenches very wet and everything much worse needed on them, but pumping in the absolutely flat ground is difficult. 10/E. Durham L.I. (43rd L.I. Bde.) on our left. 9th KRRC (42nd Bde) on our right.	

WAR DIARY
or
INTELLIGENCE SUMMARY.
(Erase heading not required.)

Army Form C. 2118.

6th Duke of Cornwall's L.I.

Place	Date	Hour	Summary of Events and Information	Remarks and references to Appendices
Trenches	Nov. 23		A quiet day. Coy in Sq A used for carrying of large quantities of RE stores (especially sandbags and revetting hurdles) each night. Work also on thickening parapet. Thick fog late in the afternoon with hard frost, when iflares and flares set in. Our snipers were active and successful when fog lifted. Careful precautions against "French fire" taken. Men wore thigh gum-boots, many changes of socks, and hot feet greased daily. Drying dugout provided in each trench, one also at HQ and one at Transport Camp.	Sheet 28.
"	24		Fairly quiet day. Weather having cleared, 14th Div. artillery (after relief of 6th R. Div.) was able to spot and so doing produced some retaliation. Parapets raised and thickened and hand bombs laid in piles. Revetment continued. Patrol investigated LRB. Cottage. N.F. found.	
"	25		A normally quiet day. Our snipers made an impression on the enemy, who seemed more cautious about showing himself. Patrols went out from Bq and B to C in front of our wire and to report on suspected enemy sniping pits and work in front of their lines. Wire was reported fairly good. No enemy seen where suspected. Relieved by 6/KOYLI at night. HQ lark G Bn. Dispositions. HQ in farm S. of YPRES-VLAMERTINGHE road. H.W. central, and one Coy in FRENCH DUGOUTS just N. of road at same part, 2 Coys to MACHINE GUN FARM M.5.A.7.7. 1 Coy, 1 Platoon Grenadiers and Machine Gunners in dugouts CANAL BANK WEST.	
"	26		Working parties totalling 370 provided to 10/DLI and 6/KOYLI at night.	
Trenches	27		Much sniping at 48 hrs relief. Later relieved 6/KOYLI in trenches.	
"	28		Very quiet day. Work continued on lines as before. Very hard frost made work and pumping difficult. Ground frozen over a foot.	

A. [signature] Lt Col.
and 6/DCLI

Army Form C. 2118.

WAR DIARY
or
INTELLIGENCE SUMMARY.

(Erase heading not required.)

6th Duke of Cornwall L.I.

Instructions regarding War Diaries and Intelligence Summaries are contained in F. S. Regs., Part II. and the Staff Manual respectively. Title pages will be prepared in manuscript.

Place	Date	Hour	Summary of Events and Information	Remarks and references to Appendices
Trenches	Nov 29.		Very quiet day. Three parties had first aid made Trenches very difficult. Relieved by 6/KOYLI at night and returned to same billets as in 2nd inst. Dispositions same except that No. 2 Platoon Grenadiers also went to MACHINE GUN FARM.	
Billets.	30		In Billets. Some shelling towards us.	

J. Browne
Lt. Col.
cmdg 6/DCLI

1577 Wt.W10791/1773 500,000 1/15 D. D. & L. A.D.S.S./Forms/C. 2118.

WAR DIARY
6ᵗʰ BATT D.C.L.I

DECEMBER 1915

Army Form C. 2118.

WAR DIARY
or
INTELLIGENCE SUMMARY.

(Erase heading not required.)

Instructions regarding War Diaries and Intelligence Summaries are contained in F. S. Regs., Part II. and the Staff Manual respectively. Title pages will be prepared in manuscript.

Place	Date	Hour	Summary of Events and Information	Remarks and references to Appendices

1577 Wt.W10791/1773 300,000 1/15 D. D. & L. A.D.S.S./Forms/C. 2118.

Army Form C. 2118.

WAR DIARY
or
INTELLIGENCE SUMMARY.

(Erase heading not required.)

6th Duke of Cornwall L.I.

Instructions regarding War Diaries and Intelligence Summaries are contained in F. S. Regs., Part II. and the Staff Manual respectively. Title pages will be prepared in manuscript.

Place	Date	Hour	Summary of Events and Information	Remarks and references to Appendices
SUPPORT TRENCHES	1		The Batt. were in support. Headquarters and 1 Coy. H. 11 Central. 1 Coy at machine gun farm. The Batt. arrived up to the trenches at ST JEAN.	B. 10
TRENCHES	2		The day was fairly quiet. Saw shells from a field howitzer fell very near H.Qrs. and we retaliated. Enemy aircraft were active and turned by our m/c guns & Rifles	
	3		Quiet on our front but on the R. and L. Enemy Artillery seemed busy. It was noticed at night that the enemy were showing artillery and shooting very lights severely followed this.	
	4		Little occurred to mark this day differently to the preceding days. The Batt. were relieved at night. The being done without loss.	
	5		The Battalion in support as the 1st, providing working parties as required.	
	6			
	7		The Battalion went up into front line trench as before.	
	8		Enemy Artillery began in the early morning from 8.15 a.m. until 9.30. Grenades were thrown by catapult & trench Mortar. Both 5th in our front trench	
	9		At 10 a.m. WEILTJE VILLAGE was shelled and small arms on our front trench was badly knocked in. A number of casualties caused. Ritchie was delayed brave Fanny Aircroft	

M.N. Mark O/c/16 2nd Lt
6 D. C. L. I.

1577 Wt. W10731/1773 500,000 10/15 D.D. & L. A.D.S.S./Form/C. 2118.

WAR DIARY
INTELLIGENCE SUMMARY.

Army Form C. 2118.

6th Duke of Cornwall L.I.

Place	Date	Hour	Summary of Events and Information	Remarks and references to Appendices
TRENCHES	9		Enemy shelled from from N.E. and a section of 5"-9" Howitzers from due E. at 11.30 a.m. Shelled S.JEAN considerably. The outfall was inspiration to S9a when several dug outs were blown in and casualties. All the shells passed over our firing line. Artillery retaliation was good.	
	10		Enemy bombed B.10 about 9 a.m., also trench mortar knock mortars fell in. At 11 a.m. S.JEAN was given much attention but no serious damage was done or any casualties. Prompt retaliation was fired both in the day when asked for. One Coy. has 2 platoons was withdrawn from S9a owing to its bad state.	
	11		The enemy have shelled at various times from 2 a.m., it was particularly fierce about 6 a.m. Shells registered on the S.JEAN ROAD frequently but not small shells. The Regimental Office was blown in but beyond 2 slight casualties no damage was done. Trench Howitzers shelled the ground behind S9a between 1.30 and 2.30 p.m. Knowing it is noticeable that they were mostly duds. The Battalion was relieved the night with only 1 casualty, it is highly probable the enemy also relieved, red lights went up in the early evening and for some hours it was exceedingly quiet. Much heavy rain was experienced in the later 7 days.	

Lt. Colonel M.N. Kaye 6th D.C.L.I.

Army Form C. 2118.

WAR DIARY
or
INTELLIGENCE SUMMARY.

(Erase heading not required.)

6th Duke of Cornwall L.I.

Instructions regarding War Diaries and Intelligence Summaries are contained in F.S. Regs., Part II. and the Staff Manual respectively. Title pages will be prepared in manuscript.

Place	Date	Hour	Summary of Events and Information	Remarks and references to Appendices
B. CAMP	12		The Batt. came back to rest, as working parties visited the trenches hats. Pioneer fatigue improved the Camp and also transport camp. General training was done.	
	13		As above	
	14		As above	
	15		As above	
	16		The Battalion on this day moved back to await orders. work was started on partly finished huts, paths, drainage by One Coy. per day. General training was done.	
	17		As above	
C. CAMP REST AREA	18		As above	
	19		During the early morning from 11.30 am. heavy firing was heard. Shortly after 7pm orders were received to "stand to". This was done the whole day and until next morning. No further orders were issued. Several enemy aircraft were observed.	
	20		Work was carried on in Camp had no one left camp until his return.	
	21		Work was carried on and general training commenced again.	
	22		As above but rather furious rainy outdoor parade training.	

M. Myers Lt Col
6. D.C.L.I.

Army Form C. 2118.

WAR DIARY
or
INTELLIGENCE SUMMARY.
(Erase heading not required.)

6th Duke of Cornwall's L.I.

Place	Date	Hour	Summary of Events and Information	Remarks and references to Appendices
C. CAMP	22		Work was done. General training	
REST AREA	23		As above	
	24		As above	
	25		Working parties were engaged during the morning cleaning Camp and on French Railway was laid. Operation orders for the expected movement came in during the afternoon. Preliminary arrangements were made; during the night 25/26 Christmas was observed by giving the troops extra food and pudding. A concert at night was provided, the men being extremely cheerful. This was cancelled.	
	26		The Operation Order No. 38 43rd Bde. received the previous day was cancelled giving some disappointment in the morning, later Orders came in and preparations was made to relieve the 49th Division	
	27		The Camp was inspected by the Corps Commander who was pleased with conditions	
A'CAMP	28		The Battalion on this day moved up to the area near VLAMERTINGHE several shells, shortly after our arrival fell within 400 yards of the Camp, doing no damage	
TRENCHES	29	4.30	The Battalion left the Camp to go to the right of the Jeketi instructions given by the	

W.W. Orr Capt. 6 DCLI

Army Form C. 2118.

WAR DIARY
or
INTELLIGENCE SUMMARY.
(Erase heading not required.)

6/2 Duke of Cornwall[?]

Place	Date	Hour	Summary of Events and Information	Remarks and references to Appendices
	29		43rd Bde. The front line trenches D.21 & D.22 were on the Ridges of this Sector held by two Coys at 3 "O'Clock". The trenches were in bad ground and considerably. Very full of water, causing much discomfort to troops although an Arch duck boards provided. It was in this area that the enemy made a gas attack on the 19th of this month. The 3rd Wor[c]k storm were relieved. Suffering many casualties. The night was very dark and the relieving was not affected without casualty. Wind N.W.	
	30		The day was generally quiet, about noon a 5.9" shell fell near our support line, the falling in the trench doing no damage. Several shells passed near Headquarters but none fell near. There were no casualties throughout the day. At night a Patrol under 2/Lieut Jenner Clarke went out and found this today to be a front so taken, (further in front condition) was taken from him & it was stated January 19th would give the idea that he may have been posted early in the year.	
	31		Artillery was active on both sides, shells passed over in section but far fell within it. No damage was caused. Wind S.E. and unfavourable to any gas attack	(signed) Frank Maud Major 6/DCLI

6TH BN DCLI

List of Officers
&
Men

20/12/15

6TH. (SERVICE) BATTALION DUKE OF CORNWALL'S LIGHT INFANTRY.

NOMINAL ROLL OF OFFICERS, WARRANT OFFICERS, N.C.O'S & MEN.

RANK & NAME.	COMPANY.	REMARKS.
~~Lieut. Col. T. R. Stokoe~~	A.	In England.
Lieut. Col. J. L. Swainson	A.	
Major. A. W. Stericker	B.	
Captain N. A. G. Quicke	C.	
Captain L. C. Heygate	A.	
Captain G. H. Forty	B.	
Captain A. H. Hopkinson	C.	
Captain H. Cartwright	D.	C.L.231 20/12/15
Lieut. R. M. Barrington-Ward	D.	
Lieut. (Hon) F. Stallard	B.	
Lieut. G. B. Brookes	C.	
2/Lieut. C. A. Orchard	D.	
2/Lieut. T. G. Lilley	B.	
2/Lieut. R. K. Spurrell	A.	
2/Lieut. J. W. Jenner-Clarke	C.	
2/Lieut. R. H. Tyack	A.	
2/Lieut. A. H. Bennett	D.	
2/Lieut. W. J. Hill	D.	
2/Lieut. T. E. Andrews	B.	
2/Lieut. E. C. Codyre	D.	
2/Lieut. M. Higman	B.	
2/Lieut. J. Truscott	B.	
2/Lieut. H. B. Paull	C.	
2/Lieut. C. E. Coley	B.	
2/Lieut. R. Oakley	A.	
2/Lieut. A. M. Reep	C.	
2/Lieut. H. S. Reynolds	C.	
2/Lieut. R. Lawry	C.	
Lieut. E. J. Morton		R. A. M. C. Attached.

(Contd

REGTL. NO.	RANK & NAME.	REMARKS.
5961	R. Sgt. Major H. Hill	
7383	C. Sgt. Major P. Fuller	
6306	" J. Bonham	
9633	" E. Whitnall	
8731	" C. Weech	
5804	O.R.Q.M.S. A. Marshall	At Base, Rouen.
8166	R.Q.M. Sgt. R. G. McVitty	
5527	C.Q.M. Sgt. E. F. Moore	
5524	" D. W. Lavie	
0608	" A. W. Bird	
0635	" A. I. Morgan	Depot, D.C.L.I., Bodmin
6902	Sgt. F. Cutler	
5702	" G. Tomlinson	
5507	" F. Genge	
2057	" C. S. J. Harris	
0423	" R. Treloar	
2037	" G. M. Silver	
7592	" E. Parkin	
2924	" H. Carter	
0970	" G. Croucher	
9562	" S. Simmonds	
9287	" C. Pearce	
2245	" S. E. Johnson	
3812	" W. Dimelow	
2108	" H. Coney	
1472	" W. H. Smith	
0751	" D. Gregory	
8742	" W. Carter	
1821	" W. G. Crabbe	
6661	" R. Chandler	
3674	" L. J. Carter	
587	" C. Stuart-Beet.	
7955	" J. C. Turpin	
0764	" W. E. Devoil	
4601	" S. H. Kingsmill	
0665	" A. Humphries	
0706	" F. Knowles	
4599	" T. G. Kingsmill	
1313	" W. Battie	
XXXX	XX XXXXXX	
6419	" D. Warren	
8871	" W. B. Millington	

(Contd)

15377	Sgt.	H. Taylor
10648	"	E. Leonard
11128	"	B. Hutton
5165	"	J. D. Candy
9838	"	A. Harrod
11632	"	C. B. Christmas
5978	"	R. Howe
14477	"	J. W. Henderson
5852	"	W. Pritchard
7552	L/Sgt.	V. Ross
9306	"	J. Elliott
6034	"	C. S. Lilley
3488	"	E. Knight
15696	"	W. Walters
11828	"	E. R. Lewin
12400	"	A. E. Russell
9154	"	E. Heathcock
10652	"	J. Elmer
10656	"	E. Stevenson
12125	"	G. H. Dowsett
10904	Sgt.	C. A. Pullen-Burry
5261	Cpl.	F. H. Bradley
4215	"	J. Downey
14003	"	H. Grimshaw
11455	"	W. J. Bartlett
10847	"	A. G. Webb
14356	"	J. Harris
11392	"	H. L. King
12473	"	O. W. Taylor
11851	"	E. Poole
10775	"	T. France
10821	"	F. Oxenham
11562	"	E. Rogers
11884	"	G. Bewsher
10914	"	W. Harvey
10870	"	T. C. Joslin
16287	"	F. Allcock
15567	"	G. Ranford
15002	"	L. Snowden
14932	"	R. E. Mason
10956	"	W. T. Samwells
10558	"	H. W. Hatcher

(Contd)

11865	Cpl.	G. H. Jones
10836	"	E. Dixon
10964	"	W. Smith
11845	"	G. Young
10288	"	G. Reeves
8444	"	A. White
21155	"	H. Hoskyns
15358	"	G. H. Tunbridge
10186	L/Cpl.	C. Murdin
11778	"	F. J. Stuart
12302	"	H. W. Stammers
10819	"	F. T. Davies
11868	"	A. Lee
19542	"	A. V. Sheppard
11418	Cpl.	N. T. Robbins
19632	L/Cpl.	J. W. Oliver
14536	"	P. J. Jones
11481	"	J. Thomas
12079	"	L. Taylor
12031	"	S. N. Wear
10672	"	J. Lown
0776	"	W. Weeks
11463	"	S. C. Hill
9282	"	J. Wilkin
14855	"	A. J. Pryor
10897	"	J. Dudman
10900	"	A. Mason
11276	"	A. O'C. Birch
10906	"	A. J. Crisp
11908	"	A. Turk
17196	"	S. J. French
17318	"	A. W. Morris
10544	"	J. Ellis
16946	"	A. Probert
11496	"	H. Swain
10537	"	W. Hopkins
5822	"	J. Browning
15066	"	G. Schofield
11242	"	E. L. Daniels
11326	"	T. Jeffs
14069	"	R. O. Goldsmith
12186	"	A. Vowles
13802	"	J. Donovan
11837	"	A. Reddick
22661	"	J. H. Golby
11484	"	B. Bundell
10713	"	A. Cole
11015	"	C. D. Smith
10708	"	G. Martin

(Contd)

10660	L/Cpl.	J. Hill	
11387	"	D. Beere	
11909	"	W. T. Robbins	
4804	"	G. Spence	
18536	"	H. Smart	
11931	"	A. E. Chambers	
11197	"	A. Lloyd	
11927	"	J. C. Quinn	
11804	"	M. Clayden	
11590	"	J. Mercer	
10567	"	J. Huggard	
10357	"	J. Jobbins	
10712	"	A. Bradley	
5606	"	G. Green	
10962	"	F. Courtney	
11934	"	A. Burling	
13065	"	P. Salt	
18635	"	B. Salmon	
15171	"	J. W. Reeves	
10711	"	A. Alexander	
12353	"	W. Youdale	
10827	"	B. S. Taylor	Acting C.Q.M.S.
10626	"	W. Dawson	
11860	"	A. E. Cross	
10502	"	G. McGuire	
9284	"	W. Hosking	
9746	"	T. Brown	
15923	"	W. G. Crowl	
12098	"	W. J. Thomas	
19714	"	A. Savage	
11700	"	F. V. Ivey	
12440	"	A. H. Stephens	
11859	"	J. Carling	
9827	"	G. Medlin	
11066	"	W. Albon	
19302	"	W. Wyke	
11704	"	C. V. Coate	
11354	"	L. W. Pillinger	
11121	"	C. A. Liggett	
12246	"	J. Jenkins	
12459	"	R. R. Troubridge	
11569	"	C. W. Hellard	
12129	"	S. Farmer	
8052	"	A. Daw	
18414	"	J. Taylor	
15736	"	A. A. Wood	
12218	"	R. F. Prince	
8987	"	A. Jones	(Contd)

11456	L/Cpl.	H. A. Collis
9080	L/Cpl.	S. Arnold
19808	"	F. Richards
9532	"	A. H. Thomas
11584	Pte.	R. H. Avery
13016	"	S. J. F. Ayles
16755	"	M. Alderson
11675	"	S. A. V. Atkins
10935	"	H. B. Allen
11502	"	R. Anderson
16751	"	J. H. Allen
11524	"	A. G. Anderson
17663	"	A. Arnold
19798	"	H. Allen
19821	"	T. Ashton
21219	"	G. Aylward
21849	"	J. Allen
21156	"	W. Aspin
12925	"	J. Alcock
10893	"	J. Allen
18659	"	W. Aldridge
12768	"	A. E. Ames
11648	"	S. Allum
11102	"	C. W. Anderson
10654	"	A. Ashman
20886	"	E. C. Adams
21281	"	W. Arthur
16910	"	W. Baylis
13479	"	W. J. Blake
10912	"	E. Block
17096	"	W. Brent
21547	"	L. Brocklebank
5908	"	G. Brundish
10869	"	J. H. Bard
10428	"	J. Brackenbury
11623	"	A. B. Bacon
12051	"	W. Billingsley
11563	"	A. Brinklow
10799	"	J. Brown
18686	"	G. H. Baston
4917	"	F. Burnett
10299	"	E. Brooks
19099	"	G. Biggs
21089	"	J. Bray
21574	"	A. Black

(Contd)

21288	Pte.	F. J. Blackburn
19532	"	J. Bould
21196	"	G. Bullock
10440	"	J. Brown
21304	"	C. XXXXX Barnes
17194	"	F. Barnard
10451	"	L. Ball
17019	"	L. H. Bloxham
17020	"	A. Bloxham
11029	"	C. Bertram
12209	"	R. Brazill
17980	"	R. Buckingham
19621	"	W. Bertram
11499	"	T. Beavis
10572	"	C. W. Birt
13539	"	H. C. Byrne
10557	"	D. Barker
10921	"	A. Battey
16930	"	H. Brand
21284	"	A. Bennett
12458	"	A. Banyard
21308	"	A. Brewer
12908	"	T. Barron
21061	"	W. Bowden
21004	"	J. Barker
19571	"	H. Bunce
19909	"	A. Bridgeman
6973	"	C. W. Bayes
11154	"	F. Burton
20863	"	A. G. Bryan
10766	"	G. H. Bowley
10698	"	J. Berryman
22161	"	A. Barnes
5468	"	J. Brand
10960	"	A. E. Braddy
5441	"	R. Baker
12226	"	A. H. Boswell
10585	"	A. Broad
20872	"	C. Budge
10617	"	H. Barrett
5222	"	J. Barry
21864	"	C. Brawn
11419	"	L. Byron
10980	"	E. Biggs
13260	"	A. G. Bailey
11408	"	L. Broadway
18806	"	W. Bloomfield
19235	"	J. Bennetts

(Contd

10779	Pte	T. J. Brooks	
11666	"	T. H. Blyth	
21194	"	G. Boxall	
11118	"	C. E. Bellinger	
12139	"	F. A. Burgess	
10550	"	H. Bromwich	
19262	"	S. Boobyer	
9497	"	J. Branby	
11214	"	A. C. Barker	
19744	"	J. Bolge	
12297	"	C. A. Blake	
5686	"	F. Brown	
9760	"	A. G. Brown	
21084	"	J. Baker	
10868	"	L. F. Chamberlain	
16697	"	G. Carr	
11071	"	T. J. Coles	
12845	"	H. Coles	
10824	"	F. Coghlan	
11736	"	A. E. Croucher	
12916	"	A. Coleman	
11836	"	B. S. Crisp	
5681	"	R. Clark	
19196	"	J. Curnow	
19764	"	C. Clothier	
19177	"	J. Cullen	
20868	"	G. Carruthers	Absentee.
19831	"	T. Coventry	
5691	"	J. Cutting	
21089	"	C. Chown	
21402	"	W. Clegg	
21536	"	T. Crowther	
2145	"	C. W. Cox	
11441	"	W. Costin	
19376	"	J. C. Chalmers	
19305	"	W. Clark	
21334	"	F. Corkhill	
19308	"	E. Cox	
21177	"	A. Coleman	
21082	"	W. Crisp	
19836	"	W. Chapman	
18831	"	J. Collick	
19829	"	A. Capp	
21110	"	G. Camp	
12177	"	D. Coward	
10439	"	R. J. Chapman	

(Contd)

21404	Pte.	S. Claridge
16871	"	J. Crocker
15671	"	S. F. Cheese
19716	"	H. Cornish
21073	"	H. Crowther
10768	"	H. Crawford
11893	"	G. Crouch
11635	"	J. Cash
13751	"	W. G. Campbell
12362	"	F. Chantler
16672	"	H. Crowhurst
11129	"	A. Clay
11357	"	D. Carr
10995	"	R. F. Collier
12171	"	J. R. Coxall
10234	"	C. Coleman
19639	"	G. Carnell
12190	"	D. Collier
10687	"	P. Dwyer
21542	"	C. Danning
10590	"	J. M. Duncan
10693	"	G. Downing
13531	"	A. Day
XXXXX		
21096	"	G. Carr
17523	"	A. Cave
13656	"	C. T. Collins
10561	"	G. Cox
8615	"	F. H. Clark
5809	"	H. E. A. Cook
10810	"	W. Cranfield
19674	"	A. Childs
19618	"	A. Clark
7294	"	J. Cook
17556	"	N. Casey
10233	"	F. Chappell
19658	"	C. Cooper
5392	"	C. J. Cox
10014	"	W. Chapping
21124	"	S. A. Clark
13658	"	W. Conlan
17160	"	W. Cassam
13635	"	H. Carroll
17219	"	W. Crews
10069	"	E. Cucksey
21147	"	J. Cross
17831	"	C. Dunstan

(Contd)

21985	Pte.	C. Dicks
5747	"	W. Daley
5797	"	W. DeLacy
17119	"	H. Dingle
17116	"	F. H. Dowrick
12482	"	J. E. Davis
9692	"	C. A. Dewson
17060	"	J. Dymond
9624	"	T. Dawkins
10823	"	G. Dives
21170	"	C. W. Dyer
10788	"	F. Doswell
12363	"	F. Dobson
11581	"	J. Dewey
10915	"	H. Dennison
21229	"	C. W. Dodd
19692	"	J. Davis
10863	"	R. Davies
10805	"	A. Dovey
19752	"	J. Dowd
19671	"	J. Downing
13777	"	J. Ducker
10852	"	W. Donnelly
10634	"	A. H. Dunning
21313	"	A. Danns
19561	"	C. Dartnell
21581	"	J. Daniels
11886	"	F. Ellis
10398	"	A. Evans
17133	"	F. Allcock
21348	"	A. J. Ellery
21317	"	F. Everett
10298	"	R. Emery
19541	"	J. Edmonds
21063	"	E. W. Emery
17212	"	C. Edyvane
13892	"	S. J. Eyre
13895	"	E. Everett
18492	"	T. C. Elder
19818	"	J. Edyvane
10202	"	J. Eames
19706	"	C. Earley
17555	"	E. Fidock
13014	"	F. J. Faulkner
10709	"	W. E. Cox
~~13842~~	~~"~~	~~E. Froggatt~~
10768	"	W. Finch

(Cont'd)

21194	Pte.	F. Fairburn
21294	"	A. Fielden
19371	"	P. J. Fraser
10465	"	A. Fletcher
16721	"	H. Farrow
13939	"	L. Franklin
19551	"	W. E. Foulser
21160	"	J. Flynn
5744	"	W. Ferris
21407	"	W. Farne
19769	"	A. Franklin
10744	"	C. Fisher
11169	"	C. Faulkner
11000	"	J. Flint
11202	"	E. W. Fellows
11360	"	W. Freeman
15893	"	F. Fulker
15904	"	G. Fairchild
13940	"	A. E. Fullard
11275	"	A. Flynn
19700	"	J. F. Fisher
19653	"	C. French
10592	"	S. J. Fee
21074	"	J. Farrar
21095	"	A. Fraser
19103	"	G. Flack
10808	"	W. Fincher
10934	"	D. P. Gordon
11654	"	J. T. Guy
14027		F. J. Goodwin
5779	"	J. Gatter
11896	"	F. G. Green
5485	"	E. C. Gentle
12044	"	A. V. Golden
17558	"	R. Gurney
14080	"	E. J. Glenn
19171	"	J. Gill
19317	"	B. Gossage
6172	"	G. Griffiths
9895	"	A. G. Greenhead
19718	"	E. Gaylor
19786	"	H. Gaskin
4750	"	J. Graham
17871	"	T. Goodman
10750	"	C. J. Green
21108	"	C. H. Green
18751	"	J. Gteen

(Contd)

6409	Pte.	A. Grovier
21374	"	J. Godfrey
17054	"	J. Grose
19834	"	S. Grove
21128	"	S. Gaunt
21315	"	R. Gillson
14048	"	A. C. Griffin
21362	"	J. Guise
13941	"	H. Garrod
14061	"	A. Gearing
11944	"	G. Gibbs
10996	"	L. George
11650	"	A. Gittens
11861	"	F. Gibbs
11544	"	S. E. Green
19559	"	F. Grieve
18556	"	E. Grenham
10602	"	H. Griffin
10504	"	A. Gregory
10638	"	H. Gooderham
10777	"	G. Goodram
5674	"	J. Greenhalf
19696	"	A. Graham
12216	"	W. Green
12207	"	A. Guerin
12231	"	T. J. Gibbs
14066	"	P. Groombridge
11210	"	P. C. Gill
8589	"	H. Galpin
11624	"	G. Goldsworthy
11273	"	R. Harris
18682	"	W. Heather
19587	"	W. Hawtin
21339	"	A. Horley
10527	"	C. Hocking
11751	"	W. J. Harmer
10798	"	A. Hurst
5424	"	W. H. Hawtin
10802	"	J. H. Hughes
11597	"	S Hovells
11891	"	A. H. Hobbs
10509	"	J. Holliday
10473	"	S. Howard
10831	"	T. Haynes
10821	"	H. House
10927	"	W. T. Hemming

(Contd)

17111	Pte.	S. Hunkin
12260	"	J. O. Hayward
17606	"	J. Hay
12803	"	E. Hillett
18470	"	J. Hackett
17131	"	F. R. Hicks
19721	"	E. Hicks
19693	"	F. Hutchins
17281	"	A. Henwood
8886	"	H. Hawthorn
4109	"	H. Higgs
21370	"	G. Howe
19791	"	E. J. Harris
16714	"	W. J. Hosking
5222	"	P. Hall
21041	"	W. Hooper
10783	"	J. Hemmings
18629	"	L. H. Hamilton
19647	"	R. Howarth
21842	"	J. Hoffman
11722	"	A. H. Herbert
17038	"	A. Heard
11262	"	A. Hooper
10377	"	F. Hamid
17290	"	C. F. Hayes
15878	"	H. Hopkins
10459	"	J. Harris
21530	"	W. Holbert
18950	"	J. Hargreaves
18855	"	H. Hazell
19630	"	A. Hives
21369		R. H. Harrison
21218	"	J. Healey
20881	"	A. Hamilton
18623	"	A. Hills
7785	"	W. Hunt
11317	"	J. Hamblyn
11201	"	H. Hardman
10719	"	H. Harris
11541	"	T. Howard
11942	"	J. Hatch
14375	"	J. D. Harris
14313	"	F. Hunt
12146	"	L. H. Hayward
12060	"	C. Hill
10425	"	M. How

(Contd)

10736	Pte.	T. Harnetty
10963	"	G. Hammond
10647	"	W. Hodges
21292	"	W. Haynes
10704	"	T. J. Hall
17629	"	E. C. Hall
22401	"	J. Hyman
21332	"	H. Hewman
21287	"	W. Howlett
12197	"	W. Harvey
12444	"	B. S. Hobbs
17870	"	C. F. Haynes
19669	"	F. Hemmens
17170	"	C. Hewitt
11209	"	W. Hill
11142	"	J. T. Holliday
8552	"	J. Hopkins
11287	"	W. J. Hall
21069	"	A. Hill
19126	"	G. Hall
21537	"	W. Harris
5825	"	E. Hodson
21470	"	S. Hooper
12399	"	J. G. Isaac
19661	"	E. Irvin
11867	"	F. G. Jones
5761	"	W. Johnson
5167	"	G. A. Johnson
12086	"	H. A. Jordan
10539	"	F. Jones
10662	"	S. Julien
11119	"	F. H. Jones
19324	"	I. Jones
11699	"	C. Johannsen
11476	"	A. J. Joseph
11555	"	C. W. Jauncey
11466	"	F. Jennings
9788	"	M. Jones
19279	"	T. Jarvis
21275	"	H. Jarvis
12446	"	F. E. Jewell
~~18517~~	"	~~A. Joynes~~
15915	"	E. J. Jones
11535	"	B. James
10939	"	H. Jarden
11670	"	F. Johnson

(Contd)

12198	Pte.	F. Johnson
21306	"	W. Joynes
11695	"	F. A. Jones
19142	"	B. Johnson
20374	"	W. Jenkins
10574	"	C. Jenkins
8703	"	C. Jenkins
11566	"	W. T. Jones
11813	"	E. H. C. Johnson
10684	"	A. Jack
17159	"	G. Julien
19553	"	G. Jennings
21347	"	R. A. Jones
11058	"	J. L. Johnston
21148	"	W. A. Jones
18641	"	W. H. Jacobs
21775	"	S. Johns
5751	"	C. Knowles
21290	"	C. Knowles
18884	"	T. A. Karn
19617	"	O. Keegan
19549	"	W. G. Knight
10925	"	A. T. Killen
21321	"	P. Kelly
14618	"	W. Kynaston
19286	"	E. Kempson
11923	"	C. Knight
17022	"	W. King
21204	"	R. J. Kelly
19720	"	C. KEARNEY
17866	"	J. C. Knight
10678	"	C. W. Kenny
11921	"	C. T. Louden
11832	"	J. A. Law
9225	"	W. Leighton
21356	"	F. Lock
3435	"	J. Lawrence
21179	"	C. Lambert
10438	"	H. Langman
18458	"	S. Langdon
11497	"	H. J. Lavis
11157	"	R. A. Lees
11155	"	J. H. Lees
11239	"	H. Longdon
10716	"	J. Little

(Contd)

21572	Pte.	F. Louth
18624	"	A. Leach
10427	"	B. Levine
17178	"	J. Lashbrook
11924	"	A. J. Leverett
14688	"	T. Lambert
10733	"	B. E. Lilley
19539	"	C. Lett
11257	"	L. G. H. Lee
10725	"	G. Leslie
11299	"	W. Lewis
19811	"	H. Lampshire
21579	"	E. A. Lennox
21872	"	H. Marsh
21187	"	J. Melbourne
10929	"	C. E. Mead
14953	"	W. J. Mignot
12948	"	W. F. Martin
11389	"	D. Murphy
10749	"	A. Moore
10930	"	F. Moment
5751	"	W. Marsh
12941	"	G. L. Maxfield
17128	"	C. Medland
4873	"	R. J. Mutch
7845	"	E. Mullender
16680	"	A. Matthews
17577	"	G. Morcombe
21113	"	A. Midgeley
10326	"	T. Melson
21092	"	H. Mann
21318	"	R. Mannell
10538	"	D. McCarthy
19552	"	W. R. Maloy
21083	"	W. Mears
21393	"	W. C. Martin
21231	"	W. McNamara
22906	"	T. McCarthy
21291	"	J. Maryan
21216	"	W. Mayor
10909	"	A. E. Mesure
17003	"	T. Mason
10741	"	W. McLean
10658	"	J. Mears
10013	"	H. Mills

Contd)

21391	Pte.	A. J. Minson
18619	"	A. J. Matthews
21015	"	J. Miles
9136	"	W. Morris
11318	"	J. Maloney
16663	"	R. Matthews
19815	"	J. Mitchell
11123	"	W. Massingham
12352	"	C. E. Milson
10703	"	J. J. Matthews
18643	"	E. Meredith
19311	"	J. Mullins
19841	"	E. W. Matthews
19556	"	M. May
9707	"	W. Mateer
11325	"	J. Meloy
19409	"	D. Maxwell
19840	"	E. C. Menear
19698	"	C. Mastin
21187	"	J. Melbourne
21400	"	H. Middleton
21887	"	R. MOOrlen
21068	"	E. Minter
10636	"	A. H. Marshall
17368	"	F. W. Marden
10948	"	J. McDonald
14979	"	T. Miller
19702	"	C. Morgan
11827	"	E. Mostell
11677	"	W. J. Millward
17340	"	D. Macarino
22447	"	J. McLlaine
21316	"	G. Milne
14941	"	T. E. Manderson
11049	"	R. Meadows
11292	"	F. J. Martin
10959	"	A. W. Mattingley
21401	"	A. Newman
10445	"	R. D. Newman
15282	"	J. Nelson
16655	"	H. C. Noy
5344	"	W. E. Nicholas
21346	"	W. Newcombe
15274	"	J. Nield

(Cntd)

21142	Pte.	D. North
12180	"	G. Nash
10612	"	J. Nicholas
18015	"	T. Nichols
19012	"	W. H. Nash
12404	"	A. Noel
18532	"	W. J. Nevitt
10424	"	C. Neale
10896	"	A. F. Osborne
15547	"	G. Oakley
19186	"	R. J. Olds
5048	"	J. Orr
19855	"	W. Older
19234	"	E. J. Olver
17149	"	W. Orams
10908	"	R. Perry
8950	"	R. Perry
10793	"	W. Payne
14801	"	T. R. Payne
10495	"	H. J. Page
10924	"	S. E. Pillbrow
14757	"	W. Pike
20897	"	J. Pike
11820	"	F. J. Pink
17123	"	M. Parkin
17798	"	D. C. Polkinghorn
9057	"	J. Pedrick
21098	"	A. Peters
21548	"	W. Papworth
19734	"	E. J. Pascoe
14809	"	H. Parsons
16677	"	C. W. Prickett
18615	"	J. Partridge
12041	"	H. Perks
10613	"	S. Price
19793	"	F. Phillips
22349	"	W. Peddle
22350	"	T. Pople
18649	"	W. J. Phillips
21078	"	E. Parsons
19620	"	G. Pratt
22085	"	W. H. Peters
11401	"	H. Pearce
11395	"	J. Percy

(Cntd)

17423	Pte.	J. Preston
15578	"	J. Porter
11303	"	E. J. Perrin
14793	"	J. Patston
19846	"	J. Piper
18571	"	A. Paterson
11170	"	F. Perrins
10586	"	W. Perkins
5486	"	W. Pascoe
14831	"	J. M. Philp
21076	"	J. W. Pearson
10853	"	F. C. Poppy
19667	"	A. E. Portingale
21344	"	J. Poulton
22399	"	G. R. Powell
12210	"	T. Palmer
21172	"	A. G. Pollard
16715	"	A. E. Prout
20880	"	J. Place
11151	"	J. Parsons
5900	"	W. Philp
21320	"	G. A. Parsons
22909	"	F. T. Parsons
10842	"	B. Perry
21219	"	J. Rochester
5730	"	H. Reynolds
5748	"	J. Read
18557	"	W. C. Roberts
18336	"	W. Roberts
10923	"	S. Roberts
19545	"	J. Rudman
9725	"	W. Ridewood
10395	"	C. Rea
12894	"	E. Richards
11298	"	G. Racknell
11676	"	W. G. Rann
10933	"	W. C. Rowe
16157	"	W. C. Rowe
17964	"	H. Raybould
21301	"	A. Reading
22449	"	T. Reeves
21097	"	G. Rich
9324	"	F. Robinson
19719	"	T. Rumbol
5195	"	W. Rosin

19699	Pte.	A. Relf
9836	"	F. Roberts
11014	"	R. Rolfe
21867	"	J. Roach
18636	"	C. Rawlinson
19230	"	A. Roberts
11892	"	H. Rush
11926	"	H. Redford
11342	"	H. Robinson
10720	"	H. Richard
15164	"	F. J. Reeves
17340	"	H. Russell
7289	"	G. Rowley
11568	"	M. Richard
10825	"	H. B. Raynor
11634	"	R. A. Rushforth
15564	"	E. Richardson
20867	"	A. Redgard
21466	"	R. S. Roberts
10875	"	H. J. Skellett
10890	"	C. Slade
14998	"	S. F. Spurrell
12369	"	R. C. Spurrell
15080	"	J. A. Simmons
19710	"	J. Smith
10822	"	J. Sullivan
11919	"	W. Shore
11596	"	J. Sawyer
10862	"	S. E. Sharpe
10512	"	J. Smith
11525	"	T. M. Smith
11841	"	W. P. Sayers
10834	"	R. W. Mead
18907	"	G. R. Souch
19691	"	W. H. Speller
18340	"	R. Stone
6468	"	C. Sansome
21533	"	F. Sculthorpe
11255	"	J. T. Saddington
9819	"	W. Smith
19550	"	C. Spinks
21293	"	F. Sharpe
21227	"	F. G. Smith

(Contd)

10449	Pte.	M. Searle
17012	"	M. Searle
10623	"	F. Stokes
19579	"	A. Skinner
12073	"	W. Stratford
11243	"	H. L. Skinner
19832	"	S. W. Salloway
21274	"	C. Shelley
11600	"	J. Snook
21229	"	J. Silcox
5939	"	E. Stannard
21065	"	W. Stuckey
10051	"	H. Swain
21087	"	J. Seeley
20871	"	J. Saunders
11855	"	H. Smith
9118	"	P. Sheldon
11589	"	G. Sims
18550	"	E. Smith
21072	"	W. Stanley
21164	"	J. Solley
19701	"	E. Sargent
19329	"	A. H. Smith
19650	"	R. Smith
11162	"	C. E. Smith
21886	"	J. Stringer
12203	"	E. Speller
19276	"	A. Sharp
18551	"	R. F. Smith
11713	"	J. Steven
21101	"	A. Slater
18217	"	P. J. Snowden
18640	"	R. W. Spurin
19331	"	R. Stevenson
11347	"	T. Stiff
21091	"	G. Schofield
8220	"	A. Scotchmer
10966	"	E. J. Samwells
10589	"	G. Smith
11683	"	T. Sturt
21321	"	P. Smith
17155	"	A. Scales

(Contd)

0770	Pte.	C. Sharman	
2199	"	J. W. Sims	
0047	"	H. Smith	
1390	"	C. Sweet	
7562	"	G. E. Silverside	
1095	"	W. Sutton	
1093	"	E. Smith	
0883	"	G. H. Sells	
2370	"	R. C. Sanger	
1510	"	J. E. Simkin	
1570	"	J. H. Sumner	
0325	"	T. Stallard	
9313	"	C. J. Sherwood	
7581	"	J. E. Sherwood	
5091	"	W. H. Saunders	
2343	"	G. Stone	
21138	"	W. Stay	
22176	"	J. Simmonds	
1913	"	F. G. Steele	
0669	"	A. E. Singler	
20874	"	P. Squires	
9682	"	J. Smith	
0649	"	P. Snow	
5899	"	S. E. Stone	Absentee
0730	"	R. H. Tozer	
0844	"	B. Taylor	
3964	"	C. E. Trevatt	
1490	"	C. Town	
16909	"	J. Todd	
17664	"	C. Tunstall	
5319	"	J. Touboulic	
6133	"	M. Tucker	
0552	"	R. Thorne	
9629	"	H. Taylor	
1742	"	G. F. Taylor	
9570	"	T. Tutton	
18589	"	A. Thompson	
29000	"	L. Thomas	
16315	"	F. E. Travers	
20884	"	A. Timmins	

(Contd)

19842	Pte.	E. Toms
11166	"	W. Tennant
8659	"	W. Turner
18536	"	W. H. Turner
11633	"	R. Todd
11165	"	W. Townsend
10350	"	A. Towse
19670	"	J. Taylor
18591	"	F. L. Turner
18545	"	G. H. Trevillion
10563	"	C. Taylor
19163	"	E. Thompson
21539	"	C. H. Taylor
22663	"	R. Trand
21580	"	F. Trevillion
19113	"	H. G. Thomas
21538	"	C. Turner
19159	"	J. Underwood
13009	"	F. C. Underhill
10909	"	W. A. Vincent
15882	"	F. Vincent
10690	"	E. Vale
10747	"	F. Vaughan
19660	"	A. G. Vernum
21326	"	G. Veale
12189	"	W. E. Wilmer
11626	"	S. Willmott
11415	"	J. Wagstaff
15706	"	T. West
18616	"	G. Warne
17806	"	H. Williams
19736	"	J. Williams
19741	"	E. Wilson
12923	"	T. W. Woodman
11868	"	A. K. Walding
21482	"	J. Willis
11522	"	W. J. Whaley
5707	"	G. R. Winter
20911	"	W. Wilkinson
10400	"	H. Warren
19135	"	R. J. Williams
11027	"	E. Wakeley
10757	"	W. Whitehead
11857	"	W. Wingrove

(Contd)

15686	Pte.	S. Ward
16886	"	H. W. Warren
19806	"	W. Walters
10480	"	W. Watkins
10881	"	J. E. Williams
20898	"	L. C. Williams
11800	"	S. F. Wilson
10450	"	W. Whell
9594	"	R. Wright
15699	"	A. C. Warren
15810	"	S. Webb
17187	"	R. H. Williams
11143	"	W. E. Webb
19578	"	H. Webb
11470	"	F. Wells
10971	"	H. E. Williams
18428	"	J. Williams
16735	"	L. White
17208	"	A. G. Watkis
15737	"	P. J. Wolton
21184	"	C. Way
15506	"	B. Woodbine
11171	"	F. Williams
11592	"	K. Westcott
12410	"	F. A. Wiggins
11793	"	R. White
10736	"	S. Walker
10975	"	F. R. Williams
10950	"	D. Wilson
11288	"	B. Whitmore
13018	"	H. H. Wyatt
16886	"	J. Warren
21405	"	A. Wright
21161	"	F. Weller
19224	"	C. Wonfer
9408	"	E. Wheeler
19600	"	H. Wakeham
11730	"	A. Warner
21169	"	T. Williamson
11109	"	F. Wood
15557	"	H. Witney
19227	"	W. Wallace
19459	"	J. Ward

(Contd)

19844	Pte.	E. Watkins
21545	"	G. Warner
19347	"	F. Willis
19728	"	F. Woolley
21571	"	C. H. Walding
19762	"	J. F. Woollcott
5505	"	W. J. Wall
19814	"	J. West
18693	"	G. Wellsman
10534	"	F. G. Walling
19882	"	J. Watkins
10855	"	S. Worby
12289	"	A. E. Worwood
21186	"	R. Yes
10958	"	F. Young
19740	"	F. Zelley
11602	"	G. Burdock
10734	"	F. Beach
21123	"	J. Ashton
10603	"	P. Addison
14695	"	J. H. Lee
11644	"	S. White
19666	"	C. East
11149	"	L. Fellows
10644	"	J. H. Rawlings
19664	"	G. Russell.

20th. December 1915.

.... Lieut. Colonel.
Commanding 6th. Battalion D. C. L. I

43 B/6

WAR DIARY or INTELLIGENCE SUMMARY

Army Form C. 2118.

Place	Date	Hour	Summary of Events and Information	Remarks and references to Appendices
Trenches in C.14.D Sheet 28 1:10000	Jan 1		A quiet day. Some slight shelling round DAWSON CITY and of CANAL BANK near Bridge 4. At night a band was heard playing behind the enemy lines.	Sheet 28
	2		Aged quiet. D22 shelled in the morning and establish in the scale of place to no advantage.	"
	3		The usual ineffective shelling. Machine gun traverses D21 & D22.	
	4		Nothing to report from the front line. The 6th Somerset L.I. relieved us the night. The batt. returned by trains and march route to Rest Camp No. 4, A.8.B.10.4. (Sheet 28) Training and refitting. Detachment sent to live at 146th. Inf. Bde Tpt Camp to clean it up.	"
Rest Camp	5		—	
	6		—	
	7		—	
	8		— . On night 8/9 relieved the 1/KSLI (64. Div) in a new sector now taken over from the 66. Div. by 14 Div. which this entails its front, headr in C.15.C. Dispositions:- Three bombing posts S. and SE. of MORTELDJE Estaminet and in front of our line. One platoon each in WILLOW WALK S.19.A and B.17.A. & Platoon S.16.B and ½ B. S.15.B with 1 Platoon Grenadiers there section (in the dunes [not]). One Company B.16. 2 Companies (less 2 platoons) and 1 Platoon Grenadiers in the Batt. HQ in CANAL BANK. 2 Platoons in CYCLIST FARM B.20.a.1.1.	
Trenches in C.15.C etc.	9		War rests. There was no communication other than telephonic with the front line. When the telephone has gone, Batt. HQ have to wait till dusk for re-establishment of communication. We were cut off for 5 hrs one [night] in the front line. Trade under relaxation wholesale.	

WAR DIARY or INTELLIGENCE SUMMARY

Army Form C. 2118.

Place	Date	Hour	Summary of Events and Information	Remarks and references to Appendices
Trenches C.15.e etc.	9 and		Following working parties, details to work nightly in front line, from CANAL BANK. 1 Officer and 50 to WILLOW WALK, 1 Officer and 30 to S.I.6.B, 1 Officer and 50 to B.16. Party also was employed on head (dim) dugouts on CANAL BANK and B.H. Hd. also supplies for X10. Work was begun on Head (dim) dugouts on CANAL BANK and B.H. Hd.	Sheet 28 (2nd Army Sheet 1) (10⋅000)
	10.		A rather lively day. The trench on the left of the Division were active with rifle fire and bombing. B.16 was shelled. Aeroplanes were much in evidence. Enemy with front line again broke many huns. A very large unexploded trench mortar bomb was brought from a front line the MORTELDJE ESTAMINET, and sent to Corps for inspection. Work resumed of relaying tracks made in last few days. Wiring - which was very unfortunate here - was pushed on.	
	11.		Quiet. Normal shelling of our trenches.	
	12.		An then usually quiet. Patrols reported that the enemy wire was in good condition.	
	13.		Artillery fairly active. Enemy shelled B.16 about 3 p.m. Retaliation obtained from our field guns firing H.E. shell. About 9 p.m. in listening post in front of B.16 Capt was a German on patrol. He showed a good deal of fight and unfortunately had to be brought to submission by a message bullet from his own rifle. He was Augustus HIRSCH, 234t Res. Regiment came to this colonies July 1915, sent to this front in November 1915, between Ypres Infantry	
	14.		at our front. We were relieved by 6th Som.L.I. in this night, and returned to Camp 4.	
Camp 4.	15.		Resting and refitting.	
	16			
	17		Working party of 250 sent up to to work and carry for R.E. in trenches.	
	18		Training	
	19			

WAR DIARY
INTELLIGENCE SUMMARY
(Erase heading not required.)

Army Form C. 2118.

Place	Date	Hour	Summary of Events and Information	Remarks and references to Appendices
Trenches C.15.c	20		Went by troops to trenches and relieved 6th Somerset L.I. in the same sector. Saw B. of E. Platoons were taken from CYCLIST FARM are running into CANAL BANK where C.coy in in support had now been put up and not its X10 in a working garrison. Night very quiet. Another very quiet day of which there is little to report. At night Sgt. C.A. Pulken Bcoy.	
	21.		6/DCLI who had already distinguished himself by a reconnaissance (when he found enough tripping wire) single handed of the German fire-trench at C.15.c.9.8. went out to secure a specimen of German carroline wire ashes by 2nd. Army. This he did not great difficulty owing to the exceptional shortness of the wire. He incountered a patrol of 3 on the way back coming from NO MAN'S COTTAGE. Shots were exchanged. He got the artillery successfully on to a German working party near CANADIAN FARM. Enemy whistlers for stretchers.	
	22		At 9 a.m. a disappearing bombardment on heavy and field guns of the HIGH COMMAND REDOUBT (C14B and C15A). Enemy retaliated on CANAL BANK and TURCO FARM.	
	23.		Quiet. Our patrols active. MORTELDJE inspected and no traces of the enemy found. ADMIRAL'S ROAD was patrolled. Exceptionally quiet night. An aeroplane fired on in the early morning (1.15 a.m.) of this day and brought down POPERINGHE and ELVERDINGHE. In the early morning an officer's patrol went out from B.6.	
	24.		telephone wire attaches to officers uniform. A patrol went out under cover of mist. They saw 3 Germans at 9 a.m. and the officer's patrol went out under cover of mist. They saw 3 Germans walking two transport etc. and a train. At 7 p.m. C.S.M. F.H. KEELING with Sgt.	

HBB
Capt LtD.C.L.I

Army Form C. 2118.

WAR DIARY
or
INTELLIGENCE SUMMARY.
(Erase heading not required.)

Instructions regarding War Diaries and Intelligence Summaries are contained in F. S. Regs., Part II. and the Staff Manual respectively. Title pages will be prepared in manuscript.

Place	Date	Hour	Summary of Events and Information	Remarks and references to Appendices
Trenches	24 Cont.		Capt. PULLEN-BURRY took out three bombing parties to deal with the enemy's bombing post which MORTELDIE arranged wires around all, but they were too early for garrison of the post which had not the time out. That post was fully reconnoitred and signs of permanent occupation found there. It will be dealt with in another way as soon as portable land-mine fires from an advanced post. Artillery dry. Heavy shelled the approaches to the trenches very persistently and regularly during the night.	
	25.			
	26.		Carey St communication trench and BURNT FARM huts damaged. We were relieved at night by the 6/Som L.I. Returned to Camp 4.	
	27.			
Camp 4	28.			
	29.			
	30.		250 working party for RE in trenches.	
	31.			

[signature] H.A. Hammersley
Lieut-Col 6th D.C.L.I.

6th D.C.L.I.
14th Div.
Vol 10

10N.

6th Batt. The Duke of Cornwalls Light Infantry.

WAR DIARY
or
INTELLIGENCE SUMMARY

Army Form C. 2118.

Place	Date	Hour	Summary of Events and Information	Remarks and references to Appendices
No. 4 Rest Camp. A 8. B. 10. 4 Suez.	January 31.		In rest.	Sheet 28 1/40,000
"	February 1		"	
"	2		We moved up (to make "bivouacs as far as BRIELEN) to relieve the 6th Somerset L.I. in trenches C.15.c. Night very quiet and relief successful.	
		10.30 a.m.	The Enemy attacked the 10th Durham L.I. on our left, taking the attack long breaches simultaneously against D.20 and D.21 trenches. The preliminary bombardment was heavy and our front line came in for a good deal of it, fortunately with few casualties owing to our front line being lightly held. It the lines the alpha and machine gun fire of the Durhams kept the attack within the limits to the enemy who got as far as our parapet. HQ and CANAL Bank Coy's stood to during the attack. A very successful bombardment by guns of all calibres of the High Command REDOUBT opposite the DURHAMS trenches. There was presumably not a prime coincidence with the enemy's attack. Rest of the day quiet.	
	3.		Quiet day. Stood to activity in the part of our own and the enemy's aeroplanes. Work continued in trenches and on CANAL BANK where a number of large French (circular iron) dugouts have by this time been completed.	
	4.		Nothing of consequence to report save desultory shelling of CANAL BANK.	

WAR DIARY or INTELLIGENCE SUMMARY

Army Form C. 2118.

6th D.C.L.I.

Place	Date	Hour	Summary of Events and Information	Remarks and references to Appendices
Trenches	February 5.		A good deal of hostile shelling. WILLOW WALK, B.16 and CANAL BANK were all shelled in the morning and afternoon. Very effective retaliation from D47, R.F.A. They seemed retaliated with Fd. Gun H.E. on enemy front line, securing 14 direct hits on his trench which the occupants were seen to leave. An enemy listening post was (defence Co. on Jany 24th) was seen at about 2 p.m.	
	6.		The enemy were still shelling fairly hard. Doubles Emplacements on WILLOW WALK and B.16 with E. Fd. Guns and 4.2 field Hows Trgs. B.R. trench trenches hit little other damage ensured. Our retaliation was again effective. A patrol under Sgt. PULLEN-BURRY places a phone [?] interval machine gun mode by the Bgde. Fld. Co. R.E. at our weakest in the enemy listening post early in the morning. (It was fused electrically at 2.45 a.m. and demolished the listening post, which — we fear — was unoccupied at the time.	
	7.		A noisy day but little damage up to D. Bridge 4 over the CANAL suffers heavily. Shelter. B.16 again damaged by shell fire. P.R.I. reports that the damage done in the early morning on land division was extensive. It was noted by us that we were relieved at night by the 16/Som. L.I. on the same night on [?] (later on relief of January – The enemy appears to observe the same interval as ourselves Six day company relief, every three days). 26 Nights of 20th, 23rd, 26th, 29th in (noted by Somerset) 1st, 4th, 7th [?] have noted no particular quiet.	

A.D.S.S./Forms/C. 2118.

6. D.C.L.I.

Army Form C. 2118.

WAR DIARY
or
INTELLIGENCE SUMMARY.
(Erase heading not required.)

Place	Date	Hour	Summary of Events and Information	Remarks and references to Appendices
	February			
Handler	7		Returned (by 'buses from BRIELEN) to No. 4 Hut Camp.	
No. 4 Hut Camp	8		In camp resting and refitting.	
"	9		"	
"	10		March to "A" hut "VLAMERTINGHE" by road. Route taken via 10E. Dickebusch, 10E. Duke L.I. in that camp. "A" huts" are on N. side of POPERINGHE-YPRES ROAD just W. of VLAMERTINGHE.	3
"A Huts"	11		In "A Huts"	
"	12		Moved early by train as far as POPERINGHE. Thence by road via WATOU to billets 1½ miles N. of HOUTKERQUE. The 20 L.I. (Light) Division (6th L.I. Bde) was late on the roads and consequent confusion made marching slow. 7th D.C.L.I. passed us in WATOU—there was an attack by day on the Divisional front/— we knew nothing of it till next day.	A.S.Ree
Billets in HOUTKERQUE (Sheet 27)	13		Billets.	
	14		" Rifle camps opened. Company route marches	
	15		"	
	16		Billets. Training + refitting.	
	17		—	
	18		Lt. Col. T.R. STOKOE rejoined from England (W.O.)	

Army Form C. 2118.

WAR DIARY
or
INTELLIGENCE SUMMARY.
(6 - D.C.L.I)

(Erase heading not required.)

Instructions regarding War Diaries and Intelligence Summaries are contained in F. S. Regs., Part II. and the Staff Manual respectively. Title pages will be prepared in manuscript.

Place	Date	Hour	Summary of Events and Information	Remarks and references to Appendices
	February			
Billets N of HOUTKERQUE Sheet 27	19		Billet.	
	20		—	
	21		—	
	22	3 a.m.	Marched off at 3 a.m. to ESQUELBECQ station.	
		9 a.m.	Entrained for the South.	
		6.30pm	Arrived at LONGUEAU, suburb of AMIENS. Went in motor lorries to VIGNACOURT where we billeted. Very cold weather, 5°F in, will snow later.	Ref: LENS II 1/100,000
VIGNACOURT	23.		In billets.	
BEAUVAL	24.	3.40 a.m.	Warned at 3.40 a.m. to march at short notice. Marched for BEAUVAL. Frozen muddy roads and steep roads made it very hard marching. Left for troops who carried full "bomb kits" and for transport accustomed for 9 months to the flat YPRES country. Billeted at BEAUVAL. Close billets, as the town was very full of troops. Snow fell all night.	
COULLEMONT	25.	10 a.m.	Marched for billets at COULLEMONT. Very trying march. Roads frozen and snow falling continuously. Detailed a company to assist transport. Roads busy thanks to disorganized French and British motor and other traffic. The 16 mile march took from 10.15 a.m. to 5.45 p.m.	
"	26		In billets.	
"	27		In billets. Thaw set in.	
SIMENCOURT	28		Marched to billets at SIMENCOURT, relieving a battalion of the 252nd of the French Inf. Regiment in the billets.	
"	29		Marched at 11 p.m. from billets to AGNY where we relieved the battalion in reserve of the 207th French Infantry Regiment. Battalion billeted through the village.	

Wt. W10791/1773 500,000 1/15 D. D. & L. A.D.S.S./Forms/C. 2118.

WAR DIARY
INTELLIGENCE SUMMARY. 6th D.C.L.I.

Army Form C. 2118.

Place	Date	Hour	Summary of Events and Information	Remarks and references to Appendices
AGNY	March 1		Quiet day. Began work with B Coy. in defences of AGNY, one Coy. on B line behind 6/Som L.I.	Ref sheet 51 B 1/40,000
"	2		Few shells into N.W. end of village. Work continued by day.	
"	3		Nothing to report.	
"	4		" by night.	
"	5		One Coy moved up to CHEMIN CREUX dugouts (French Map 1/5000) to work on B line and CT's under 10/D.L.I.	
"	6		Quiet day. Work continued.	
"	7			
"	8			
"	9			
"	10		Relieved 6/Som. L.I. in trenches G1 - G12. Two Coys and ½ Grenadier Coy front line. One Coy and ½ Grenadier Coy in support. Later assisted by 1 Coy 10/DLI to work on B line.	
Trenches	12		Quiet day.	
"	13		— Some shelling of G11 & G12.	
"	14		— More active sniping.	

WAR DIARY or INTELLIGENCE SUMMARY.

6th D.C.L.I.

Army Form C. 2118.

Place	Date	Hour	Summary of Events and Information	Remarks and references to Appendices
Trenches	March 15		Nothing to report	Sheet 51.B 1/40,000
—	16		55th Division on our right carried out a short on enemy saps opposite their left Batt., a Territorial Batt. of the King's (Liverpool) Regt.	
—	17		Quiet day. Relieved by 6th Som. L.I. at night and marched back by Coys. to BERNEVILLE.	
BERNEVILLE	18		In billets. Resting and refitting. Supplies Town guards and fatigues.	
—	19			
—	20			
—	21			
—	22			
—	23		Relieved 1st Som. L.I. in trenches G1–G2. Three Coys and ½ Grenadier Coy in front line. One Coy & ½ Grenadier Coy in support. The latter were assisted by 1 Coy 1st Som. F.I. to work on B line. Every weather fine arose. One casualty while relieving – Capt. M. a Buck. Relief complete at 11.20 p.m. If very quiet day. No Artillery fire on either side. At night machine guns getting but no casualties. (Pol. of Moore closes which so wells in have being covered) Snowed all night to a depth of 3 inches.
Trenches	24			

Private 6th D.C.L.I.

WAR DIARY
INTELLIGENCE SUMMARY.   1st D.C.L.I.

Place	Date	Hour	Summary of Events and Information	Remarks and references to Appendices
Trenches	25th		Weather fine. Snow still on ground. Enemy fired two (2) 4.2 shells into side of Communication Trench (Gun St) Our aeroplanes fairly active.	Sheet 51.B 1/40000
"	26		Weather still fine + snow still on ground. Quiet day there being little Artillery or machine gun fire. Carrying parties of 40 men detailed to R.E.	
"	27		Enemy shelled our front line with Trench mortar + about 20 77s + shells. We retaliated with Trench mortar (47A) 12 rounds of Shrapnel + 12 rounds. H. Explosive. Rained very hard most of the night.	
"	28		A quiet day. Enemy shelled Battalion dump carrying two (2) Casualties in 1st Somerset L.I. Dark night soft ground slight rain + machine gun active	
"	29		Enemy shelled front line with Trench mortar + about 6 77 into still damaging front parapet. Weather fine. Relieved by 1st Somerset L.I. + completed by 6.50 p.m. Enemy quiet while relief was taking place. 10 Casualties billets in ANZIN.	

WAR DIARY
or
INTELLIGENCE SUMMARY. 6 D C L I

Army Form C. 2118.

Place	Date	Hour	Summary of Events and Information	Remarks and references to Appendices
AGNY	30th		Weather fine. H Q + 2 Coys (B+C) + Grenade Coy billeted in AGNY preparing village defences. 2 Coys (B+C) Coys 'A'+'D' in Brigade Reserve in dug-outs on Chemin Creux. 'A' Coy furnishing working parties for 6th Somerset L.I. + 'D' Coy furnishing working parties for 10th Durham L.I. Enemy quiet during day. Two machine guns were very active at Anquet from C15 10 p.m. but the machine guns were very active at Anquet from C15 10 p.m.	Sheet 51B 1/40000
"	31		Weather fine. Battalion billets + working as on the 30th. Very little enemy activity. Heavy machine gun fire at night from about 8 to 10 p.m.	

To A.G. Office
  Basra

I forward herewith War Diary
for the month of April
marked Recent, Registered post

5-5-16   Hallard / Capt
                        Comdg 6/D.C.L.I

WAR DIARY
or
INTELLIGENCE SUMMARY.

Army Form C. 2118.

XIV
1/ D.C.L.I   Vol 12

Place	Date	Hour	Summary of Events and Information	Remarks and references to Appendices
AGNY	1916 APRIL 1st		Weather fine. AGNY shelled heavily by enemy between 1.20 & 1.50 p.m. with little success, beyond damaging a few dug-outs. Between 7.30 & 8.30 p.m, enemy machine guns active as usual. No casualties.	
"	2		Weather fine. AGNY again shelled by enemy (Shrapnel). Our own & enemy & our own machine guns active between 7.30 & 8 p.m. Owing to enemy hollow observation from BEURAIN, AGNY is becoming a popular spot for retaliation.	
"	3		Weather fine. CHATEAU AGNY shelled about 11 a.m. with about 30. high shrapnel. Night quiet.	
"	4		Weather dull. Enemy quiet. Machine guns less active during the evening. Relieved French somewhats at dusk.	
In Trenches	5		Weather fine. Enemy quiet, but at 9.30 p.m to 10 heavy shrapnel were fired into French G 8 – 9 mounds between each shot. Retaliation asked for. Enemy labels to be using dummy flashes. Officers patrol reports very lights were	12N

Army Form C. 2118.

WAR DIARY
or
INTELLIGENCE SUMMARY.

(Erase heading not required.)

1st D.C.L.I.

Place	Date	Hour	Summary of Events and Information	Remarks and references to Appendices
In Trenches	5th (Continued)		fires (dummies) were sent up 200 to 500 yds behind front line. Wireline fires fairly active between 8 & 9 p.m.; Trench mortars active against A.G.N.Y. No 2. Soft Trench Howitzers - one bursting in Soft head, shattering one of our bombs with many fragments but did not detonate it. A New Zealand Officer (Lummis) was severely or seriously hurt. A Spy! He has been listening to enemy runners. He turns out to be another officer, the suicide of an officer. – Capt. Quake.	
— " —	6.		Weather fine. Enemy very quiet during day, night. Quite a lot of shown in old trenches S. of CHEMIN CREUX, in order to draw enemy's fire & remove the trenches. No result.	
— " —	7.		Weather fine. At G.11. parapet & parados badly damaged by enemy Trench mortars. An officer reports that he keeps account of running fire in G.4. from his dug-out.	
— " —	8.		Weather fine. Moderate trench gun fire. At 1.30. a.m. our 18-pdrs fired 3 Shrapnel Shells into enemy working parts at G.3. Cries of wounded were heard.	

Army Form C. 2118.

WAR DIARY
or
INTELLIGENCE SUMMARY.   6th D.C.L.I.
(Erase heading not required.)

Instructions regarding War Diaries and Intelligence Summaries are contained in F. S. Regs., Part II. and the Staff Manual respectively. Title pages will be prepared in manuscript.

Place	Date	Hour	Summary of Events and Information	Remarks and references to Appendices
In Trenches	9th		Weather fine. Moderate machine gun fire. Enemy quiet during the day.	
"	10		Weather fine. Machine gun fire, Artillery active. Our Intelligence Sergeant - S.C. Queen-Berry - shot by sniper. Relieved by Somerset L.I. + Battalion then moved to BERNEVILLE.	

Army Form C. 2118.

WAR DIARY
or
INTELLIGENCE SUMMARY.

6th Bn D. of Corn? L.I.

(Erase heading not required.)

Place	Date	Hour	Summary of Events and Information	Remarks and references to Appendices
BERNAVILLE	April 11		Rest in Billets	
"	12		Rest in Billets	
"	13		Rest in Billets	
"	14		Rest in Billets	
"	15		Rest in Billets	
"	16		Rest in Billets. Relief postponed until night of 14-15. owing to bombardment of the CH^T. MAIGRE by the CH^T. MAIGRE	
"	17		Companies paraded at 4.30 pm to relieve the 6th Somerset Light Infantry in the front line trenches. The relief was carried out without incident and completed about 11.30pm	
"	18		Several showers of rain fell during the day. The enemy shelled Trench G.12. Hys. Enemy Machine Guns were active during the night. No casualties	

Capt 6th D of Corn L.I.

Army Form C. 2118.

WAR DIARY
or
INTELLIGENCE SUMMARY.
(Erase heading not required.)

Instructions regarding War Diaries and Intelligence Summaries are contained in F.S. Regs., Part II. and the Staff Manual respectively. Title pages will be prepared in manuscript.

6th Bn of Gloster R.

Place	Date	Hour	Summary of Events and Information	Remarks and references to Appendices
	April 19th		Weather. Pouring practically the whole of the 24 hours. Enemy Machine Guns active at night. No Casualties.	
	20th		Weather. Rain fell very heavy during the night. Enemy shelled S.12 and Communication Trench S.1 Street but was silenced by our 18 pounders of A.4.Y. Battery. No Casualties.	
	21st		Weather. A few showers of rain fell during the day. During the afternoon the French Trench Mortar Batteries registered on the CHAT: MAIGRE; the enemy retaliated on S.12. Our 18 pounders retaliated for the shelling of and trench mortaring of S.12. No Casualties.	
	22nd		Weather Dull. There was considerable hostile machine gun fire during the night. An enemy's working party was heard in front of Trench S.12. They were fired on by one of our Lewis Guns which prevented further work. Casualties one man accidentally wounded.	

L.D.Mitcal
Lieut Col Comdg 6 Glosters

WAR DIARY
or
INTELLIGENCE SUMMARY.

(Erase heading not required.)

C. N. D. of Corps L. L.

Place	Date	Hour	Summary of Events and Information	Remarks and references to Appendices
	April 23rd		Weather fine. French 6.12 came in for it usual amount of shelling at about the usual hour. Enemy's Machine Gun again active during the night. Reply by 6" howitzers opened during 9ft H2 Bde relieving on our left. No casualties.	
	24th		Weather fine. Enemy shelled Mill in AGNY firing 68 shells round 14 direct 4 direct hits. Relief carried out without incident and completion at 8.30pm. No casualties.	
AGNY	25th		Weather fine. Enemy shelled the outskirts of AGNY with little success	
-"-	26		Weather fine. Enemy's machine guns been active during the night. Casualties nil.	
-"-	27th		Weather fine. Enemy shelled AGNY between 6.30pm and 9pm with little success beyond damaging a few buildings. Machine guns active. Casualties one man wounded.	
-"-	28		Weather fine. Enemy shelled the outskirts of the village. No casualties.	

Army Form C. 2118.

WAR DIARY
or
INTELLIGENCE SUMMARY.
(Erase heading not required.)

6th D. of Corn. L.I.

Place	Date	Hour	Summary of Events and Information	Remarks and references to Appendices
AGNY	April 29		Weather fine. Enemy shelled AGNY for two and half hours. The Church was evidently the objective and appeared to suffer very much. The hill also came in for some attention and a few other buildings. About 40 heavy shells 5"9, and 200 small shells were counted. Casualties 1 killed 6 wounded	C.O. D.O. Army L.I. ...
	30		Weather fine. Coys paraded at 4.30 pm to relieve 6th Somersets in the front line trenches. Relief was carried out without incident and completed at 9.10 pm. Occasionally Machine Guns were active during the evening. Casualties 1 man wounded	

WAR DIARY
or
INTELLIGENCE SUMMARY.

Army Form C. 2118.

Place	Date	Hour	Summary of Events and Information	Remarks and references to Appendices
ACN1	1916		Weather fine. The Batts relieved the [illegible] in the front line trenches. Relief complete at 9 p.m. Occasional firing of enemy machine guns during the night. Casualties Ort. F. Sadler, one O.R. wounded by Afers.	
[illegible]	2nd		Weather fine. Enemy machine guns active as usual and several howitzer shells off-[illegible]. Several of our bombs burst prematurely in working party. One of our bombers hit.	
"	3rd		Weather fine. Enemy fired howitzers the whole of our front line, also sent over to one of our [illegible] the heavy torpedoes, this is our first experience of these, looking much like [illegible] of iron suspended to [illegible]. machine guns much during the night. Casualties 2 wounded.	
"	4th		Weather fine. French 6" gun came on to our front trench which without doing any [illegible]. 18 [illegible] rifles [illegible] dropped these casualties one [illegible].	

Army Form C. 2118.

WAR DIARY
or
INTELLIGENCE SUMMARY.
(Erase heading not required.)

Instructions regarding War Diaries and Intelligence Summaries are contained in F.S. Regs., Part II. and the Staff Manual respectively. Title pages will be prepared in manuscript.

C^in^C of Coys L.I.

Place	Date	Hour	Summary of Events and Information	Remarks and references to Appendices
Francelus	1916 6th May		Weather fine. During the day our French mortars were active, machine guns were quiet during the night	
"	6th		Weather fine. A very quiet day. Apparently during the night there was very little machine gun or rifle fire. The Batn was relieved by the 6th Som L.I. the relief was completed without incident about 1.20 a.m. Casualties Nil	
DAINVILLE	7th		Weather fine. The Battn marched by Coys to Rest Billets at DAINVILLE, and arrived there about 3 am. Casualties Nil	
"	8th		Rest in Billets	
"	9th		Rest in Billets	
"	10th		Working Party of 100 All Ranks for 59 Coy R.E.	

J. Marriott

Army Form C. 2118.

WAR DIARY
or
INTELLIGENCE SUMMARY.
(Erase heading not required.)

Instructions regarding War Diaries and Intelligence Summaries are contained in F. S. Regs., Part II. and the Staff Manual respectively. Title pages will be prepared in manuscript.

1st Bn. Royal Scots to S [?]

Place	Date	Hour	Summary of Events and Information	Remarks and references to Appendices
DAINVILLE	1916 11th May		Rest in Billets	
"	12th		The Batln. relieved the 6th Devon R.S. in the front line trenches. Enemy opened at 10 am. remainder 10 minutes without at. The Rely. was completed without incident about 1 AM	
Fonchies	13th		Weather several showers of Rain fell during the day. The enemy were exceptionally quiet and there was very little machine gun fire. Casualties nil	
"	14th		Weather. Rain at intervals during the day. Enemy trench mortars were active about 6.10 at 3.15 am. The material damage was slight. Enemy machine gun active during the night. Casualties 3 men wounded in head. The shell intermittently and there slow	
"	15th		Weather fine. The situation has been comparatively quiet, practically no Machine gun or Rifle fire during the night. The Germans gave a display of Very lights. well behind their lines about 9.15 pm distance about 6 miles. Casualties nil	

Army Form C. 2118.

WAR DIARY
or
INTELLIGENCE SUMMARY.
(Erase heading not required.)

Instructions regarding War Diaries and Intelligence Summaries are contained in F. S. Regs., Part II. and the Staff Manual respectively. Title pages will be prepared in manuscript.

Place	Date	Hour	Summary of Events and Information	Remarks and references to Appendices
Trenches	April 16 May		Weather fine. B.H.Q. shelling carried out a mance shot on Enemy wh. appears quiet. Never really quiet. Our Lewis gunnon disposed of a working party of about 6.10 Enemy machine gun and rifle fire away the night. Apparently not Casualties Nil	
-"-	17"		Weather fine. The enemy sent over a few whizzbangs on to our second line & which our artillery replied and silenced them. Machine gun and rifle fire were quiet during the night. Casualties Nil	
-"-	18"		Weather fine. Except for a few trench mortars the day was fairly quiet. The batt. was relieved by the 6" bon L.F. a nothgn. was completed about 9p.pm. Casualties One Officer accidentally wounded.	
ACNY	19"		Brigade Reserve	
-"-	20"		Brigade Reserve	
-"-	21.		Brigade Reserve. The Enemy shelled ACNY pretty in retaliation for our shelling BEAURAIN yesterday. Casualties Nil	

Army Form C. 2118.

WAR DIARY
or
INTELLIGENCE SUMMARY.

(Erase heading not required.)

1st Bn Rif Brig? L.J

Place	Date	Hour	Summary of Events and Information	Remarks and references to Appendices
Army	1916 22 May		Brigade Reserve	
"	23"		—	
"	24"		The batt'n relieved the 6th Som L.I. in the front line. Finches the first Coy farmesic at 6.15pm remainder at 10 moments interval. The Relief was completed without incident at 8.10pm	
Trenches	25"		Weather Raining the whole of the 24 hours. Enemy very quiet. A few French mortars came over on B.11 & B.12. Casualties nil	
"	26"		Weather fine. Enemy active with trench mortars on B.10-11&12. At very heavy mortar is used about 150 lb. An1 Bty sent over french mortars retaliation. The afternoon was fairly quiet. The night was very dark and opening very little. Machine Gun and Rifle fire W.E. were kept on Enemy working party with good effect. Casualties 2 shell shock.	

1577 Wt. W10791/1773 500,000 1/15 D. D. & L. A.D.S.S./Forms/C. 2118.

Army Form C. 2118.

WAR DIARY
or
INTELLIGENCE SUMMARY.
(Erase heading not required.)

1st Battalion L.S.

Place	Date	Hour	Summary of Events and Information	Remarks and references to Appendices
Trenches	May 27th		Weather fine. Enemy began active with trench mortars in G.29-11-12. He also strafed this sector heavily on the forward A.H. line. Retaliated. The night was exceptionally quiet. Casualties 2 other ranks.	
	28th		Weather fine. Early this morning just after stand to the enemy working party commenced work on the FISCHER ROAD. The artillery soon opened and succeeded in dispersing them. A few small bombs were thrown onto our B.S. line near CAMP STREET. Enemy not quiet during the night. Casualties nil.	
	29th		A few showers of rain fell during the day. The M.G. fire was unusual amount of trench mortar A.M.; 10 came in for the usual amount of trench mortar fire and H.13th from practically all during the night.	
	30th		Weather fine. The enemy was quiet during the day. The Battalion was relieved by the 1/7 Hants L.I. relief completed without casualties.	

Army Form C. 2118.

WAR DIARY
or
INTELLIGENCE SUMMARY.

(Erase heading not required.)

6th Rifle Corps B.E.F.

Place	Date	Hour	Summary of Events and Information	Remarks and references to Appendices
DAINVILLE	3.1. 1916		Weather fine. After the relief the Battn. marched by coys to our billets at DAINVILLE. arriving there about 3.30 a.m.	

1577 Wt.W10791/1773 500,000 1/15 D.D.&L. A.D.S.S./Forms/C. 2118.

WAR DIARY or INTELLIGENCE SUMMARY

Army Form C. 2118.

Place	Date	Hour	Summary of Events and Information	Remarks and references to Appendices
DAINVILLE	1st June 1916		Weather fine. The Battn. was relieved in the front line trenches by the 6th Som L.I. The relief was completed without incident and the Battn. marched by coys to rest billets at DAINVILLE arriving there about 2.30 am. Casualties Nil	
"	2nd		Rest in billets. 100 men working party were supplied to Bde. signals	
"	3rd		"	
"	4th		"	
"	5th		"	
"	6th		"	
"	4th[?]		The Battn. paraded by coys at 9.15 p.m. & relieved the 6th Som L.S. in the front line trenches. Relief was completed without incident about 1.30 am. Casualties Nil	

WAR DIARY
INTELLIGENCE SUMMARY

Army Form C. 2118.

6th Bn. L.L.S.

Place	Date	Hour	Summary of Events and Information	Remarks and references to Appendices
Trenches	June 8th 1916.		Weather fine. A heavy trench mortar was in action firing on G.10, G.11, G.12 and O.S. Mine. Most of the shells fell in the O.S. LINE, including two direct hits; they were no plinos and the explosions were very violent, the weight of the projectile is thought to be 100lbs. Our Stokes and 3" Mortars retaliated. Between 9 and 10.30am enemy search 28 LINE from Batt. HQ to GOAT ST with H.E. Casualties NIL.	
Trenches	9th		Weather fine. At 9.00am G.S.10 and GIRL STREET were heavily shelled with H.E. Shrapnel about 105 m.m. No serious damage. Six rounds were fired in retaliation over G.10. Enemy craters firing. A patrol went out from the night of C.1 and came in on the Left of G.2. There was nothing to report. Casualties NIL.	
"	10th		Weather fine. Our Stokes Gun registered on tops opposite Girl Street. Between 8 and 9am enemy shelled front line trenches of centre Coy. About 40 rounds of fairly heavy shells were fired at the G.S. and G.B. LINES. No damage. Our artillery retaliated on each instance with the desired effect. Hostile machine guns were active during the night, also occasional rifle fire was much more in evidence. A double trench was very active the whole night along G.B.4.5. and 6. Our Lewis guns replied vigorously to enemy machine guns. We threw 10 bombs by the West Hopper at Enemy sap, two of which appeared to drop right into the sap. Their machine guns ceased firing after this.	

WAR DIARY
or
INTELLIGENCE SUMMARY.   D. C. L. I.

Army Form C. 2118.

(Erase heading not required.)

Place	Date	Hour	Summary of Events and Information	Remarks and references to Appendices
Trenches	June 11th		Weather dull. Artillery on both sides has been comparatively quiet. Enemy snipers were very active from ridge opposite C.12. There was the usual enemy machine gun activity during the night, to which our teams gave replies. No casualties	
"	12th		Weather fine. Enemy shelled C.3 and C.5 line with 4.2". About 30 rounds in all were fired. C.5.3 and part of BATE STREET were knocked in. About 65m the enemy searched the C.S. line with 4.2" shells. An enemy machine gun opposite C.1 was active & otherwise the night passed very quietly. There was hardly any reply for the bosch was relieved by the 8th J.B. L.I. the relief was completed about 1am 13th without incident. Casualties NIL	
A.P.N.Y.	13th		In Brigade Reserve	
"	14th		"	
"	15th		"	
"	16th		" Casualties 1 killed	
"	17th		" Casualties 1 wounded	
"	18th		The battn relieved the 6th Somt L.I. in the front line trenches, the relief was completed without incident. Opposite C.3m. There was very little machine gun fire during the night. No Casualties	

Army Form C. 2118.

WAR DIARY
or
INTELLIGENCE SUMMARY. 1' D. C. L. I.

(Erase heading not required.)

Instructions regarding War Diaries and Intelligence Summaries are contained in F. S. Regs., Part II. and the Staff Manual respectively. Title pages will be prepared in manuscript.

Place	Date	Hour	Summary of Events and Information	Remarks and references to Appendices
Trenches	June 19th		Weather fine. Artillery have been very quiet on both sides during the day, the night was very quiet. Enemy machine guns were slightly active on A.C.N.Y. at 12 midnight. The battn was relieved by the 11th Royal Lancashire Regt. On completion the battn march by coys to ARRAS and arrived in Billets about 8.15 am 20th. Casualties NIL	
ARRAS	20th		Coys paraded at 10 p.m at 15 minutes intervel and relieved the 1st Hampshire, 5th Division, in J.2. sub sector. The relief was complete without incident about 12.40am 21st Casualties NIL	
Trenches	21st		Weather fine. Enemy trench mortars our front line in two places, our artillery retaliated with the usual effect. The night was very quiet there being hardly any machine or rifle fire. Casualties NIL	
" "	22		Weather fine. A quiet 24 hours, slight trench mortaring of front lines, practically no machine gun or rifle fire during the night. Casualties Nil	
" "	23		Weather. Heavy thunder storm which lasted about 2 hours. The 24 hours have been fairly quiet. At 8.10 pm our artillery fired about 12 HE shrapnel with good effect, there has been considerable anti aircraft activity no Casualties.	

A.Melor Lunt/Col
6/c 6th D.C.L.I

Army Form C. 2118.

WAR DIARY
INTELLIGENCE SUMMARY.

(Erase heading not required.)

6th D.T.M.B.1.

Place	Date	Hour	Summary of Events and Information	Remarks and references to Appendices
Trenches	June 24		Weather fine. At 7am our Artillery commenced and were bothering. Enemy retaliated indiscriminately with trench mortars 4.4 mm and some 5.9" shells on front trenches, they registered down the BAILLEUL ROAD and also REDOUBT LINE. They (also?) at times swept for our batteries. Our Artillery and Trench mortars appear to have shot with great effect - put enemy's retaliation has been futile in comparison. Enfer were fairly active on the night of 7.9" Crater. The night passed quietly. Casualties NIL.	
Trenches	25th		Weather very showery. Enemy Snipers more active. Our T.Ms & 4.5's were very active & their fire intense. At 4pm Six 5.9" shells fell behind Support Line 9.2. About 18pm & again at 4:30pm. The enemy's retaliation was very feeble. Stokes firing rapid at 4:30pm. Casualties NIL.	
Trenches	26th		Weather very showery. At 11pm & again at 11:30pm a combined shoot was carried out with Trench Mortars & 18 pdrs on enemy trenches, good effects were observed, wire being cut in many places. Enemy's retaliation meagre, a few rounds of 77mm shells & fire from "Lucky Elizabeth" (T.M.). Enemy offensive the very minimum of shelling, numerous very lights being sent up. Casualties NIL.	

N Arthur Lieut/Col
c/o 6/KAR R.I.

WAR DIARY
or
INTELLIGENCE SUMMARY.

Army Form C. 2118.

6 K.O.Y.L.I.

Place	Date	Hour	Summary of Events and Information	Remarks and references to Appendices
Trenches	June 27th		Weather showery. Enemy's Trench Mortars have shewn increased activity along the whole of this sector. He hit Heavy T.M's opposite our front line heavily. CHANTECLER Crs. Road at 2.45am. Enemy flare carried fuzes S.99. No casualties. Enemy wiring have drawn much gunfire, but the explosion has returned enemy's work considerably. From our third 5.9 shells fell between SUFFOLK AV & AUGUST AVENUE. Certain amount of damage done to trenches by enemy T.M's Guns. Since fresh about 60 rounds in retaliation to round trench falling between J.10 & J.10f. Casualties. 2 WOUNDED.	P. Adam Lieut/Col o/c 6 KOYLI
Trenches	28th		Weather showery. A very heavy Trench Mortar shell which was thin, fell in rain Cr. in G.T.99. The noise of a similar detonator fired the Bailleul Road was registered a with 97mm shells about 2.30pm. Enemy Heavy T.M's were active all day, beside the shells fired lately 4 during August Avg: 8 the top of J.17, others round about J.9.5 CRATER. Down in one of our day sentry posts. Our retaliation with field guns & field trench G's does not yet seem to shewed effect. CASUALTIES 2 WOUNDED.	
Trenches	29th		Weather showery & unsettled. Enemy artillery & Trench Mortars during the whole day, except at 3am when he opened a barrage on our trenches & approaches, then fire was a rise for the first 10 minutes & after that continued intermittently for half an hour. It is thought that the outburst may have been a retaliation for our previous day's shelling, or that signified our standing Patrols with drawn. CASUALTIES 1 KILLED, 2 WOUNDED	

Army Form C. 2118.

WAR DIARY
or
INTELLIGENCE SUMMARY. 6th D.L.I.
(Erase heading not required.)

Army/tet
c/o C.H.L.L.I

Place	Date	Hour	Summary of Events and Information	Remarks and references to Appendices
Trenches	June 30th		Weather fine. The enemy much quieter even with Trench Mortars. Very little to report. Less rifle & machine gun fire during the night; fewer "Very Lights" was sent up. Our standing patrols afforded that there was no movement of enemy in "No Man's Land". CASUALTIES. 1. SHELL SHOCK.	

WAR DIARY.

for

JULY 1916.

6th Bn. Duke of Cornwall's Light Infantry.

Army Form C. 2118.

WAR DIARY
or
INTELLIGENCE SUMMARY.   6th D.L.L.I.

(Erase heading not required.)

Place	Date	Hour	Summary of Events and Information	Remarks and references to Appendices
Trenches	July 2nd		Weather fine. Coloured lights & searchlights were reported at intervals during the night. Between 3 & 4 pm every five fifteen 77mm. shells exploded on Angres & "Jay" avenues. Lamps picked up were "Blinds". About 7 pm. enemy trench mortars along our front between "The Trench Road" & our retaliated. Our patrols report no enemy movement in "No Man's Land". Our snipers claim to have hit German officer wearing light blue cap.	Ashley
Trenches	2nd		CASUALTIES. TWO WOUNDED.	
			Battle fire. CASUALTIES from 10.55 – 11.45 a.m. enemy active with 77 mm & trench mortars. Firing smoke, 2 few gas shells were included. Searchlights again seen during night. At 8 pm every flew a camouflet well out in front of J.10.1. N.Z. Tunnelling Coy. report no damage to any gallery. Snow storm made much more than the same. Chain ours. Patrols report no movement of enemy. CASUALTIES NIL	
Trenches	3rd		Weather fine. This morning enemy fired at our front line with 77 mm & 105 mm shells doing considerable damage to trenches. Standen (patrols report no aggressive movement) between the lines, but considerable wiring activity ahead. G.6.c.40.10. Our snipers claim seven hits during last 12 days. CASUALTIES 1 SHELLSHOCK.	
	4th 5–18 July		Relieved by D.L.I. Two Companies in ARRAS. Working Parties provided for N.Z. Tunnelling Coy. & R.E.s.	

1577 Wt.W10791/1773 500,000 1/15 D.D.&L.   A.D.S.S./Forms/C. 2118.

WAR DIARY
or
INTELLIGENCE SUMMARY. 6 D.C.L.I.

(Erase heading not required.)

Army Form C. 2118.

Place	Date July	Hour	Summary of Events and Information	Remarks and references to Appendices
Trenches	19th		Weather cloudy. Quiet 24 hours. CASUALTIES. NIL.	
"	20th		Weather fine. Night was very quiet, no enemy patrols were encountered. T96 was considerably damaged by heavy trench mortar firing from G6 c 95-05. CASUALTIES. NIL.	
"	21st		Weather cloudy. Situation remains normal. A new track was found last night leaving the small crater near the enemy line, heading up to three small craters near Sap 99. Some D1 wire was discovered in front of T99 M out from the German line towards our wire & the trench S.E. CASUALTIES. NIL.	
"	22nd		Weather fine. Enemys artillery searched from trench mortar at I.101. Hostile rifle fire was at our aeroplanes. In the night of this section was very heavy this morning. Small crater opposite T.100 was investigated again last night & found to be empty. CASUALTIES. 1 WOUNDED.	
"	23rd		Weather fine. Night very quiet. Patrols report no movement in front of enemy wire. Hostile T.M.s bombarded this had during the morning. Considerable damage done round CRATERS, T96, T.95 + AUGUST AVE. CASUALTIES. 1 SHELLSHOCK.	
"	24th		Weather fine. Enemy fired about 50 Heavy T.M.s during afternoon behind the 3 craters also occasional 77mm, rifle grenades. Good deal of damage done. The little dummy right. 4th from Geneva Gate (96). Also at 9.30pm which T.1 was being bombarded hostile T.M.s were also seen from especially right by Patrol report enemy wire intact, but ours very much damaged in front of CUTHBERT, CLARENCE. Craters. CASUALTIES. 1 KILLED 1 WOUNDED SHELLSHOCK 1.	

WAR DIARY or INTELLIGENCE SUMMARY

Army Form C. 2118.

Place	Date	Hour	Summary of Events and Information	Remarks and references to Appendices
Tranchee	25th		Weather cloudy. Past twenty hours was very quiet. Nothing of importance occurred.	CASUALTIES 1 KILLED
"	26th		" "	NIL
"	27th		Fine. About 2pm enemy shelled Iq6 with 150mm & Heavy T.M.s. very little damage. Our retaliation with howitzers excellent. Relieved by 5th & 9th Leicesters. Marched to LOVE2.	"
"	28th		Marched from LOVE2 to SOMBRIN weather very hot.	
"	29th		" " SOMBRIN to BONNIERES " " "	
"	30th		" "	
"	31st		Halts at BONNIERES	

43rd Brigade.
14th Division.

1/6th BATTALION

DUKE OF CORNWALL'S LIGHT INFANTRY

AUGUST 1916

WAR DIARY.

AUGUST 1916.

6th Bn. Duke of Cornwall's Light Infantry.

Army Form C. 2118.

WAR DIARY
or
INTELLIGENCE SUMMARY.
(Erase heading not required.)

Place	Date Aug	Hour	Summary of Events and Information	Remarks and references to Appendices
BONNIERES	1st	7 a.m.	Marched to LE MEILLARD arrived there 10.30 a.m	
LE MEILLARD	2		Training	
do	3		— do —	
do	4		— do —	
do	5		— do —	
do	6		— do —	Reference map ALBERT 1/40000
do	7	1 a.m.	Transport left 10 a.m. for ALBERT (E15.a.3.5).	— do —
		2.30 p.m.	Marched to CANDAS + entrained MERICOURT	
near ALBERT	8		marched to Camp near ALBERT (E15.a.3.5) Training. BIDES	
do	9		do. had news that Major J.L. Swanson D.S.O. had died of wounds whilst attached to, + commanding 1/4 King's Own.	
do	10		Training	

Alban
LtCol
cmdg 1/5t D.C.L.I.

WAR DIARY
INTELLIGENCE SUMMARY

Army Form C. 2118.

Place	Date 1916 Aug	Hour	Summary of Events and Information	Remarks and references to Appendices
near ALBERT	11		Training	
do	12	4 pm	Marched to MONTRUBAN to relieve 6th Somerset L.I. in support trenches. Relief complete 8 p.m. C.O. + 22 officers only, went up with the battalion, 2nd in Command with Reserve of 13 officers, 2 W.C.O.'s + Squadrons, remained at Moreford Camp.	
MONTAU BAN	13		In support. Furnishes carrying parties for water, rations, transport, & 2nd in Command, & Reserve officers. Intermittent shelling moved to ALBERT. 3 O.R. casualties.	
	14		In support. Furnished carrying parties for water, rations & Intermittent shelling. 20 O.R. casualties.	
DELVILLE WOOD	15	6 a.m	Relieves 6th Somerset L.I. in forward French. 'B' Coy, 'C' Coy (less 2 platoons) & 'D' Coy in front line. 'A' Coy in LONGUEVAL ALLEY, + 2 platoons 'C' Coy in TRONES WOOD in support. Intermittent shelling by enemy all day. Buffs on left, & R. Berks on right.	

6 ROYL D.C.L.I

WAR DIARY
INTELLIGENCE SUMMARY

Army Form C. 2118.

(Erase heading not required.)

Place	Date	Hour	Summary of Events and Information	Remarks and references to Appendices
DELVILLE WOOD	16		During day, shelling mostly intermittent — both sides. From 7 to 9.30 p.m. our Troops & Huns fired bombardes N.E. corner of wood. French that was in minor enterprise, trenches against enemy post about S.18.b.95.65. Sheet 57c S.W. This could not be undertaken, as our heavy shells dropped short on our own trench, inflicting about 23 casualties on raiding party. Enemy bombard went during night.	Sheet 57c S.W. Section 2.B 1:20000
— do —	17	6 am	C.O. & Coy Commanders went to Bde. H.Q. to go into details of attack ordered for following day (18th). Awaiting their absence, Bn Commanders by 2i/c in Command, 'Coys by their 2nd in Command, who were ordered up for this purpose. Heavy bombardment of enemy's position from 8 am to 8 p.m., when intermittent bombardment was substituted. Our position heavily bombarded by enemy all day. C.O. & Coy Commanders returned from Bde. H.Q. about 10 p.m.	

J. Allen
Lt. Col.
cmdg 16th D.C.L.I.

WAR DIARY or INTELLIGENCE SUMMARY

Army Form C. 2118.

Place	Date	Hour	Summary of Events and Information	Remarks and references to Appendices
DELVILLE WOOD	1916 Aug 4	2 am	Bn in Carnoy returned to Mansfort Camp.	
		6 am	On our right 6th Somerset L.I. & on left 6th K.O.Y.L.I. Heavy bombardment of enemy trenches when attack was launched. Intense bombardment by field guns from 2:45 to 2:50 p.m. — 'B' Coy with one platoon of 'A' Coy on the right, 'D' Coy on the left & Blythshire in reserve in perfect order, under cover of our barrage. 3 platoons of 'A' Coy followed immediately in support, while 'C' Coy (in reserve) was thrown in at 3 p.m. The heavy casualties suffered by 'D' Coy were caused chiefly by machine gun fire from the left flank. At 6 p.m. sent to relieve 7th Buffs. Heavy casualties. Length of line (approximately 500 yds) the extreme right of the position only was transferred, largely owing to the initiative & gallantry of 4th Group — & a block established. The line was reorganised in DEVIL'S TRENCH (front portion), & the captured portion on right was held by Bombers & the remnants of 'B' & 'C' Coys. About 150 prisoners fell in. Heavy Casualties in Officers & other ranks.	

A. Allen Lt.Col.
Cmdg 6th D.C.L.I.
29/6/1933

Army Form C. 2118.

WAR DIARY
or
INTELLIGENCE SUMMARY.
(Erase heading not required.)

Place	Date 1916 Aug	Hour	Summary of Events and Information	Remarks and references to Appendices
DELVILLE WOOD	19th		b Reserve Officers to replace casualties were ordered up from POMMIERS REDOUBT. Our original line, & the captured Position, were held by snipers & Lewis Guns during Enemy bombarded trenches intermittently during the day. From 7.30 to 9 P.m. he maintained a heavy barrage, which caused a few casualties.	
two FRICOURT	20th	4.30 a.m	Relieved in DELVILLE WOOD by 8th Rifle Brigade. March to Reserve Camp to refit & (F.8. & Centre). Casualty list completed, which show from 15th inst. to date; 7 officers killed — Lt E.A. Freeman; Lt P.G. Collins; 2/Lt W. Stigman; 2/Lt A.N. Bennett; 2/Lt C.V.R. Wise; 2/Lt N.B. Pawle; 2/Lt P. Riley; also 7 wounded. Other ranks 69 Killed; 233 Wounded; 30 missing.	References ALBERT 1: 40,000
do	21		Resting & refitting. This Bn — well Lt Somerset L.I - hour less before B.G. Cox of when expressed his pleasure at the Bns achievements & states that they had done "brilliantly".	
do	22		Resting & refitting	

Lt/Col
17th R.C.L.I

[signature]

WAR DIARY or INTELLIGENCE SUMMARY.

Army Form C. 2118.

Place	Date	Hour	Summary of Events and Information	Remarks and references to Appendices
Nr FRICOURT	1916 Aug 23rd		Resting & refitting	
do	24th		do. In Reserve to 42nd Inf Brigade. All ranks confined to camp. Bn to be in readiness to move at half hours notice, on receipt of orders.	
do	25		Resting & refitting. Moved to Montauban Defences (6 Relieve 1st KOYLI. w11.30 p.m	
MONTAUBAN Defences	26	4am	Relieve 1st K.O.Y.L.I. in support working party furnishes 16 Bg. R.B. 5. O.R Casualties.	
do	27		In support. Working + carrying parties furnishes K Brigade. machine Gun Coy, & to 10th D.L.I in front line.	
do	28		In support. Water rations carrying parties furnishes to Koybi in front line. 1 Officer – 2/Lt G. B. Clarke killed. 7. O.R Casualties	

J Salter
Lt Col
Cmd 6 D.C.L.I

WAR DIARY
INTELLIGENCE SUMMARY.
(Erase heading not required.)

Army Form C. 2118.

Place	Date	Hour	Summary of Events and Information	Remarks and references to Appendices
MONTAUBAN Defences	Aug 29		In Support. Carrying parties furnished to 5th KSLI & 9th Rifle Brigade	
do	30		In support. At 6.30 p.m. relieved by 9th Bn. Surreys (?) Inf. Bd. Reference map ALBERT 1:40000. Marches to F.B.C.S.O. where B5. weeks & has tea at 11 p.m. Marches to Camp D.12.d.30 (N.E. DERNANCOURT)	
near DERNANCOURT	31	12.45 a.m.	Arrives in Camp. At 9 a.m. marches to Mericourt, entrains at 2 p.m. detrains at 6 p.m. marches to BUIRE + arrives 10 p.m.	

Arthur Lt Col
comdg 6th D.C.L.I.

W A R V   D I A R Y.
****

for the month of

SEPTEMBER 1916.
****

6th Bn. Duke of Cornwall's Light Infantry.
****

WAR DIARY
INTELLIGENCE SUMMARY.

Army Form C. 2118.

(G.D.C.L.T)

Place	Date 1916	Hour	Summary of Events and Information	Remarks and references to Appendices
AUMONT	Sept 1		In Billets. Training	
"	2		do —	
"	3		do —	
"	4		do —	
"	5		do —	
"	6		do —	
"	7		do —	
"	8		do —	
"	9		do —	
"	10		do —	
"	11		Marched out 2 p.m. for LALEN arriving	
LALEN	12	4.15 a.m / 4.15 p.m	There 4.15 p.m. Left for AIRAINES + entrained there at 6 a.m. arriving MERICOURT 11.30 a.m + marched to Camp at nr ALBERT	Reference Map ALBERT 57.d.S.a.3.S. 1/40000
nr ALBERT	13		In Camp. Training	S.J.Mircer Lieut Comdg 1st C.L.T.B. 9

Army Form C. 2118.

WAR DIARY
or
INTELLIGENCE SUMMARY.
(Erase heading not required.)

(1st D.C.L.I.)

Place	Date	Hour	Summary of Events and Information	Remarks and references to Appendices
near ALBERT	Sept. 14	7.30 p.m.	Weather fine. Marches to Camp at T.13.c (near BERCORDEL)	Ref. Map ALBERT 1:40000
near BERCORDEL	15	7.30 a.m.	Marches to Bivouac at POMMIERS REDOUBT F.6.11.6. Arrives there 9.30 a.m. At 12 noon, moves up to MONTAUBAN DEFENCES.	APPENDIX I
MONTAUBAN DEFENCES	"	12.5 p.m.	Orders to move up to YORK ALLEY & CRUCIFIX ALLEY, + to be ready to move forward at short notice to reinforce 42nd Brigade if required.	Ref. Map France Sheet 57cSW Edition 2A APPENDIX II
YORK ALLEY	"	5.30 p.m.	Ordered to relieve Troops (?) holding GAP TRENCH, between T.2.c & 5 & T.1.b.1.13, + consolidate position. At 5.30 p.m. moves up to this position in support to 10th D.L.I. & 1st Som.L.I., who had moved up to hold front line near BULLS ROAD. The night was spent in consolidating. Direction was difficult to keep as the night was very dark + the [...]	APPENDIX III Missing Capn. L.P.C. Lomax

WAR DIARY or INTELLIGENCE SUMMARY

Army Form C. 2118.

6th D.C.L.I.

Place	Date	Hour	Summary of Events and Information	Remarks and references to Appendices
YORK ALLEY	Sep 15	5.30 p.m.	Continued from —— which cut up with the heavy shelling. An officer (2nd Lt A.W. Reap) reconnoitred the route, & guided the battalion — which had to advance in single file — with great skill. There was little shell fire, & no casualties. Retreat was completed by 12.30 a.m. (night 15th/16th). Ration parties were sent back to CRUCIFIX for rations & water. No water was obtained, & rations (for about half of the battalion only) were scarcely fairly got up. As soon as the parties had lost their way. During the move up orders were received at about 12 p.m. that the 43rd Brigade would attack (at a time to be notified later) this battalion being ordered to act in support. the 6th Som LI were to attack on the right, the 10th D L I on the left. The 6th KOYLI (less 2 Coys) to remain in Brigade Reserve.	S.A.A. letter Coys 6,7,8,9,of.../...day APPENDIX IV

Army Form C. 2118.

WAR DIARY
or
INTELLIGENCE SUMMARY.
(Erase heading not required.)

6th D.C.L.I.

Place	Date	Hour	Summary of Events and Information	Remarks and references to Appendices
GAP TRENCH	1916 Sept 15/16	about 2 a.m.	Weather fine but murky. Orders were received that at 9.25 a.m. attack was to be launched. This was to be preceded by a bombardment when light & wet permitted. Barrage to lift at 9.45 a.m. At 9.25 am (Zero Time) battalion advanced over	APPENDIX V
"	16		the open space in one wave, to occupy line on or near BULL'S ROAD. The line was extremely wandering, the drain in west of the parapets. The preliminary bombardment, which began directly west of light parapets — about 6.45 a.m — was very weak & made two observable increases in the intensity was noticeable at zero. The heavy artillery barrages the village of GUEDECOURT but this village appeared to be very weakly held, as beyond occasional sniping, little fire came from it. Heavy machine gun fire however came from both flanks of the village, causing	

P.J. Miers Capt.
Cmdg. 6th D.C.L.I.

WAR DIARY
INTELLIGENCE SUMMARY.

Army Form C. 2118.

6th D.C.L.I.

Place	Date	Hour	Summary of Events and Information	Remarks and references to Appendices
BULL SWIFT TRENCH	Sept 16		(Cont'd) — only a few casualties during the advance. Most of the fire was high & the enemy Artillery — worthy of the name — was very rarely dangerous. During the advance of the 6th Som.L.I. the 16th D.L.I., the machine gun fire (from the flanks of the villages) was more accurate, & these two battalions suffered many casualties in consequence.	
		10.20am	A message was sent from this battalion to 6th Som.R. as follows:- "Am very often to have machine gun barrage on our right flank. It seems useless to pour more men into it. Our artillery ought to be informed. Can you get on to them". No reply was received to this message. Consequently at 10.30.am the advance was again continued, but owing to the [?] in the advanced battalions (6th Som.L.I.	1st D.C.L.I. 6 Som L.I. 6 D.C.L.I.

Army Form C. 2118.

WAR DIARY
or
INTELLIGENCE SUMMARY.
(Erase heading not required.)

(H.D.C.L.I.)

Place	Date	Hour	Summary of Events and Information	Remarks and references to Appendices
A.A. & TRENCH BULLS ROAD	Sep 16 1916	10.20 am	Continued — 10th D.L.I.) it was decided to advance the battalion in two lines one wave. The formation adopted was waves of half companies in extended order, with a distance of 100 yds between waves. Notwithstanding this, each wave suffered heavily through the terrific machine gun fire, but they reached the advanced position & intermixed with the (1st Somm L.I. & 10th D.L.I.) Two Vickers machine guns with them became so supposed heavily.	
		11 am	At about this time the machine gun fire became so intense on the right flank, it was suspected that the sweeper on our right had not advanced. Consequently, a patrol of 2 men was dispatched to round the crest, to ascertain if such was the case. This patrol did not return, they have	29 Officers 1st 15 LoE Bomb. 10th DLI Roy.

1577 Wt.W10791/1773 500,000 1/15 D. D. & L. A.D.S.S./Forms/C. 2118

WAR DIARY
or
INTELLIGENCE SUMMARY.

Army Form C. 2118.

1st D.C.L.I.

Place	Date	Hour	Summary of Events and Information	Remarks and references to Appendices
EAST of FRICOURT BULLS ROAD	1916 Sep 16	11 a.m.	[receiving Cavalries —] [recomming cancelled. At 12 noon another patrol of two men was despatched for the same purpose, one man returned on our right & wounded, gun fire still very heavy].	MM Nissen Corps 16/9
"		11.15 a.m.	A message was sent to Brigade that, Signals has been made to our Aeroplane, that Machine Gun barrage was being up the advance, that Tanks had broken down, that severe masses of enemy on left GUEUDECOURT, to warn artillery.	APPENDIX VI
"		1.30 p.m.	Brigade replies to "Hang on where you are unto Durham has been cleared up on Divisional right".	
"		1.40 p.m.	What appears to be a counter attack in four waves developes W of GUEUDECOURT – this IS about this Conference. This was broken up by our Artillery & broken up, the enemy appeared	APPENDIX VII

WAR DIARY
or
INTELLIGENCE SUMMARY.

Army Form C. 2118.

1st D.C.L.I

Place	Date	Hour	Summary of Events and Information	Remarks and references to Appendices
Buus Road	Sep 16	1.40pm	Continued — to various units in trenches. During the afternoon, enemy aircraft became very active, reflying unusually low. At the same time, enemy artillery fire became heavy on all our lines – 5.9", 4.2" Shells being used freely. Casualties from this source were but slight.	Appx A Ct Miller bittn
"	"	4 pm	See after, Sep 16th 8.30 p.m	
		6.10pm	Orders were received to resume the attack at 6.55 p.m The 43rd Brigade being reinforced by two battalions of the 42nd Brigade — the objective being the capture of GIRD SUPPORT TRENCH & if this proves successful, the attack moves to continue on GUEUDECOURT. It proved very difficult in the short space of 45 mins allowed to O.C's Companies to organise, as casualties had been heavy in	Appendix VIII

Army Form C. 2118.

WAR DIARY
or
INTELLIGENCE SUMMARY.

(Erase heading not required.)

1st D.C.L.I

Place	Date	Hour	Summary of Events and Information	Remarks and references to Appendices
BULLS ROAD	Sep 15th	6.10 pm	Continued — both Officers & other ranks, owing to battalion becoming mixed. However at 6.55 pm the whole line advances with the utmost serenity, but an intense machine gun fire however from both flanks, causing excessive casualties. Every Company Commander had either been killed, or wounded, + only two very junior Officers remain in the firing line. After advancing 200 yds the attack melts away, the remainder were crawled back.	Sgd Major Comdg 6th Bn D.C.L.I
		7.40 pm	After consultation with the 1st Som.L.I + 10th D.L.I, a defensive line consisting of all units in the Brigade, were established in BULLS ROAD. This was reinforced by 4 Yorks Guns. Our casualties were 15 Officers and 10 – t 294 other ranks, but of those SfO all A...... who took part in the operation.	

WAR DIARY or INTELLIGENCE SUMMARY.

(6th D.C.L.I.)

Army Form C. 2118.

Place	Date	Hour	Summary of Events and Information	Remarks and references to Appendices
BULLS ROAD	Sept 16	8.30 p.m.	Orders were received from Brigade cancelling attack on GUEUDECOURT, but attack on GIRD SUPPORT was to be proceeded with. This order was issued at 6.15 p.m but did not reach B.H.Q before 8.30 p.m.	APPENDIX IX
		4.20 p.m.	Brigade message states that our Artillery has been ordered to bombard GIRD SUPPORT. That Division on right (Guards) has been ordered to advance & take LES BOEUFS at all costs. (1st Som L.I were ordered to advance in conjunction with the 6th Koyli). Planning of the Chenes was considered reasonable. The 6th Koyli, Planning this Corps at his disposal. The 10th D.L.I were ordered to make every effort to get in touch with left of (1st Som L.I) & the 6th DCLI were to be offered to be assistance if necessary. At 4.25 pm a message was received from (1st Som L.I) which stated that assistance at 4 pm was suggested but	APPENDIX X at 9.10 p.m 6/7 K.O.Y.L.I Reported 16/9/16 Casualty 16 officers & 67 O.R's APPENDIX XI

Note:— Omitted from Sep 16th 4 p.m & now inserted here.

Army Form C. 2118.

WAR DIARY
or
INTELLIGENCE SUMMARY.
(Erase heading not required.)

1st D.C.L.I.

Place	Date	Hour	Summary of Events and Information	Remarks and references to Appendices
BULLS Rd ROAD	1916 Sep 16	4.20 pm	Continues moved hy & occupy GIRD TRENCH at dusk	
"	Night 16/17		After this has been consolidated, all west of the Bapaume Road is wire retrieved.	
"	17	5am	Bn relieved at by 10th Yorkshire Regt (21st Division), on completion of relief, moves back in single column to bivouac in POMMIERS REDOUBT, Flat 1.b.	Ref map ALBERT 1:40000
Near BERCORDEL		4.30 pm	Moved to Camp at F.13.c. (near BERCORDEL)	
	18	9 am	Marches to RIBEMONT & went into Billets, arrives there 12 noon.	
RIBEMONT	19		Training (9 ruus)	
"	20		" (" ")	

WAR DIARY or INTELLIGENCE SUMMARY.

(Erase heading not required.)

6th D.C.L.I.

Army Form C. 2118.

Place	Date	Hour	Summary of Events and Information	Remarks and references to Appendices
RIBEMONT	21		Training (In huts)	
"	22	6.30 am	Moves to SUS ST LEGER (N.24.a.) per Motor Busses arriving there 3.30 p.m.	Ref map FRANCE 51c 1:40000
SUS ST LEGER	23		In huts. Training.	
"	24		do	Motor Buses 6" D.C.L.I.
"	25		do	
"	26		do	
"	27		do. Returns to ARRAS per Motor Lorries, arriving References Trench Map there 9 p.m. Went into Brigade Support, Companies being ARRAS disposed of as follows:- "A" Coy. In support to 6th KOYLI. S.I.B. N.W.3 right of Balgone Sector. "C" Coy. In support to 10th D.LI. horsing Edition 3.C left of 1:10000 Brigade Sector. "B" Coy Garrison of ACHICOURT DEFENCES. "D" Coy Neuville Garrison of RONVILLE DEFENCES. Battalion H.Q. No 8 Rue Vitasse de Pasteur ARRAS Sector held by Brigade G.3's V.O.8. to M.10.C.4.5 51B. S.W.1. Edition 2.C. 1:10000	

Army Form C. 2118.

WAR DIARY
or
INTELLIGENCE SUMMARY.   6th D.C.L.I
(Erase heading not required.)

Place	Date	Hour	Summary of Events and Information	Remarks and references to Appendices
ARRAS	28		In Brigade Support. Situation very quiet. Slight Shelling occasionally during the day, & moderate machine gun fire during the night	O.C. Messrs Stops Bailey & Stops
do	29		— do — do —	
do	30		— do — do —	
			Note:- List of Code Calls	
			14th (Light) Division	
			attached herewith.	APPENDIX XII

"A" Form.   Army Form C. 2121.

MESSAGES AND SIGNALS. No. of Message _____

Prefix....Code....m. Office of Origin and Service Instructions.	Words	Charge	*COPY OF ORDERS* *This message is on ajc of:* ....Service. *Appendix I* (Signature of "Franking Officer.")	Recd. at....m. Date............ From............ By............
	Sent At....m. To.... By....			

TO	SPIN			

Sender's Number ⁕ B.M.18	Day of Month 15	In reply to Number		AAA
The	Brigade	will	move	to
area	N.E.	of	MONTAUBAN	as
follows	aaa	SPED	and	SPUR
to	YORK	ALLEY	and	CHECK
LINE	between	THRONES	WOOD	and
CRUCIFIX	ALLEY	aaa	SPED	will
move	off	at	11.15 a.m.	SPUR
at	11.30 a.m.	Distance	of	50
yards	between	platoons	aaa	SPOT
will	move	at	11.45 a.m	to
MONTAUBAN	ALLEY	between	BERNAFAY	WOOD
and	S.27.b.	Central	aaa	Same
distance	between	platoons	aaa	SPIN
will	move aaa	into	MONTAUBAN	DEFENCES
at 12.0 noon	/ SPY	and	SIT	to
MONTAUBAN	at 12.15 p.m.	aaa / BRIGADE	H.Q.	moves
to	MONTAUBAN	S.28.a. 4.0.	at 11.30 a.m. aaa	

From	SPAR			Acknowledge
Place				
Time	10.55 a.m.			

The above may be forwarded as now corrected.   (Z)   (Sd.) C.R.Congreave, Capt.

.... Censor.   Signature of Addressor or person authorised to telegraph in his name.

⁕ This line should be erased if not required.

"A" Form. Army Form C. 2121.
MESSAGES AND SIGNALS.   No. of Message_____

COPY OF ORDERS

Appendix II

TO SPIN

Sender's Number	Day of Month	In reply to Number	
B.M.19	15		A A A

Move	up	on	receipt	of
these	orders	to	YORK	ALLEY
and	CHECK	line	between	THRONE
WOOD	and	CRUCIFIX	ALLEY	aaa
SPOT	on	right	SPIN	on
left	aaa	Be	prepared	to
move	forward	at	short	notice
to	reinforce	SLAY	if	required
aaa	Send	Officer	forward	to
reconnoitre	state	of	affairs	in
front	aaa	SPED	and	SPUR
are	moving	forward	to	squares
T.7.a.c & d	and	S.12 b.		

From SPAR
Place
Time 1.25 p.m.

"A" Form. — MESSAGES AND SIGNALS. — Army Form C. 2121.

COPY OF ORDERS

Appendix III

Folio 1.

TO: SPIN

Sender's Number: B.M. 20. **Day of Month:** 15   AAA

SPAR	will	relieve	SLAY	as
early	as	possible	to-night	as
follows	aaa	SPED	and	SPUR
will	relieve	battalions	of	SLAY
in	front	line	holding	it
with	three	companies	each	in
front	line	and	one	company
each	in	rear	aaa	SPED
will	be	on	the	right
SPUR	on	left	aaa	SPIN
will	relieve	troops	holding	GAP
TRENCH	between	T.2.c.8.5	and	
T.1.b.1.1½ aaa		The	above	lines
are	to	be	consolidated	
tonight	aaa	SPOT	will	dig
themselves	in	on	a	line
about	150	yards	in	rear

"A" Form.   Army Form C. 2121.
MESSAGES AND SIGNALS.

Prefix....Code....m.	Words	Charge	This message is on a/c of:	Recd. at....m.
Office of Origin and Service Instructions.		COPY OF ORDERS		
	Sent		.........Service.	Date...........
	At....m.		Appendix III	From...........
	To........			
	By Folio 2.		(Signature of "Franking Officer.")	By............

TO   2.

Sender's Number	Day of Month	In reply to Number	
B.M.20	15		A A A

of	GAP	TRENCH	aaa	Battalions
to	be	prepared	for	further
attack	on	GIRD	TRENCH	and
GIRD	SUPPORT	tomorrow	aaa	Troops
of	S C A N	are	remaining	in
SWITCH	TRENCH	aaa	Tools	S.A.A.
Rockets	and	Flares	will	be
taken	over	from	SLAY	and
365	picks	and	565	shovels
will	be	dumped	from	Bde.
tool	carts	at	the	CRUCIFIX
aaa	Units	may	draw	on
them	in	addition	to	their
own	tools	which	they	will
make	arrangements	to	get	aaa
Bde.	H.Q.	will	be	established
in	YORK	TRENCH	immediately	WEST

From	SPAR	of	the	CRUCIFIX
Place		aaa	Acknowledge	
Time	5.40 p.m.			

The above may be forwarded as now corrected.   (Z)

....   C.R. Congreatt............
Censor.   Signature of Addressor or person authorised to telegraph in his name.

* This line should be erased if not required.

COPY OF ORDERS   *Appendix IV*
S P I N   Copy No. 2

      43rd L/I Bde. O.O.   No. 67.

(1) The 43rd L/I Bde. will continue the attack tomorrow at an hour to be notified later.

(2) The attack will be carried out by the 6th Somerset L.I. on the right and the 10th Durham L.I. on the left
The 6th D.C.L.I. will be in support.
The 6th K.O.Y.L.I. (less two Companies) will be in Brigade Reserve.

(3) 4 Brigade M.Gs. are allotted to each Battalion except the 6th K.O.Y.L.I. 4 guns will be in reserve. These guns will move into position tonight. O.C.Battalions will give permission to the Machine guns and Trench Mortars of the 43rd. Infy. Brigade to leave the trenches they now occupy when they are satisfied the 43rd Bde. guns are in position.

COPY OF ORDERS   Appendix IV

(4) O.C. Battalions will order all TANKS still capable of movement to proceed at once to rendez-vous south of FLERS in the sunken road known as FLERS AVENUE.
Units will at once inform the Brigade how many tanks are still capable of action & also give registered number of each tank or name of commander. Location of any disabled tanks to be forwarded to the Brigade.

(5) Artillery boards if available to be erected behind new front line.

(6) Active patrolling is to be carried out during the night & every effort made to establish ourselves in GIRD Trench if found only lightly held or unoccupied.

(7) Further orders for the attack will be issued as soon as possible.

                         (Sd.) C.R. Congreave, Capt.

COPY OF ORDERS — Appendix V

SECRET.   Copy No. 2.

43rd Bde. Operation Order No. 68.

(1) In continuation of O.O. No. 67, the 6th Somerset L.I. and 10th Durham L.I. will attack GIRD SUPPORT at 9.25 a.m. this morning.

(2) Boundaries of the attack will be as follows:-

   6th Somerset L.I. from N.33 c.4 2 to ~~N.26.e.6.9.~~ N.32 C.3.8.

   10th Durham L.I. from N.32 b 3 8 to N 26 c. 6.9.

(3) Special mopping up parties will be left behind in GIRD TRENCH to deal with any dugouts.

(4) The attack will be preceeded by a bombardment as soon as light permits. Barrage will be on approximate line N.33 c. 7.4. to N.32 a. 1.9. Owing to line being inclined to our jumping off place and to enable Infantry on the left to get up to within attacking distance the

Folio 2   COPY OF ORDERS   *Appendix V*

Barrage will lift at 9.45 a.m. on 14th Division front and at 9.55 a.m. on 41st Division front.

At 9.25 a.m. Infantry to creep forward as close to Barrage as possible ready to assault moment barrage lifts. Barrage will creep back about 50 yards per minute until it establishes a protective barrage N.E. of GIRD SUPPORT Heavies lift on GUEUDECOURT.

At 9.25 a.m. 6th K.O.Y.L.I. and 6th D.C.L.I. will advance to present line on or about BULLS ROAD occupied by 6th Somerset L.I. and 10th Durham L.I. 6th K.O.Y.L.I. on the right.

(5)   At 10.30 a.m. the Barrage will lift off GUEUDECOURT and the 10th Durham L.I. will assault the village and establish themselves in a line NORTH of the village in touch with the 41st Division about N.25.d.5.0. At the same time the 6th Somerset L.I. will advance on the right of the 10th Durham L.I. with their right resting about N.33 Central in touch with the Guards Division & their left in touch with the 10th Durham L.I.

At 10.30 a.m. the 6th K.O.Y.L.I. and 6th

Folio 3 COPY OF ORDERS Appendix V

D.C.L.I. will advance and occupy GIRD SUPPORT and will be prepared to give any support required for the attack on the final objective.

(6) In the event of the attack on GIRD SUPPORT being unsuccessful the O.C. 6th Somerset L.I. will have a direct call on the 6th K.O.Y.L.I. for assistance, and in the same way the 10th Durham L.I. a call on the 6th D.C.L.I.

(7) TANKS will probably assist in the operations.

(8) Objectives gained will be at once consolidated.

(9) Red Flares will be lit on reaching objectives and when called for by aeroplanes.

(10) Acknowledge.

16/9/16.

                                                Captain
Brigade Major,
43rd Infantry Brigade.

"A" Form
Army Form C. 2121.
MESSAGES AND SIGNALS.

COPY OF ORDERS
Appendix VI

TO: S P A R

Sender's Number: C.A.32
Day of Month: 16
AAA

Enemy	M.G.	barrage	still	holding
up	advance	aaa		
Have	signalled	same	to	aeroplane
aaa	Tank	broken	down	out
of	action	aaa	Reported	by
Officer	in	front	line	that
he	saw	several	masses	of
Germans	to	left	of	GUEUDECOURT
aaa	Probably	a	counter	attack
aaa	Please	warn	artillery	aaa

From: SPIN
Place:
Time: 11.15 p.m.

(Z) (Sd.) E.C.Codyre Lt.

"A" Form.   Army Form C. 2121.

MESSAGES AND SIGNALS.

COPY OF ORDERS

Appendix VII

TO: S P I N

Sender's Number: B.M.24
Day of Month: 16

A A A

Hang	on	where	you	are
until	situation	has	been	cleared
up	on	Divisional	right	aaa
Barrage	is	being	put	back
on	GIRD	Support	and	GIRD
trench	in	front	of	SPUR aaa
SPED	to	report	if	barrage
satisfactory	or	if	he	would
like	it	brought	further	along
GIRD	trench	toward	him	aaa
Further	orders	will	be	issued
later	for	continuance	of	attack

From: S P A R
Place:
Time: 11.45 a.m.

(Sd.) C.R.C.

"A" Form. Army Form C. 2121.

MESSAGES AND SIGNALS. No. of Message _____

Prefix ...... Code ...... m.	Words	Charge		Recd. at ...... m.
Office of Origin and Service Instructions.	COPY	OF ORDERS a/c of:		Date ......
	Sent		...... Service.	From ......
	At ...... m.	Appendix VIII		
	To			
	By Folio 1.	(Signature of "Franking Officer.")		By ......

TO { S P I N

Sender's Number	Day of Month	In reply to Number	
* B.M.25	16		A A A

Orders	have	been	received	that
43rd	Bde.	reinforced	by	two
~~battalions~~	of	42nd	Bde.	will
~~resume~~	the	attack	this	evening
~~Creeping~~	barrage	lifts	off	G I R D
Trench	at	6.55	p.m.	At
this	hour	all	units	of
the	43rd	Bde.	will	advance
~~and~~	endeavour	to	capture	GIRD
Support	leaving	adequate	mopping	up
parties	in	. GIRD	Trench	These
positions	are to be	consolidated	at	once
Two	battalions	42nd	Bde.	attached
43rd	Bde.	will	carry	out
the	attack	on	GUEUDECOURT	They
will	move	from	SWITCH	line
at	such	an	hour	as

From	SPAR			
Place				
Time				

The above may be forwarded as now corrected. (Z) (Sd.) C,R,C,

...... Censor. Signature of Addressor or person authorised to telegraph in his name.

* This line should be erased if not required.
T. & W. & J. M. Ltd., London. W 14042/M44. 75,000 12/15. Forms C 2121/16.

"A" Form. Army Form C. 2121.

MESSAGES AND SIGNALS.

COPY OF ORDERS

Appendix VIII

AAA

to	arrive	in	G I R D	Support
at	7.25	p. m.	At	7.35
p. m.	the	barrage	on	GUEUDECOURT
will	lift	and	infantry	will
assault	Officers	patrols	will	be
pushed	well	ahead	of	Battalions
of	42nd	Bde.	to	ascertain
whether	GIRD	Support	has	been
captured	If	it	has	been
unsuccessful	these	two	Battalions	will
establish	themselves	on	BULLS	ROAD
and	consolidate			
Situation	reports	are	to	be
at	once	forwarded	to	the
43rd	Bde	If	Battalions	of 42nd
Bde.	are	already	distributed	side

"A" Form
MESSAGES AND SIGNALS.

Army Form C. 2121.

This message is on a/c of: **COPY OF ORDERS**

By Folio 3.

Appendix VIII

TO (3)

AAA

by	side	the	Battalion	at
present	on	the	right	will
attack	on	the	right	If
one	behind	the	other	the
senior	battalion	will	attack	on
right				

From 43rd Bde.
Place
Time 4.20 p.m.

"A" Form
MESSAGES AND SIGNALS.
Army Form C. 2121.

Prefix......... Code......... m. Words | Charge — COPY OF ORDERS — This message is on a/c of:
Office of Origin and Service Instructions.
Sent At......... m.
To.........
By Folio 1.
Appendix IX
(Signature of "Franking Officer.")
Recd. at......... m.
Date.........
From.........
By.........

TO	S P I N			

Sender's Number. * B.M.34	Day of Month 16	In reply to Number		A A A
Reference	my	B.M.25	the	attack
on	GUEUDECOURT	will	not	now
take	place	aaa	Battalions	of
the	43rd	Infy.	Bde.	will
endeavour	to	establish	themselves	in
GIRD	Support	as	previously	
ordered	aaa	S L E D	on	right
S L I M	on	left	will	occupy
Switch	line	each	sending	forward
2	companies	to	G A P	trench
aaa	immediately	on	arrival	O.Cs
S L E D	and	S L I M	will	send
forward	Officers	patrols	to	get
in	touch	with	units	43rd
I.B.	and	reconnoitre	situation	aaa
In	the	event	of	the
43rd	Infy.	Bde	attack	on

From.........
Place.........
Time.........
The above may be forwarded as now corrected. (Z)
Censor. Signature of Addressor or person authorised to telegraph in his name.
* This line should be erased if not required.

"A" Form
MESSAGES AND SIGNALS.

Army Form C. 2121.

This message is on a/c of: COPY OF ORDERS

Appendix IX

By Folio 2.

GIRD	Support	being	unsuccessful	SLED
and	SLIM	will	consolidate	themselv
on	BULLS	road	gaining	touch
with	Divisions	on	each	flank aaa
SPY	will	at	once	send
up	four	remaining	Vickers	guns
to	GAP	Trench	aaa	If
GIRD	Support	is	captured	these
guns	will	be	sent	forward
to	assist	in	holding	the
line	aaa	If	unsuccessful	they
will	take	up	a	position
to	cover	BULLS	road	

From: SPAR
Place: —
Time: 6.15 p.m.

(Sd.) C.R.Congreave, Capt.

"A" Form
MESSAGES AND SIGNALS.
Army Form C, 2121

Prefix_____ Code_____ m. Words Charge
Office of Origin and Service Instructions.

COPY of ORDERS

Appendix X

(Signature of "Franking Officer.")

TO: SPED SPOT
    SPIN SPUR

Sender's Number: B.M.28
Day of Month: 16.
AAA

Our	Artillery	have	been	ordered
to	heavily	bombard	GIRD	SUPPORT
from	N.33.c.4.1.	and	thence	in
a	North	Westerly	direction	aaa
The	Division	on	your	right
have	been	ordered	to	advance
At	4.0 p.m.	the	above	bombardment
will	lift	If	O.C.	SPED
considers	there	is	reasonable	chance
of	advancing	in	co-operation	with
the	Division	on	his	right
he	will	do	so	and
occupy	GIRD	SUPPORT	forming	a
defensive	flank	towards	GUEUDECOURT	O.C.
SPOT	will	get	into	touch
with	SPED	placing	two companies	at
disposal	of	SPED	aaa	The

"A" Form
Army Form C. 2121.

MESSAGES AND SIGNALS.

Prefix	Code	m.	Words	Charge	This message is on a/c of:	Recd. at	m.
Office of Origin and Service Instructions.			COPY OF ORDERS				
			Sent At	m.	Service.	Date	
			To		Appendix I	From	
			By Folio 2.		(Signature of "Franking Officer.")	By	

TO

Sender's Number.	Day of Month	In reply to Number	
* B.M. 28	16		AAA

Division	on	your	right	has
orders	to	take	LESBOEUF	at
all	costs	aaa	SPUR.	will
make	every	effort	to	get
in	touch	with	SPED	left
as	soon	as	possible	aaa
SPIN	is	to	be	applied
to	if	necessary	for	this
to	be	done	aaa	SPIN
to	get	at	once	into
touch	with	SPED		

From SPAR
Place
Time 2.30. p.m.

The above may be forwarded as now corrected. (Z) (Sd.) C.R.Congreave, Capt.

Censor. Signature of Addresser or person authorised to telegraph in his name.
* This line should be erased if not required.

COPY OF ORDERS — Appendix XI

S P I N

I do not think that we are in touch with Spurs right. My left is on the Sunken Road.

Some of your men in the front line (Gird Trench is just behind it) are in touch with mine.

(Sd.) T.F.Ritchie, Lt-Col.
Sped.

I am not going to advance at 4 p.m. as suggested in B.M. 28 but will try to occupy all Gird Street at dusk.

Recd. 4.25 p.m.

Appendix XII

List of Code Calls
of the
14th (Light) Division

Divisional Headquarters.		SOME
41st Infantry Bde	HQ.	SCAN
7th KRR		SKEW
8th KRR.		SKIN
7th RB.		SCOT
8th RB.		SCUD
42nd Infantry Bde	HQ.	SLAY
5th Oxf & Bucks LI.		SLED
5th Shropshire LI		SLIM
9th KRR		SLOT
9th RB.		SLUG
43rd Infantry Bde	HQ.	SPAR
6th Som LI		SPED
6th DCLI		SPIN
6th Yorks LI		SPOT
10th Durham LI.		SPUR
11th Liverpool Regt (Pioneer Bn)		STEP
41st Bde MG Coy		SKY
42nd " " "		SLY
43rd " " "		SPY

WAR DIARY

of

6TH BN DUKE OF CORNWALL'S LIGHT INFANTRY.

October 1st 1916 — October 31st 1916.

WAR DIARY
INTELLIGENCE SUMMARY. 6th D.C.L.I.

Army Form C. 2118.

Place	Date	Hour	Summary of Events and Information	Remarks and references to Appendices
ARRAS	1916 Dec. 1st		In Brigade Support. Situation very quiet. Slight shelling occasionally during the day, & moderate machine gun fire during the night.	Relief Orders 6th D.C.L.I.
"	2nd		— do —	
"	3rd		— do — Relieved by 6th K.O.Y.L.I. R/k Then relieved 10th D.C.L.I in trenches left of H Sector. H33 to H42, all Coys in front line. 1 Coy 6th K.O.Y.L.I. in support in RONVILLE, + 1 Coy 6th K.O.Y.L.I. in Saney RONVILLE DEFENCES. B/n H.Q. in RONVILLE. Relief complete by 10 P.M.	
In Trench	4th		Weather fine. Situation quiet. Sewing up front line wire.	

WAR DIARY
or
INTELLIGENCE SUMMARY. 6th D.C.L.I.

(Erase heading not required.)

Army Form C. 2118.

Place	Date	Hour	Summary of Events and Information	Remarks and references to Appendices
In Trenches	Oct 5th		Heavy French mortars by enemy on left of sector. Casualties. 1 man killed & 5 wounded. Slight damage to support line. Clearing front line & rebuilding damaged trenches.	
	6th		During night enemy machine gun active, to which he replied. Every so often a few Trench Mortars came over, doing little damage. Clearing wine at front line. A few M.M. shells fired at Ronville. Enemy artillery dropping a large number of shells in South end of RONVILLE (G 34 Central to G 34 d. 8. 8.) Enemy has 5.9" shells firing in groups of 8, at half hour intervals. Very little damage. Suffered claim to have hit a man seen watching our aeroplane from Hd 36. Watching parties were observed at G 35 d. 4. & later at G 36 C 15.90 Both were driven by our fire from aeroplane during the evening.	References. Trench maps ARRAS 51 B NW.3 2 cm to 1 1:10000 Neuville Vitasse 51 B SW.1 2 cm to 1 1:10000

WAR DIARY / INTELLIGENCE SUMMARY ('D' D.C.L.I)

Army Form C. 2118.

Place	Date	Hour	Summary of Events and Information	Remarks and references to Appendices
Trenches	1916 Dec 8th	6.30 a.m.	Our work relieved in CHALK MOUND, but no enemy Patrols were seen. Trenches were fairly active during the night. Rifle Grenades were fired from enemy Sap at G.35.c.2.65.13 during the night. Enemy fight heavy between 11-11.30 p.m. also during the afternoon, to which our Artillery replied by firing 3 salvos of 6 rounds each. Enemy then became quiet. Orders were received to continue patrolling up to 16th inst. Endeavoring the wire from their r. 15 before patrols, for a smoke attack to be made within a few days. Towards morning the night became quiet.	Aitken /Lt. Col. Comdg /10 D.C.L.I.
	9th		The morning slight tracer harassing, to which we replied promptly. Relieved by 10th D.L.I. Regt began at 2 p.m., completed by 8 p.m. Bn marched to 10th D.L.I. in Divisional Reserve. Cavalry Barracks ARRAS.	
ARRAS	10th		In Divisional Reserve. Training. Officers & N.C.O's 30. men attended to work assigned training. Hodge St Commercial French.	

1527 Wt. W10791/1773 500,000 1/15 D D.D.& L. A.D.S.S./Forms/C. 2118.

Army Form C. 2118.

WAR DIARY
or
INTELLIGENCE SUMMARY.   6th D C L I
(Erase heading not required.)

Place	Date	Hour	Summary of Events and Information	Remarks and references to Appendices
ARRAS	11th		In Divisional Reserve. Training, furnishing parties to refain HOOGE St + reserve line Spoil.	O. i/c 1st Li...
-do-	12		-do- -do- -do- also furnishing party to	
			Carry in T.M. ammunition to Trenches.	Relieve 1st ...
-do-	13		-do- -do- -do-	
-do-	14		-do- -do- -do-	
-do-	15	5pm	Relieved 10th D.L.I. in Kemmel, relief complete at 7.30pm. Bn. relieved by 1st K O Y L I. Very slight enemy machine gun activity during the night. Our T.M's harrassed enemy front line from 2pm to 2.30pm. Aeroplane - ours & theirs - very active during afternoon. Two Balloons seen behind enemy lines seen afternoon.	

1577 Wt.W10791/1773 500,000 1/15 D. P. & L. A.D.S.S./Forms/C. 2118.

WAR DIARY or INTELLIGENCE SUMMARY

L. D. C. L. I.

Place	Date	Hour	Summary of Events and Information	Remarks and references to Appendices
In Trenches	1916 Oct 16"		Enemy rifle fire active during the night. About 10.45am enemy snipers front line Topper trenches. No casualties. A very late somme (E. end). He also dropped 5 9" shells in RONVILLE (South end) Our Artillery retaliated with 18 pdr. Our Snipers claim to have hit a man at M.5.a.2.4. at 11.10 am. Enemy placed a board above his trench with Red, White & Black above a board opposite a house G.36.c.1.7. At 10.30 am enemy aeroplane dropped a bomb about 300yds from our right company H.Q. and at M.4.6.19. Snipers busy with spurts of fire on enemy trench between 11 – 11.30pm.	Arteries L.G.S. L.T.G. L.T.G.
"	17		Heavy Trench Mortars on our front. The Support line. Our Heavies & Field Artillery were also active – The Letem firing on enemy front line support, especially H.40 – H.42. 2 Bombs called Rum which Black about 6 x 7 ½ lbs about 3 ½ x 1 ½ inch to edge of trench at about G.35.d.7.3. Lin three bombs from our line & the first then they are close together, rather deeper than they cushy are Artillery aircraft busy during the morning. Enemy burst in our lines at G.35.C.4.2. Elater	

WAR DIARY
INTELLIGENCE SUMMARY. (1 D.C.L.I)

Army Form C. 2118.

Place	Date	Hour	Summary of Events and Information	Remarks and references to Appendices
In trenches	1916 Oct 17		Continued shelling warters at the top of Hunter St. A few also landed along H 4c. About 8 am our light trench mortars fired about 20 rounds about M.46.9.2, + about 10 rounds about M.5. a. 6.7. Our Heavy Mortars fired 5 rounds on M.5. 6.3.9. Heavy artillery with T.M. fire + T Mortars. 2nd of our aeroplanes forced an Enemy line. Enemy Balloons up at about M.6.d. Numerous Pieces seen. Our heavier fired Artillery snipped shells on Tilloy + Beaurains during the morning. Our Trench Mortars were also active cutting enemy wire. Enemy Trench Mortars our front line rather busily between H37 + H40.	Walker Lt Capt 17/10/16
"	18			
"	19		Enemy Trench Mortars our front line + communication Trenches between H 39 + H 4c + also on H 37, 38. ARRAS also shelled by hostile fine active during the night.	

WAR DIARY of INTELLIGENCE SUMMARY.

6th D.C.L.I

Place	Date 1916 Oct	Hour	Summary of Events and Information	Remarks and references to Appendices
In trenches	20		Enemy shelled with 77 m/m shells about G.35, d.8.9. Our T.M.'s were employed in cutting enemy wire, traces of press satisfactory. Enemy T.M. active during the morning. Much damage done to trenches, but no casualties. Enemy bombing in the afternoon. He trained our trench about H.35. One of our aeroplanes flying low over enemy lines forced down by machine gun fire, but landed in our lines. Four enemy aeroplanes seen but no aeroplane. They were visibly damaged, but was down.	Reliefs of 6 Som L.I
"	21		Our front line shelled by 77 m/m Stokes guns and rifles at 3.25 pm on G.36.c.15.10. 140 m/m aeroplane seen returning from behind enemy lines. Three helps from friendly action during the night. Relieved by 10th D.L.I 6th Som L.I. Relief complete by 7.30 pm. 1 Coy in support to C 10 KOYLI theory	
ARRAS	22		In Brigade Reserve. 1 Coy in Support to C 10 KOYLI heavy	

WAR DIARY
INTELLIGENCE SUMMARY. 6 D.C.L.I

Place	Date	Hour	Summary of Events and Information	Remarks and references to Appendices
ARRAS	23		Continued night shells. 1 Coy in support to D.L.I. having left ceaton, 1 Coy (Commn) ACHICOURT DEFENCES. 1 Coy in support RONVILLE DEFENCES. BHQ Nº 8 Rue De Pasteur ARRAS. Situation quiet	Attack of 9th Corps
"	24		In Brigade support. Situation quiet.	
"	25		"	
"	26		"	
"	27		" Relieved by 35th Brigade (12th Division) 1st Essex, 1 Suffolk, 1st Norfolk. Relief complete by 3.30 am Bn marched to AGNEZ LEZ DUISANS + buses there left for IZEL LES HAMEAU at 1 pm arriving there about 2.30 pm.	

WAR DIARY
INTELLIGENCE SUMMARY. Lt D.C.L.I

Army Form C. 2118.

Place	Date	Hour	Summary of Events and Information	Remarks and references to Appendices
TEL LEZ HAMEDU	Oct 28th		In billets. Training	Aircraft Co. Lewis Gun C/O
"	29		- do -	
"	30		- do -	
"	31		- do -	

Vol 19

Confidential

War Diary
of
6th D.C.L.I.

From 1st November   To 30th November 1916.

Volume 19

19ᴺ

Army Form C. 2118.

WAR DIARY
or
INTELLIGENCE SUMMARY. 6th Ser. BTD. E.L.

(Erase heading not required.)

Instructions regarding War Diaries and Intelligence Summaries are contained in F. S. Regs., Part II. and the Staff Manual respectively. Title pages will be prepared in manuscript.

Army Form C. 2118.

Volume 19

Place	Date	Hour	Summary of Events and Information	Remarks and references to Appendices
12.E.L. LEZ-HAMEAU	1-11-16		The Battalion was quartered in Billets. Work carried out TRAINING in the vicinity	In the Field. Commdg. 6th (L) Bn. E.L.I. J. Walker Lieut Col
"	2-11-16		Do	
"	3-11-16		Do	
"	4-11-16		Do	
"	5-11-16		Do	
"	6-11-16		Do	
"	7-11-16		Do	
"	8-11-16		The Battalion paraded at 10.45 a.m. and started at 11 a.m. to march to MONCHAUX and MONTS-en-TERNOIS, where they arrived about 3.15 p.m. "B" & "D" Coys and the Regt transport were billeted in the former and "A" Coy in the latter named village. The Battalion was billeted and settled by about 3 to 5 p.m. The march was a very trying one owing to the heavy rain which lasted the whole of the day.	
MONCHAUX & MONTS-en-TERNOIS	9-11-16		The Battalion was quartered in Billets. The whole day was spent in drying out clothes and equipments, also cleaning same	
"	10-11-16		The Battalion was quartered in Billets. Work carried out TRAINING in the vicinity	
"	11-11-16		Do	
"	12-11-16		Do	

Army Form C. 2118.

WAR DIARY
or
INTELLIGENCE SUMMARY. 6th (Sv) Btn. D.C.L.I.

(Erase heading not required.)

Place	Date	Hour	Summary of Events and Information	Remarks and references to Appendices
MONCHEAUX & MINTS-en-TERNOIS	13-11-16		The Battalion was quartered in Billets. Work carried out TRAINING in the vicinity	
"	14-11-16		Do	
"	15-11-16		Do	Do
"	16-11-16		Do	Do
"	17-11-16		Do	Do
"	18-11-16		Do	Do
"	19-11-16		Do	Do
"	20-11-16		Do	Do
"	21-11-16		Do	Do
"	22-11-16		Do	Do
"	23-11-16		Do	Do
"	24-11-16		Do	Do
"	25-11-16		Do	Do
"	26-11-16		Do	Do
"	27-11-16		On the 27th inst. "A" Company paraded at 2pm and moved to MONCHAUX where they were billeted	
MONCHAUX	28-11-16		The Battalion was quartered in Billets. Work carried out TRAINING in the vicinity	
"	29-11-16		Do	Do
"	30-11-16		Do	Do

Vol 20

War Diary

6th D. C. L. I.

December 1916

Army Form C. 2118.

WAR DIARY
or
INTELLIGENCE SUMMARY. 6TH (SER) BATT D-C-L-I

(Erase heading not required.)

Place	Date	Hour	Summary of Events and Information	Remarks and references to Appendices
MONCHEAUX	DECR 1916 1ST		The Battalion was quartered in Billets. Work carried out - TRAINING in the vicinity.	MAP REFERENCE SHEET 51 B&C. 1/40,000
do	2ND		do	
do	3RD		do	
do	4TH		do	
do	5TH		do	
do	6TH		do	
do	7TH		do	
do	8TH		do	
do	9TH		do	
do	10TH		do	
do	11TH		do	
do	12TH		do	
do	13TH		do	
do	14TH		do	
do	15TH		The Battalion paraded at 8.45 A.M. and proceeded by March Route to GRAND RULLECOURT, via HOUVIN-HOUVIGNEUL, ETREE-WAMIN & LE CAUROY. Arriving at 1.15 P.M. and was billeted by 1.45 P.M.	do
GRAND RULLECOURT	16TH		The Battalion paraded at 1 P.M. and proceeded by March Route to WANQUETIN via, BARLY & FOSSEUX. Arriving at 4.15 P.M. and was billeted by 4.45 P.M.	do
WANQUETIN	17TH		The Battalion paraded at 3.15 P.M. and proceeded by March Route to ARRAS via, WARLUS & DAINVILLE, to relieve the 8TH (S) BN ROYAL BERKSHIRE REGT. who were quartered in the CAVALRY BARRACKS ARRAS. The Lewis Gun company arrived at the Cavalry Barracks at 5.45 P.M. The whole Battalion were quartered by 6.45 P.M. MacCauley MAJOR.	do

COMMANDING 6TH (S) BTH D-C-L-I.

K.M.c FIELD
DECR 1916

WAR DIARY or INTELLIGENCE SUMMARY. 6TH (S) BTN D.C.L.I.

Army Form C. 2118.

Place	Date	Hour	Summary of Events and Information	Remarks and references to Appendices
CAVALRY BKS ARRAS & TRENCHES.	1916 18TH		The Battalion relieved the 9th (S) Batt. ESSEX REGIMENT in TRENCHES in the H.2. Sub-sect. The relief was carried out without incident and completed by 5.45 p.m. (51.B 1/40,000) During the evening THREE CASUALTIES were reported from "C" Company. ONE KILLED and TWO WOUNDED (OTHER RANKS) by enemy Trench Mortar. Heavy Trench Mortar on "C" Company sector through the night.	MAP REFERENCE
TRENCHES	19TH		Heavy Trench Mortaring by enemy on left. Coys. sector #3 "C" Coy. Remainder quiet.	—do—
—do—	20TH		Heavy Trench Mortaring by enemy on left Coys sector i.e. "C" Coy. Three casualties reported. WOUNDED (Other Ranks) TWO "C" Coy. & ONE "D" Coy by T.M. ONE "D" Coy by Rifle fire. Remainder quiet.	
—do—	21ST		Slight Trench Mortaring by enemy on left Coys sector. Remainder quiet. Casualties NIL.	
—do—	22ND		Quiet day. Casualties ONE ⊕ other Rank WOUNDED "B" Co.	
—do—	23RD		Quiet day. Nothing to Report. MAJOR M.E. McCONAGHEY D.S.O. 2ND BTN ROYAL SCOTS FUSILIERS. assumed command of the Battalion vice Lieut. Colonel T.R. STOKOE to ENGLAND.	
TRENCHES & CAVALRY BKS	24TH		The Battalion was relieved in TRENCHES by the 10TH (S) Battalion DURHAM LIGHT INFANTRY. The relief was carried out without incident and completed by 8 P.M. The Battalion on relief returned to the CAVALRY BKS ARRAS where they were in DIVISIONAL RESERVE. The Battalion was quartered in the CAVALRY BKS by 2 + 5 P.M.	—do— —do—
CAVALRY BKS ARRAS	25TH		WORKING PARTIES & CARRYING PARTIES.	—do—
—do—	26TH		COMPANY TRAINING under COY COMMDRS.	do
—do—	27TH		—do—	do
IN THE FIELD 31st December			—do—	

M. McConaghey Major
COMMDG. 6TH (S) BTN D.C.L.I.

WAR DIARY

INTELLIGENCE SUMMARY. 6TH (S) BATTN D.C.L.I.

Army Form C. 2118.

Place	Date	Hour	Summary of Events and Information	Remarks and references to Appendices
CAVALRY BKS ARRAS.	1916 DECR 28th		WORKING PARTIES & CARRYING PARTIES. "C" COMPANY paraded at 12.30 P.M. and proceeded to TRENCHES in support to the 10/D.L.I. WORKING PARTIES and CARRYING PARTIES. COMPANY TRAINING under Coy Commdrs.	App 1/Appdx
—do—	29th		do	
—do—	30th		do	
CAVALRY BKS ARRAS & VICINITY.	31st		The Battalion relieved the 6th (S) Battn SOMERSET LIGHT INFANTRY as follows:— BRIGADE RESERVE, and the quarters as follows:— "A" Company from quarters in Cavalry Barracks to Billets in ARRAS. "B" — — — — ACHICOURT DEFENCES. "C" — From Support Line H.2 Labyrinth where they had been in Support to the 10/D.L.I. to Billets in ARRAS. 2 platoons Gun teams and reserve in support 6.10/D.L.I. "D" — From quarters in Cavalry Barracks to Billets in ARRAS. RONVILLE DEFENCES. This relief was carried out without incident and completed by 5 H. 5 P.M.	

IN THE FIELD.
31st DECR 1916.

GWM Taylor Major.
COMMANDING 6TH (S) BTN D.C.L.I.

Vol 21

21N.

War Diary

6th DCLI

January 1917.

Army Form C. 2118.

SHEET 1.

WAR DIARY
or
INTELLIGENCE SUMMARY. 6th (S) Btn D.C.L.I.

(Erase heading not required.)

Instructions regarding War Diaries and Intelligence Summaries are contained in F.S. Regs., Part II. and the Staff Manual respectively. Title pages will be prepared in manuscript.

Place	Date	Hour	Summary of Events and Information	Remarks and references to Appendices
ARRAS.	JANY 1917 1st		The Battalion relieved the 6th Bn SOMERSET LIGHT INFANTRY in Brigade Reserve on the 31st of December 1916. About 10.30 a.m. on the 1st January orders were received from Head Quarters 43rd Inf Brigade to relieve the 10th Bn DURHAM LIGHT INFANTRY in the "H"2 Sub-Sector Trenches. At 3 p.m. the relief was carried out without incident and completed by 6.30 p.m. The night was quiet. CASUALTIES NIL.	Reference Map:- TRENCH MAP ARRAS 51.B.N.W. 1/10,000. NEUVILLE VITASSE 51B.S.W. 1/10,000. See copies of S.O.'s N° 1 & 6 attached
TRENCHES H.2. S.W.Sec	2nd		IN TRENCHES Quiet day " " NIL	
H.2. Subsector	3rd		" " " " "	
"	4th		" " " " "	
"	5th		" " " " " CASUALTIES ONE Other Rank wounded Sgt "B" Coy "D.Coy"	
"	6th		"B" Coy and the 18th Bombing Platoon of the 10/D.L.I. came in to the H.2. Sub-Sector and carried out a RAID on the enemy's trenches. The enemy shelled our Sector rather heavily with 5.9" and Mizz Bangs through the day. Our line considerable damage to the trenches. CASUALTIES ONE OFFICER 2nd Lt E.P.GAY badly wounded by a piece of shell from a Mizz Bang striking him on the head artefact. The night was quiet except for 8 slight enemy Machine Gun fire.	
TRENCHES H.2 & Brigade Reserve ARRAS and VICINITY	7th		Quiet day 2nd Lieut E.P.GAY died of Wounds on the night of the 6/7 at H.B.A.R.C. Message received from O.C. 2 3rd C.C.S. on 7th inst. The Battalion was relieved in trenches by the 10/D.L.I. and Hildreth to Brigade Reserve. The relief was carried out without incident and completed by 8.30pm. The Battalion was quartered in Brigade Reserve as follows:- "A" Company IN BILLETS IN ARRAS. "C" Company ACHICOURT DEFENCES "D" - " - RONVILLE	
IN THE FIELD 31st January 1917				Rowland [signature] Lieut Col Comm'd 6th (S) Btn D.C.L.I.

SHEET 2.

Army Form C. 2118.

WAR DIARY
or
INTELLIGENCE SUMMARY. 6/7(S) Bn D.C.L.I.

(Erase heading not required.)

Instructions regarding War Diaries and Intelligence Summaries are contained in F. S. Regs., Part II. and the Staff Manual respectively. Title pages will be prepared in manuscript.

Place	Date	Hour	Summary of Events and Information	Remarks and references to Appendices
ARRAS & VICINITY	Jany 1914	8 pm	The Battalion in Brigade Reserve. "A" + "D" Coys supplying Working and Carrying Parties.	TRENCH MAP ARRAS 51B.N.W. 1/10,000 and
— do —		9:20	do	
— do —		10:20	do	
— do —		11:20	do	
— do —		12:20	do	
— do —			do	NEUVILLE VITASSE 51B.N.W 1/10,000
Arras and Trenches	13th		The Battalion relieved the 10/D.L.I. in H.2 Sub-sector Trenches after being relieved in Brigade Reserve by the 6/K.O.Y.L.I. The relief was carried out without incident and completed by 5.30 p.m. The night was quiet.	
H.2.Sub-Sector.	14th		The day was very quiet. The water who lossy and therefor situation was difficult to carry out.	
— " —	15th		Quiet day except for a few Verner Bombs fired onto the left Coy arcts.	
— " —	16th		Quiet day. A few Wrizz Bangs fell on Ronvilles in the vicinity of the Water Tower.	
— " —	17th		A few Verner Bombs were fired on our left Coy arcts and about six Trench Mortars fell in the Right Coy sector near Trenches H.34 and H.35.	
— " —	18th		The enemy Trench Mortars the Right Coy sector near H.34 and H.35 also burst about. Three rounds of Shrapnel over the Reserve line behind Trenches H.34 and H.35. Owing to the Snow which fell heavily in the early morning of the 17th inst. the Trenches have fallen in in several places. Three places have been cleared and repaired at night.	
In the Field. 31st 1-2-1917	19th		Quiet day. (Receipt for a list of enemy French Motors Sound ring Range at Niblet letter M.10/K3 ... attached hereto Sect. Intell-Staff)	

WAR DIARY or INTELLIGENCE SUMMARY

Army Form C. 2118.

SHEET. 3.

6th(S) Bⁿ D.C.L.I.

Place	Date 1917 JANY	Hour	Summary of Events and Information	Remarks and references to Appendices
TRENCHES H.2.Sub.Sector ARRAS	20th		Quiet throughout the day, but during the night the enemy fired several Trench Mortars on to our left Company Sector which fell near H.9 and H.7.2. Trench.	Reference Maps: FRENCH MAP ARRAS 51.B.N.W. 1/10.000 NEUVILLE VITASSE 51.B.S.W. 1/10.000
"	21st		Quiet day. The Battalion was relieved by the 10/D.L.I. The relief was carried out without incident and completed by 12.15 p.m. The Battalion returned to the Country Barracks ARRAS, where they were settled in quarters by 1.30 p.m.	
CAVALRY B^{KS} ARRAS	22ND		Company and Working Parties were furnished on per Brigade Orders. Company Training was carried out under Company Commanders. Half the Battn. were bathed and received a clean change of underclothing at the COLBAS COMMUNAL BATHS.	
"	23RD		As for 22nd inst. CASUALTIES One killed and One wounded. Other Ranks D.C.M. caused by a German Shell bursting near the squad whilst they were forming under the trees near the Riding School.	
"	24TH		Carrying two other parties to per Brigade Orders Companies Training in the Replote Rooms under Company Commanders.	
H.2. Sub.Sector	25TH		The Battalion relieved the 10th/Bⁿ D.L.I. in Trenches H.2 Sub Sector before 2 p.m. This relief was carried out without incident and completed by 12.30 p.m. The day was quiet. Slight Machine Gun fire during the night.	
"	26		Quiet up to about 2 p.m. when the enemy opened a Heavy Trench Mortar bombardment on Trenches H.39. 40 and 41. Damages them very badly. This bombardment lasted until about 4.30 p.m. CASUALTIES. Captain F.C. Harrison O.C. D.Coy. WOUNDED and One Other Rank wounded Col. R. Roy^t. R^t. No. 7973.	
"	27th		Quiet day, except for a few enemy shells which fell at or near the supporting line.	

In the Field 31.1.1917
(signed) Lieut Colonel
Commanding 6th(S) Bⁿ D.C.L.I.

WAR DIARY
INTELLIGENCE SUMMARY.

Army Form C. 2118.

C.J. 13 Bn. Duke of Boris L.I.

Place	Date JANY 1917	Hour	Summary of Events and Information	Remarks and references to Appendices
TRENCHES H.2. Sub-Sector	28th		The day was quiet except for a few Trench Mortars which fell near the firing line H.1 & H.2 Trenches about 10pm. The night was quiet.	Reference Maps:- Trench Map 51B.N.W. 1/10000 ARRAS 51B.S.W. 1/10000 NEUVILLE VITASSE
"	29th		Quiet day except for a few Minnie Bangs which Silenced the Support line between H.07 S.83 and HAMILTON STREETS. Between 11am and 12 Noon.	
"	30th		Enemy active from 7am to 10am with Minnenwerfers and from 3pm onwards on old German supports line between H.05 first line new HAMILTON STREETS and SYNTON STREET. About 50 fell behind the support line near HAMILTON STREET, and A.1 which also fell behind the support line near HAMILTON STREET. The enemy also fired about 250 Rifle Grenades about 2.30am. These fell in the front line near H.41 Trench. The enemy was not very active with Trench Mortars on the Left Company Sector between 7am and 9pm. These fell in the front line between HALIFAX and HAZEBROUCK STREETS (H.41 Trench.) Casualties: Other Ranks 1 Killed 1 Wounded	
Billets Sub-sector ARRAS & vicinity	31st		The night was quiet. The Battalion was relieved in the line by the 10/D.L.I. The relief was carried out without incident and completed by 3.15 pm. On Relief the Battalion went into Brigade Reserve and was quartered in ARRAS and the vicinity as follows. Battn Hd Qrs. "B" and "C" Coys.} IN BILLETS IN ARRAS "A" Coy. ACHICOURT DEFENCES. D.L. RONVILLE.	

In the Field
31st January 1917

[Signature] Lieut Colonel
Commanding 13th (S) BN D.L.I.

SECRET.

6TH. (SERVICE) BATTALION DUKE OF CORNWALL'S L.I.

OPERATION ORDER No. 46.

Copy No. 2

Ref.Map. Trench Map. ARRAS 51.B.N.W. 1/10,000.
" " NEUVILLE VITASSE 51 B.S.W. 1/10,000.

1. The Artillery of the Corps has been ordered to carry out a bombardment of the enemy's Front system of trenches opposite the right of "I" and left of "H" Sectors on 6th January 1917.

2. In connection with this bombardment, the 43rd. Infantry Brigade will carry out a raid in co-operation with the 28th. Infantry Brigade on the left.

3. This raid will be carried out by the 10th. Durham L.I. at Zero hour.

4. Frontage of Raid.
   From Sap X.26 (M.5.b.20.85) to junction of enemy Front Line with SUNKEN ROAD at G.35.d.6.1.

5. Objects of Raid.
   (a) To obtain information as to the effects of the bombardment.
   (b) To ascertain to what extent a view of the ground to E. and S.E. is obtainable from enemy's Lines.
   (c) Capture of Prisoners.

6. Penetration.
   The Raiding Party will penetrate first and second German trenches, and if possible will push forward a strong patrol to German third trench to about M.5.b.53.60.
   Blocks will be established at flanks of xxxxxxxxxxxxxxxxx trenches temporarily occupied.

7. Composition of Raiding Party.
   The party will consist of Three detachments "A". "B" and "C", their strength being respectively 75, 50, and 25 men. Each detachment under an officer.

   Detachment "A" will clear, block and hold German First Line Trench from N.5.B.20.86. to G.35.d.6.1.

   Detachment "B" will clear, block and hold German Second Line Trench from M.5.b.36.65. to M.5.b.80.95.

   Detachment "C" will reconnoitre German Third Line trench at about M.5.b.53.60.

8. Preparations for wirecutting on January 5th.

   Field Artillery, Medium Trench Mortars and Stokes Mortars will continue their wire cutting at the following places :-

   (a) Between M.5.b.20.85. and G.35.d.6.1.
   (b) At M.5.a.8.9.
   (c) At M.5.a.00.25.

9. Artillery and Infantry Co-operation on January 6th.

(a.) VI. Corps Heavy Artillery in conjunction with "H" and "I" Groups Field Artillery and Medium Trench Mortars will bombard enemy Front system of trenches between M.5.a.6.6. and G.35.b.20.90. from 11.15.a.m. to return of Raiders.

Error of day and exact ranges will be tested from 8.0. a.m. to 11.0.a.m.

(b) At Zero ~~minus 10 minutes~~ Field Artillery barrage enemy first trench from M.5.a.6.6. to G.35.d.75.30.

From Zero until return of Raiders the following time table will be strictly adhered to.

ZERO. "A". "B" and "C". Detachments get out of their trenches in two waves. "A" detachment forming the first wave and "B" and "C" the second.
The leading wave will advance as close up to the barrage as possible.

Zero plus 7 minutes. Barrage creeps back 50 yards per minute to German Second Trench.
"A". "B". and "C" detachments occupy German First trench.

Zero plus 12 minutes. "B" and "C" Detachments commence advance to German Second Trench.

Zero plus 17 minutes. Barrage creeps back 50 yards per minute to German Third Trench.
"B" and "C" detachments occupy German Second Trench.

Zero plus 22 minutes. Barrage creeps back 100 yards and remains stationary. "C" detachment goes forward to reconnoitre German Third Trench.

Zero plus 32 minutes. Detachments "B" and "C" leave German Second Trench and return to German First Trench. Barrage lifts back to German Third Trench.

Zero plus 42 minutes. Detachments "A". "B" and "C" leave German First Trench and return to our own lines. Barrage creeps back to German Second Trench.

(c) From Zero to return of Raiding Party Flank Barrages will be formed :-

(i) On the right from M.5.a.85.70. to M.5.b.0.2.
(ii) On the left from G.35.d.75.30. to M.6.a.05.90.

10. Machine Gun and Stokes Mortar Co-operation on January 6th.

(a) 2 Guns will barrage enemy trenches between M.5.a.70.60. and M.5.a.8.8. from the direction of RONVILLE (G.34.d.)

(b) 2 Guns in G.29.c. and 2 Guns in the vicinity of ACHICOURT MILL (G.35.d) will sweep the BRICKWORKS.

The above barrages will commence and will be intense from Zero minus 5 minutes to Zero plus 5 minutes and again at Zero plus 40 minutes to cover withdrawal of Raiders.

- 3 -

(c) O.C. 43rd. Trench Mortar Battery will place Four Guns to fire respectively on points :-

1. G.35.d.70.10.
2. M.5.a.90.82.
3. M.5.a.78.81.
4. Craters at M.4.b.90.20. and M.5.a.00.25.

Fire will be opened at Zero minus 10 minutes and will continue until Zero plus 50 minutes with frequent bursts of rapid fire between Zero minus 5 minutes and Zero plus 5 minutes.

11. O.C. 10th Durham L.I. will arrange for Smoke Candles to be thrown commencing at Zero minus 2 minutes.
(a) Between G.35.c.70.30 and G.35.d.00.25. if wind is blowing from N. or N.N.W.
(b) Between M.4.b.70.42. and M.4.b.98.60. if wind is blowing from N.W.

12. The signal that raiding Party are returning will be one green Rocket fired from hostile front line and will also be the signal for Field Artillery, Stokes Mortars and Machine Guns to open intense fire on their box barrage lines to cover withdrawal.

13. Advanced Brigade Headquarters will be situated at new dugout under construction at HETSAS STREET at about G.34.b.68.20.

14. ZERO HOUR is 3.8 p.m.

15. Watches will be synchronised at Left Battalion Headquarters - RONVILLE at 9.30.a.m. and 12.30.p.m. the 6th inst.

16. (a) Between Zero and Zero plus 50 minutes the Garrisons of H.1. and H.2 Sub-sectors will co-operate with bursts of rapid fire from rifles, Lewis Guns and with Rifle Grenades against enemy trenches opposite their front.
(b) The 42nd. Infantry Brigade will co-operate as in (a) in addition to employing Trench Mortars and Field Artillery.

17. Infantry co-operation, Garrison H.1. Sector.

(a) O.C.Centre Coy. will detail one Platoon to man Support Line between HOLBORN and HULL STREET and to fire bursts of rapid fire on enemy lines between M.5.a.5.5 and M.4.b.5.0.
O.C.Right Company will detail one platoon to man Support Line between HULL and HAVELOCK STREET and to fire rapid bursts on enemies lines between M.4.b.5.0. and M.4.b.9.2.
Platoons will be in position at Zero minus 5 minutes and open fire at ZERO.

(b). 2/Lt.BIRNE will maintain Rifle Grenade Fire from Front Line between HUNTER STREET and HORACE STREET on enemy's front line to immediate front, to left of G.35.d. 8.4.

(c). Lewis Gun Officer will detail 1 Lewis Gun to each Platoon mentioned in (a), and fire short bursts between M.5.a.4.3. & M.4.b. 9.2.
L.G.5 at top of HAMILTON STREET will fire along SUNKEN ROAD M.4. b.c.0.

18. Dispositions.

(a). The front line will be vacated from HORACE STREET to HULL STREET. On the rest of the sub-sector front usual day sentry posts and Lewis Guns will remain in front line.

- 4 -

(b) Single Sentry Posts will be established over each group of occupied dug-outs, and will be responsible for observation.

(c) Supporting Company will occupy Cave G.34.D.3.78. by 10.a.m. 1 Platoon "C" Coy. attached to "A" Coy. will rejoin Supporting Coy. by 9.0. a.m.

(d) Headquarter Details will parade under 2/Lt.MATHESON at 9.0. a.m., and be accommodated in Cave G.34.d.3.78. by 9.30. a.m.

(e) Intelligence Officer will dispose his Snipers in positions suitable for observation.

19. MEDICAL ARRANGEMENTS.

(a) M.O. attached 10th. D.L.I. will establish an advanced Dressing Station in the Dug-out in Support Line between HAZEBROCK and HALIFAX STREET.

(b) 9 Stretcher Bearers (R.A.M.C.) will be stationed in Dug-out in HUNTER STREET near Patrol Line.

Sufficient accommodation for above Stretcher Bearers will be provided in Dug-outs named. Dug-out under (a) will be evacuated by 9.0.a.m.

(c) Evacuations will take place by HOOGE and HUNTER STREET. Walking cases will proceed direct by shortest route to Dressing Station, RONVILLE. An emergency Dug-Out will be provided in HOOGE STREET, near R.S. Line, for walking cases.

20. Raiding Party D.L.I. will be in the line by 10.0.a.m. O.C. D.L.I. will establish his H.Q. at Centre Coy.H.Q.

21. Special attention is drawn to probable use of Gas Shells by the enemy.

22. There will be no movement after 11.0 a.m., and no traffic along HOOGE STREET after 9.15. a.m.

23. Normal dispositions will be resumed at conclusion of raid.

24. Advanced Battalion Headquarters will be established at telephone exchange in HOOGE STREET near Reserve Line.

25. ACKNOWLEDGE.

      (Sd). R.C.CODYRE,   Captain &
5th. January, 1917.   A/Adjt. 6th. D.C.L.I.

****

```
Copy No. 1... C.O.,              Copy No. 8... Signalling Officer,
         2.. 2nd. in Cmd.                 9.   L.G. Officer,
         3... A/Adjt.                    10.   Sniping Officer.
         4... O.C. "A" Coy.              11.   Bombing       "
         5.   "   "B"  "                 12.   Brigade.
         6.   "   "C"  "                 13.   Adjt., 10th. D.L.I.
         7.   "   "D"  "                 14.   R. S. M.
                                         15.   O. O. File.
```

****

Vol 22

War Diary.

6th D.C.L.I.

February 1917.

Army Form C. 2118.

SHEET 1. FOR FEBRUARY 1917

WAR DIARY
or
INTELLIGENCE SUMMARY. 6th (Ser) Bn. D.C.L.I.

(Erase heading not required.)

TRENCH MAP ARRAS
57B.N.W.3
EDITION 6A
1/10,000

5/0 1/10,000

Place	Date	Hour	Summary of Events and Information	Remarks and references to Appendices
ARRAS & VICINITY	1917. FEBY 1ST.		The Battalion was in Brigade Reserve and quartered as follows:— Battn Hd Qrs. "B" and "C" Companies In Billets in ARRAS. "D" Coy. RONVILLE DEFENCES "A" Coy. ACHICOURT DEFENCES. "A" "B" & "C" Companies supplied working parties as per Bn instructions. CASUALTIES:— Two Other Ranks "B" Coy. WOUNDED.	
"	2ND		Same as for 1st inst. CASUALTIES	
"	3RD		The Battn was relieved in Brigade Reserve by the 6/3 Bn Somerset L.I. and on relief went in to Divisional Reserve at the Cavalry Bks ARRAS	
CAVALRY BARRACKS			The Battn was completed and the Battn settled in Billets by 3.30 p.m.	
CAVALRY BKS & BERNEVILLE	4TH		The Battn was still in Divisional Reserve but moved from the Cavalry Bks ARRAS to the Village of BERNEVILLE where they were billeted. The move was carried out as follows:— "A" Coy paraded at 5 pm and moved off to Station at five minutes interval "B" Coy. 5.15 pm "C" Coy. 5.30 pm "D" Coy 5.45 pm. All Coys 6 pm. All Coys marched by Platoons at 5 minutes interval. The move was completed and the Battn settled in billets by 8.30 pm	
BERNEVILLE	5TH		The Battalion carried out TRAINING and Company Commanders and Specialist Officers	
"	6TH		"do" for the 6th inst. with the exception of 4 Officers and 200 other Ranks who were working under the supervision of the O.C. 278 Company R.E.	

IN THE FIELD
1-3-1917

[signature] Lieut. Colonel
COMMANDING 6th (S) Bn D.C.L.I.

SHEET 2.
FOR FEBRUARY 1917.

WAR DIARY
INTELLIGENCE SUMMARY. 6TH (S) BTN D.C.L.I.

Army Form C. 2118.

Place	Date FEBY. 1917	Hour	Summary of Events and Information	Remarks and references to Appendices
BERNEVILLE	7TH		The Battalion carried out TRAINING under Company Commanders, and Specialist Officers. A Working Party consisting of 4 OFFICERS and 200 OTHER RANKS was furnished by the Battn to work under the supervision of the O.C. 278 Company R.E's.	S/C 4/6/100
-"-	8TH		As for the 7TH inst.	
-"-	9TH		-"- do -"-	
-"-	10TH		-"- do -"-	
BERNEVILLE to ARRAS	11TH		The Battalion moved to Billets in ARRAS VIA WARLUS and DAINVILLE, by Platoons + Detachments. The First Platoon (No 1 "A" Coy) leaving BERNEVILLE at 10.30 a.m. The Remainder followed at FIVE Minute interval. The Battalion (less the Working Party) were settled in Billets in "INFANTRY BARRACKS" RUE BAUDIMONT by 2.30.p.m. The WORKING PARTY arriving and were quartered in the same place by 4.30 p.m.	TRENCH MAP ARRAS 51B N.W. EDITION 6.A. 1/10000
ARRAS.	12TH		The Battalion furnished DAY and NIGHT WORKING PARTIES. amounting to 4 OFFICERS and 500 Other Ranks. Spare Officers N.C. O's + Men were instructed in MUSKETRY, LEWIS GUN, BOMBING, RAPID WIRING + TRENCH ORDERS.	
-"-	13TH		As for the 12th inst.	
-"-	14TH		-"- do -"-	
-"-	15TH		-"- do -"-	
-"-	16TH		-"- do -"-	
IN THE FIELD 1-3-1917	17TH			

Kleinhfd
LIEUT COLONEL.
COMMANDING 6TH (S) BTN D.C.L.I.

WAR DIARY

Army Form C. 2118.

SHEET. No. 3.

INTELLIGENCE SUMMARY. 67 (S) Bttn D.C.L.I.

For FEBRUARY 1917

Place	Date Feb.y 1917	Hour	Summary of Events and Information	Remarks and references to Appendices
ARRAS.	18th		The Battalion furnishes DAY and NIGHT WORKING PARTIES amounting to 14 Officers and 500 Other Ranks. Spare Officers, N.C.O.s & Men were instructed in MUSKETRY, LEWIS GUN, RAPID WIRING & TRENCH ORDERS.	TRENCH M/AP ARRAS 51B.N.W.3. EDITION 6.A. 1/11,000
—"—	19th		As for 18th inst.	
—"—	20th		do	
—"—	21st		do	
—"—	22nd		do	
—"—	23rd		do	
ARRAS at H.1 Sub-Sector Trenches	24th		The Battalion relieved the 6th (S) Btn K.O.Y.L.I. in the H.1. Sub-sector trenches. The relief was carried out without incident and completed by 3 p.m.	TRENCH M/AP 619 NEUVILLE VITASSE 1/10,000.
TRENCHES H.1. Sub Sec.	25th		The night 24/25 was fairly quiet. The day was quite except for a few MINNIE BANGS which fell behind the FRONT LINE in the vicinity of H.32. H.33 TRENCHES.	
—"—	26th		The enemy bombarded our SUPPORT LINE behind H.32 and H.33 TRENCHES with MINNIE BANGS & MEDIUM TRENCH MORTARS for about FIFTEEN MINUTES as the following times 8-4.5.a.m. 2.p.m & 6.p.m. No material damage was done.	
—"—	27th		The enemy Aeroplanes one of our Working Parties belonging to the MONMOUTHSHIRE REGT which was working near the SUPPORT LINE behind H.33. from about 6.45 p.m. to 7. P.m. Immediately preceding this a RED FLARE was sent up in the German Line about H.33. Whether Sigs MINNIE BANGS & TRENCH MORTARS opened fire.	

Harold W Wood
Lieut. Colonel
Commdg. 6/S) Btn D.C.L.I.

IN THE FIELD
1. 3. 1917

Army Form C. 2118.

WAR DIARY
or
INTELLIGENCE SUMMARY. 6 TH (S) B TN D.C.L.I.

(Erase heading not required.)

S.J.1 6 st Mar.

Instructions regarding War Diaries and Intelligence Summaries are contained in F.S. Regs., Part II. and the Staff Manual respectively. Title pages will be prepared in manuscript.

Place	Date	Hour	Summary of Events and Information	Remarks and references to Appendices
TRENCHES H.I. Sub Sector	1917 27/4		At about 8.30 p.m the Enemy except the Battalion Dump near the junction of the BUQUOY - ACHICOURT - BEAURAINS ROAD were very carrying THREE CASUALTIES. "C" Coy. From about 8.40 p.m to 9 p.m. there was a considerable amount of activity on our LEFT (about a mile or so away) during which the enemy put a few WIZZ BANGS on the LEFT Company sector which fell between the FRONT & SUPPORT Lines behind H.32 TRENCH. The remaining hours of darkness was quiet.	FRENCH MAP. NEUVILLE VITASSE. 51E 1/10,000.
" "	28 TH		AEROPLANES:- Between the hours of 2 p.m. and 4 p.m. ENEMY AEROPLANES were very active over the H.I. Sub Sector. THE ENEMY'S ANTI AIR-CRAFT GUNS were firing at OUR AEROPLANES at a longer range than usual. The day was very quiet except for a few WIZZ BANGS and light TRENCH MORTARS which fell on our SUPPORT LINE behind H.27 TRENCH. between 1.30 p.m to 2 p.m. One of our SNIPERS silenced a German Sniper who was Sniping from a LOOPHOLE about M.10.a.6.6. The night was quiet.	

In the Field
1.3.1919

Kurtful
Lieut Colonel.
Commanding 6 TH (S) B TN D.C.L.I.

CONFIDENTIAL.

WAR DIARY
of
6th Service Battalion Duke of Cornwall's Light Infantry.

from 1st March 1917 to 31st March 1917.

VOLUME 23.

****

Army Form C. 2118.

WAR DIARY
or
INTELLIGENCE SUMMARY. 6th (S) Btn. Duke of Corn'ls L.I.

SHEET 1.
MARCH 1917

(Erase heading not required.)

Instructions regarding War Diaries and Intelligence Summaries are contained in F.S. Regs., Part II. and the Staff Manual respectively. Title pages will be prepared in manuscript.

REFERENCE MAP
TRENCH MAP ARRAS 51B NW 510
NEUVILLE VITASSE 51BSW I.1/H/000

Place	Date March 1917	Hour	Summary of Events and Information	Remarks and references to Appendices
TRENCHES H.1.Sub-Sector	1st		The Battalion was in the Lyns (H.1 SUB-SECTOR TRENCHES) This day was quiet except for slight shelling and Machine Gun fire. The hours of darkness were quiet.	
H.1.Sub Sector and DAINVILLE	2nd		Quiet day. The Battalion was relieved by the 6th Btn SOMRS & SHRS L.ght INFANTRY. The relief was carried out without incident and was completed by about 3. to 5 pm. On relief the Batn. marched 4 Platoons to billets in DAINVILLE where they were at Bills at 6.30 pm. and were Bivouaced Thieves.	
DAINVILLE and ARRAS.	3rd		The Battalion marched 4 platoons from DAINVILLE to ARRAS and were billeted in the RUE-FRED 8 R.10 D6 - GEORGE where they were settled by 8.30 pm. (BRIGADE RGSR/S)	
ARRAS	4th		The Battalion was in BRIGADE RESERVE and furnishes 500- Officers and Other Ranks for WORKING PARTIES to work or certain work ordered by Brigade. Training was carried out under Company arrangements in the following subjects Rifle Exercises, Physical Training, Musketry, Saluting, and Lewis Gun.	
	5th		do for the 4th inst	
	6th		do	
	7th		do	
ARRAS and H.1.Sub-Sect.	8th		The Battalion furnishes a Working Party of 150 Officers & Othr Ranks from "A" Coy and was relieved the 6 B.S L.I in the LYNS (H.1 Sub-Sector) The relief was completed without incident and completed at 2.50pm.	

31st March 1917.   Wheeler Lt Col   Commdg 6/D.C.L.I

Army Form C. 2118.

WAR DIARY
or
INTELLIGENCE SUMMARY.

SHEET 2.   6/D.C.L.I.
March 1917

(Erase heading not required.)

Place	Date	Hour	Summary of Events and Information	Remarks and references to Appendices
TRENCHES H.2. Sub Sec.	March 1917 9th.		The day was quiet except for about five or 9 shells which fell in the vicinity of the Bn. Dump situated just behind the Support Line behind Trenches 28 & H.29. The night was quiet except for Machine Gun fire at odd times.	
—	10th.		Slight shelling along the Support Line by Whizz Bangs and Medium Trench Mortars. The night was quiet. Patrols were sent out from the three Forward Line Companies. CASUALTIES Gnr Ranti ONE. L/Cpl PARKHOUSE "B" Coy.	
—	11th.		Very quiet day. A few Medium Trench Mortars fell in rear of the Support Line behind Trench H.31. During the night between the hours of 4pm. and 9pm. the enemy put over several gas shells some of which fell in the village of ACHICOURT, but caused no damage.	
—	12th.		Quiet day. A few Whizz Bangs fell near the Bn. Dump and along the Support Line. During the night the enemy again fires Gas shells some fell in ACHICOURT. Machine Guns were active on our Communication Trenches.	
—	13th.		The forenoon was quiet except for a few Whizz Bangs which fell along HAIG STREET. During the afternoon the enemy shelled the vicinity of Bn. Hd Qrs with 5.9's from 3pm to 5pm. Machine Gun were active during the night.	
—	14th.		The forenoon was quiet. The Battn was relieved by the 1/12th London Regiment (R.F.) The relief was carried out without incident and completed by 4.30pm. On relief the Battn moved in Platoons to billets in BEAUDIMONT BARRACKS ARRAS where they were settled by 6.30.p.m.	[signed] Major Commdg 6/D.C.L.I.

31st MARCH 1917.

Army Form C. 2118.

WAR DIARY
or
INTELLIGENCE SUMMARY. 6TH BTTN D.C.L.I

SHEET. 3.

(Erase heading not required.)

REFERENCE MAP
51G NEUVILLE VITASSE.

Place	Date	Hour	Summary of Events and Information	Remarks and references to Appendices
ARRAS	March 1917 15th		The Battalion was Quartered in the BEAUDIMONT BARRACKS and furnished working parties amounting to 500. Officers and Other Ranks for work under Brigade Orders. The Battalion moved to billets in the Rue FREDERICK-des-George by platoon and was settled by 8.30 p.m.	
-	16th		In Billets in Rue FREDERICK des George and furnished 500 for Working Parties in the 15th remainder of the Battn training under Company Commanders Lieut Col VVV SANDFORD relinquished Command of the Battalion. As for 15th and 16th inst.	
RONVILLE and H.2. Sub Sector	17th		Furnished Working Parties as for 15th. About 11.30 p.m. Orders were received from Brigade to recall All Working parties and "STAND BY" for further orders. At 2.15 p.m. orders were received from Brigade to send two Companies to RONVILLE VILLAGE in Support to 6/S.L.I. who were moving forward. Two Companies whilst Battn (6/S.L.I.) were occupying the Old German Trenches in front of H.2. Sub Sector Trenches "THE BRICKFIELDS" "D" and "C" Coys moved off to platoons and were clear of billets by 3.15 p.m. At 3.20 p.m. orders were received for the remaining Two Companies HQ15 the Gro to move to RONVILLE VILLAGE ("E"A" and "B" Coys) and the former two Coys ("C"D") were to move forward and occupy the Old W/Com Hd Trenches in H.2 Sub-Sector. So the whole of the 6/S.L.I. were now occupying the Old German Trenches and had established Hear Battn Hd Qrs at the BRICKSTACK.	

21st MARCH 1917.

Ed Miller Major
Commdg 6/DCLI

WAR DIARY

Army Form C. 2118.

SHEET 4.

INTELLIGENCE SUMMARY. 6TH BTN D.C.L.I.

(Erase heading not required.)

Place	Date	Hour	Summary of Events and Information	Remarks and references to Appendices
ARRAS – RONVILLE & Sub Sector & Sub Sector	March 1917 18th		The Battalion was now situated as follows: "C" & "D" Coys Old British Front Line, H.Q. Subsects. Two Companies "A" & "B" Coys in cellars in RONVILLE VILLAGE. Batt'n HD QRS & DETAILS were quartered in BLUFF CAVE. The two Coys in Ronville carried TRENCH STORES, S.A.A, GRENADES, RATIONS & WATER for the 6/S.L.I. throughout the night.	
H.Q. Sub-Sectr. RONVILLE & Old German Trenches.	19th		Orders were received from Brigade about 10.30 a.m. that the Battalion would relieve the 6/S.L.I. in the Old German system of trenches by 6 p.m. The relief was carried out without incident and completed by 5.50 p.m. Coys were placed as follows. "C" & "D" Coys "FRONT LINE" "A" & "B" Coys "SUPPORT LINE" BHQ HdQrs THE BRICK STACK. The enemy shelled the whole Btn sector heavily during the night also the approaches to same. The Machine Guns were very active. CASUALTIES 1. Other Rank WOUNDED.	REFERENCE 1/47 51/G NEUVILLE VITASSE.
"	20th		Battalion holding Old German Trenches dispositions of Coys as for 19th. Intermittent shelling with 5.9s & WHIZZ BANGS throughout the day and night. Machine Guns were very active. CASUALTIES Other Ranks Killed 1. Wounded 8.	
"	21st		Fairly heavy shelling and Machine Gun fire through the day. Casualties Other Ranks 4 Wounded. The Batt'n was relieved by the 6/S.L.I. The relief was carried out without incident and completed by 7.30 p.m. On relief "A" & "B" Coys took up position in the Old British Front Line. "C" & "D" Coys in cellars in RONVILLE. Bt'n Hd Qrs & DETAILS in BLUFF CAVE.	

5th MARCH 1917.

W. Rueger Major

Comm'g 6/D.C.L.I.

SHEET 5.

Army Form C. 2118.

WAR DIARY
or
INTELLIGENCE SUMMARY. 6TH BTN D.C.L.I.

(Erase heading not required.)

Place	Date	Hour	Summary of Events and Information	Remarks and references to Appendices
H.Q. SUB SECTOR RONVILLE CAVES.	March 1917 22ND		The Battalion was quartered as for the 21st inst. and furnished 4 50 Officers and Other Ranks for Working Parties under Brigade Orders.	
	23RD		As for 22nd inst. (Digging Trenches at night)	
ARRAS	24TH		The Battalion was relieved by the 7/3 Battn. K.R.R. Corps. The relief was carried out without incident and was completed by 2.50 pm. On relief the Battn. moved by platoons to Billets in the RUE-des-FOURS.	
"	25TH		Furnished a Working Party of 4 50 Officers & Other Ranks as for 23RD inst. The Battalion was quartered as for 24th and furnished a Working Party of 2 Officers and 160 Other Ranks. The remainder of the Battn. carried out TRAINING under Company Commanders.	
"	26TH		As for 25th inst. plus ONE Officer and 50 Other RANKS. Working party at Rue Dump	
"	27TH		As for 26th inst.	— do —
"	28TH		do for 27th inst.	— do — CASUALTIES Two Other Ranks wounded.
"	29TH		do	— do — CASUALTIES Two Other Ranks wounded.
"	30TH		do	— do —
"	31ST		do	— do —

31st MARCH 1917.

M Mileson Major
Commanding 6/D.C.L.I.

WAR. DIARY

6th. D.C.L.I.

Volume 24

April 1917.

Army Form C. 2118.

WAR DIARY
or
INTELLIGENCE SUMMARY. 6TH (S) BTN D.C.L.I
(Erase heading not required)
For April 1917.

SHEET .1.

Reference Maps
Trench Map ARRAS 51.B.N.W.
NEUVILLE VITASSE 57.C.S.W.

Place	Date	Hour	Summary of Events and Information	Remarks and references to Appendices
ARRAS	1917 April 1st		The Battalion was quartered in ARRAS and furnished Working Parties amounting to 450 Officers and Other Ranks for Work at night (DIGGING) under Brigade arrangements. Spare Officers and Other Ranks carried out TRAINING under Company arrangements.	
" "	2ND		As for the 1st inst. with the exception of "C" Company who were detailed as "MOPPERS UP" to the 10th Battn D.L.I. and proceeded to DAINVILLE at 7 am. to train with that Battalion. They rejoined the Battn about 5.30pm.	
ARRAS TRENCHES	3RD		The Battalion relieved the 8TH (S) Battn K.R.R.C. in the Old German Trenches and were situated as follows :- FRONT LINE. "A" Coy. LEFT – "B" Coy. RIGHT with the PRUSSEN N59. "C" Coy. in support to "A" Coy. "D" Coy. in support to "B" Coy. Both "C" Coy & "D" Coy were accommodated in dugouts in the vicinity of the BRICK STACKS and were used for working and carrying parties. The relief on this occasion was not completed till 6pm and was carried out without incident. CASUALTIES ONE Officer 2nd Lt. CARTER Wound	
TRENCHES	4TH		"A" Coy & "D" Coy. moved forward and occupied the ASSEMBLY TRENCHES in front of the PRUSSEN WEG which were almost completed. Pushing out Covering parties well forward so as to enable "C" & "D" Coys. + a Strong Working Party of the 6/S.L.I. to complete same. CASUALTIES ONE OFFICER 2nd Lt. R. M. PADDISON Missing. Our Artillery heavily bombarded the Enemy's Trenches + Back areas, throughout the day and night. The Enemy making slight Retaliation. Patrols Snipers + Machine Gun were very active	P Flevarda Lt Col. Commando 6/D.C.L.I

Army Form C. 2118.

SHEET 2.

WAR DIARY
or
INTELLIGENCE SUMMARY. 6TH (S) Btn. D.C.L.I.
From 5th April to

(Erase heading not required.)

Reference Map
NEUVILLE VITASSE 51B S.W.

Place	Date 1917 April	Hour	Summary of Events and Information	Remarks and references to Appendices
TRENCHES	5th		As for War Diary.	
"	6th		— do —	
"	7th		— do —	
"	8th		This Battalion was relieved in the Front Line Trenches by the 6th (S) Battn K.O.Y.L.I. on the RIGHT and the 10th (S) Battn D.L.I. on the LEFT. "C" Coy. who were detailed to act as "Moppers Up" to the 10/D.L.I. left the Support Line at 2pm and took up their position in the Front Line Trench to 3.15.pm. and awaited the arrival of the 10/D.L.I. where orders they were under until further notice. "A" Coy. and "B" Coy. on relief returned to the Support Line and took up position with "D" Coy in the Old German Trench immediately in rear of the KRIEGER STELLUNG (between the PRUSSEN WEG and Z 18.a.15. WEG Communication Trenches) The relief was carried out without incident and completed by 4.pm. The Battalion who now in Brigade Reserve.	
"	9th		The Battalion remained in Brigade Reserve in this position until 12.30pm when orders were received from Brigade HQrs to advance and take up position in the "E" and "F" Lines (Assembly Trenches) and establish Battn HQrs in Box Trench at the junction of GINGER STREET. For further details, please see NARRATIVE on the Operations of 9th and 10th attached	

E.J. Lewis Lt Colonel
Commdg 6/D.C.L.I.

SHEET 3.

WAR DIARY
or
INTELLIGENCE SUMMARY. 6¼(S) Btn D.C.L.I

Army Form C. 2118.

(Erase heading not required.)

Place	Date 1917 April	Hour	Summary of Events and Information	Remarks and references to Appendices
TRENCHES & The CAVES RONVILLE.	10th		For details, Please see the NARRATIVE of the Operations on 9th and 10th attached. The Battalion were practiced in DUNEDIN CAVES by 8PM remaining there for the night.	MAP REF. 51.B 1/20000
	11th		Orders were received at 6AM that the attack would be renewed and that the Battalion was to advance on the German front line system by 10AM. Orders were received about 9.30 AM that the attack was cancelled and that the Battalion would remain in Caves. About 3.30 PM orders were received from Brigade that the Battalion would march to MONTENESCOURT and be relief of the Caves by 10PM. They proceeded by French Route and arrived in Billets at 4.30 AM.	MAP REF. 51.C 1/40000
MONTENESCOURT	12th		Orders were received from Brigade at 5.20PM that the Battalion recruits evacuate Billets by 6PM and march to MANIN Area. The Battalion proceeded by French Route. HABARCQ - NOYELLE VION - MANIN & arriving in Billets at 10.30 PM.	
BEAUFORT	13th		Routine and Inspections	
BEAUFORT	14th		Orders were received at 1.30 AM that the Battalion would vacate Billets by 7.30 PM and move to WARLUZEL.	E.J. Hewitt Lt Col Cmdg 6th DCLI

Sheet 4.

Army Form C. 2118.

WAR DIARY
or
INTELLIGENCE SUMMARY.
(Erase heading not required.)

6/5/DCLI

Marker S/C
FRANCE.

Place	Date	Hour	Summary of Events and Information	Remarks and references to Appendices
WARLOZEL	14th		The Battalion proceeded by Branch Route via GRAND RULLECOURT to WARLOZEL arriving there and all troops billeted by 10.15 P.M.	
	15th		Church Parade	
	16th		Training	
	17th		Training	
	18th		Training	
	19th		Training	
	20th		Training	
	21st		Training	
	22nd		Regt. P.A. Sergt. y t. P.S. Corpl joined for duty as Scouts in Command. Church Parade. Warning note received from Brigade about 5.30 P.M. that the Battalion should be prepared to move at short notice.	
WARLOZEL &	23rd		Order received from Brigade about 2.30 P.M. that the Battalion should march to SAULTY. Men at 5 P.M. they proceeded by March Route via COUTURELLE and arrived	
SAULTY			at SAULTY and billeted by 6.45 P.M.	
SAULTY &	24th		Order were received from Brigade at 6.30 A.M. that the Battalion should proceed at 5.27 A.M.	
BAILLEUVAL			to BAILLEUVAL. They proceeded by March Route at 7.30 A.M. via ARRAS – DOULLENS Road	
BAILLEUVAL	25th		arriving in Billets at 10.30 A.M.	
do	26th		Standing by. Resting. No orders	

A5834 Wt. W4973/M687 750,000 8/16 D/D. & L. Ltd. Forms/C.2118/13.

Army Form C. 2118.

WAR DIARY
or
INTELLIGENCE SUMMARY. 6TH (S) Batn D.C.L.I.

SHEET 5.

(Erase heading not required.)

Instructions regarding War Diaries and Intelligence Summaries are contained in F. S. Regs., Part II. and the Staff Manual respectively. Title pages will be prepared in manuscript.

Place	Date April 1917	Hour	Summary of Events and Information	Remarks and references to Appendices
BAILLEUVAL and "W" CAMP M.12.C.	27th	5 A.M.	The Battalion Paraded (less "Tn0 DETAILS") at 4.45 a.m. and moved off at 5 A.M. for "W" Camp Telegraph Hill M.12.C. where they arrived at 9.45 a.m. and relieved the 9th Batn "DURHAM LIGHT INFANTRY" at 10 A.M. The Battalion was in DIVISIONAL RESERVE.	Ref. Map 57B. FRANCE
"W" CAMP	28th		TRAINING was carried out under Company Commanders	
—do—	29th		The Battalion paraded "As STRONG AS POSSIBLE" at 8-30 a.m. for repairing roads under the O.R.E. Casualties Two. Ord. Ranks O.Ry. KINROSS/HOWARD/.	
—do—	30th		As for the 29th.	

J.B. Fell
Lt. Col.
15 May 1917

E.S. Lewis Lieut. & Adjt.
Comdg. 6th (S) R.D.C.L.I.

NARRATIVE OF OPERATIONS
of the 6th. Batt. D.C.L.I.

on 9th and 10th April, 1917.

9th, Zero Day. The Battalion less "C" Coy. attached 10th D.L.I. as Moppers up and one Platoon of "D" Coy. under 2/Lt. Matheson, who were employed during operations to carry up Brigade stores,was when in position as Brigade Reserve in the old German Front Line.   Battalion H.Q. in KRIEGER STELLUNG (M 5a 8.1).   At 12.30 pm. orders were received for the Battalion to proceed to the Front and E Lines (Assembly Trenches) as support to the 6th Batt. Som. L.I., who had advanced.

Ref: MAP
Neuville
  Vitasse
51b SW 1.

Battn. Headquarters in Box Trench at the Junction of Ginger St.
The Battn. was in position in F. and E. Lines by 2 pm. About 2.35 pm. orders were received for the Battn. to advance in the direction of N 15 CENTRAL and assist the 6/S.L.I. who had been held up.
2nd Lt. Bell, M.C. was at once dispatched to get in touch with the 6th. S.L.I., whose H.Q. were found to be at N 8 C 8 2 and on his reporting the Battalion at once moved forward in ARTILLARY formation, picking up "C" Coy. in HOP TRENCH, who had completed their mopping up, and passing through the 10th Battn. D.L.I., who were consolidating the BLUE LINE.
The Battn. then took up a position in Trenches and SHELL Holes in rear of the 6th. S.L.I. H.Q.
At about 5.15 pm. the 6th. S.L.I. being still held up orders were received for the 6th. D.C.L.I. in conjunction with the 6th. S.L.I. to attack and capture the BROWN LINE.
A and B Coys. were immediately pushed forward on the Right Flank of the 6th. S.L.I. with D Coy. in support on the right Flank and C Coy. in reserve.
Immediately on advancing the leading Companies came under heavy Machine Gun Fire from the High Ground to the RIGHT of Wancourt and from the vicinity of the SUNKEN ROAD about (N 22 a 5.4)
They suffered heavy casualties and were forced to fall back into the German Communication Trench (N 9 C 55.45) to N 15 d 30.7 F 20 which they eventually held for the night with C Coy. in Reserve in Trenches at N 8 G 80.05 to N 8 d 80.40.
D Coy. who had come up to the Right of A and B Coys. did not come under such heavy machine Gun owing to configuration of the ground, pushed forward and occupied a German Trench N 15 C 20.45 to N 15 D 10.60 which they held for the night as a defensive flank.
As soon as the trench was occupied BOMBING parties were sent in the direction of Wancourt along which trench the enemy had retreated.
The enemy took up a position before a large DUMP in the SUNKEN ROAD and barricaded the approach to this with WIRE and about 100 boxes.
A Lewis Gun dispersered them from the position and they fell back.
A Lewis Gun position was established to guard the DUMP and an Ammunition DUGOUT containing a large quantity of S.A.A. etc.
The DUGOUT was evidently one of enemy's chief sources of supply, for during the night four parties of men attempted to get to the place, but were driven off
An enemy attack was also made during the night on the right flank of the Company, but was driven off.   One officer and two men being taken prisoners.

Narrative of Operations　　　　　　　　　CONTINUED
　　　of the 6th. Battn. D.C.L.I.　　　　　　Page 2.

10th April.　　The next morning, the Dump and DUGOUT were bombed and
　　　　　　　cleared of the enemy, after which a company of the 6th
　　　　　　　S.L.I. came up for the purpose of clearing the SUNKEN
　　　　　　　Road.
　　　　　　　Orders were received that the 10th D.L.I. and 6th. KOYLI
　　　　　　　were to advance through the 6th S.L.I. and 6th D.C.L.I.
　　　　　　　at 11.30 am. to attack the BROWN LINE and that the DCLI
　　　　　　　were to bring covering fire to bear on the enemy's Trenches
　　　　　　　from all suitable places.　This was done.
　　　　　　　About 12.25 pm. orders were received for the Battalion to
　　　　　　　advance with their Right Flank on the SUNKEN ROAD and to
　　　　　　　get in touch with the 10th D.L.I. on the left, and that
　　　　　　　the 41st Brigade were to advance on the right of the
　　　　　　　Battalion.　A. B. and C. Coys. were ordered to advance
　　　　　　　down the Communication Trench, N 9 C 55.45 to N 15 d
　　　　　　　30.70 as far as possible, until they got in touch with
　　　　　　　D Coy., who had received orders to push up the Hill with
　　　　　　　their Right Flank on the SUNKEN ROAD, so as to cover the
　　　　　　　right flank of the Battalion.
　　　　　　　As soon as this Company advanced, they came under heavy
　　　　　　　MACHINE GUN fire and were unable to proceed.
　　　　　　　Meanwhile a report was received that the right flank of
　　　　　　　the 10th. D.L.I. was a long way to the left of WANCOURT.
　　　　　　　About this time the 41st. Brigade, instead of coming up
　　　　　　　on our RIGHT flank, swung over to the left and passed
　　　　　　　through A. B. and C. Coys. on their way to attack the
　　　　　　　BROWN LINE.
　　　　　　　About 4.45 pm. orders were received through O.C. 6th.
　　　　　　　S.L.I. that the Battalion was to withdraw and return to
　　　　　　　Quarters in the DUNEDIN Caves in Ronville.

CASUALTIES.　　Total Casualties during the above operations.

　　　　　　　　　　　　4 Officers.
　　　　　　　　　　　　96 Other Ranks.

　　　　　　　　　　　　　(sd). C. B. Scott, Capt.
　　　　　　　　　　　　　　　　Cmdg. 6/ Batt. D. C. L. I.

April 13th, 1917.

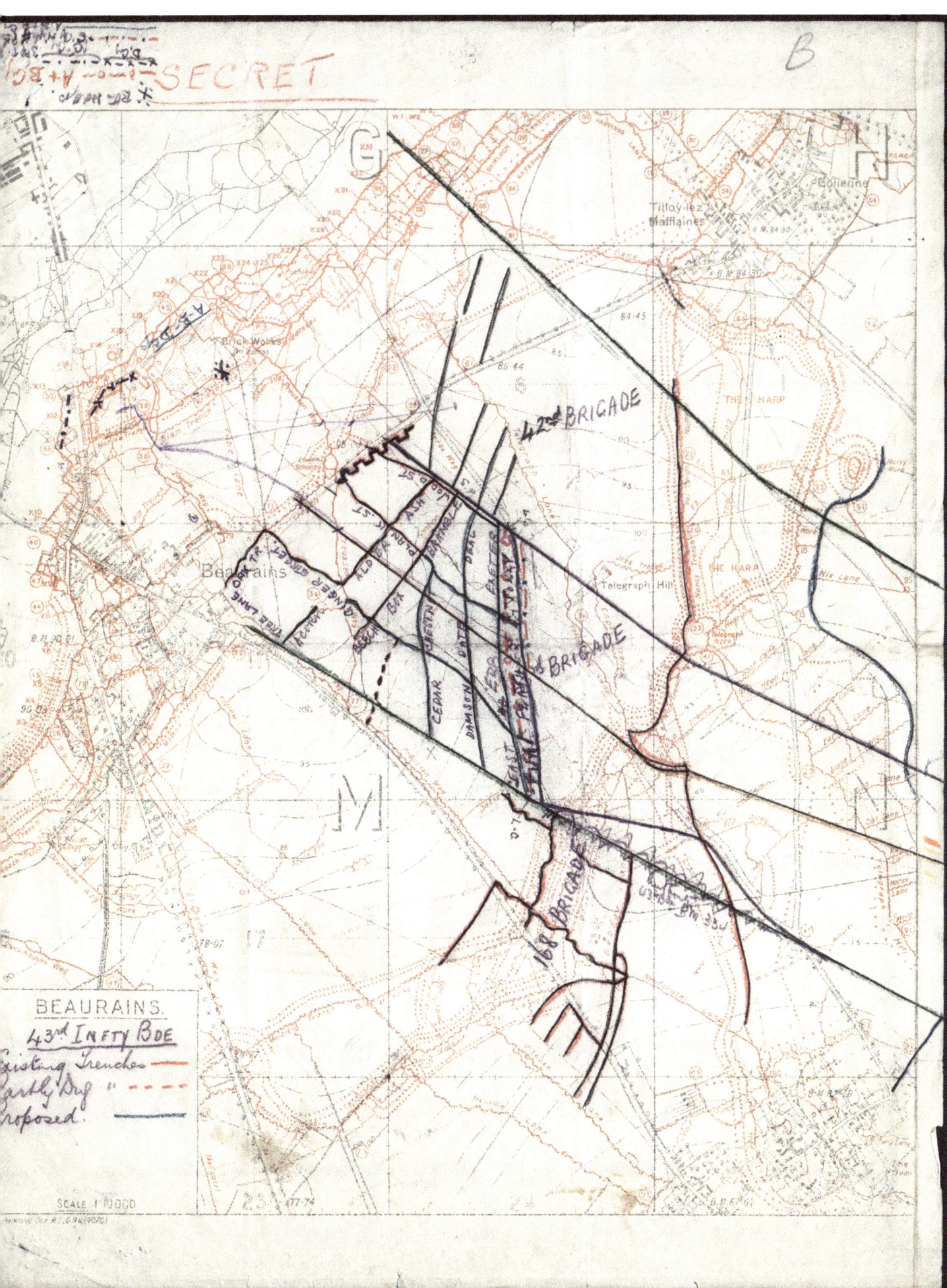

WAR   DIARY.

For Month of MAY 1917.

6th (S) Battalion Duke of Cornwall's Light Infantry.

Army Form C. 2118.

WAR DIARY
or
INTELLIGENCE SUMMARY. 6TH (S) Batt. D.C.L.I.

SHEET. 1.

(Erase heading not required.)

Instructions regarding War Diaries and Intelligence Summaries are contained in F.S. Regs. Part II. and the Staff Manual respectively. Title pages will be prepared in manuscript.

Place	Date	Hour	Summary of Events and Information	Remarks and references to Appendices
Y. CAMP TELEGRAPH HILL M.12.C.	May 1917 1ST		The Battalion Paraded "As Strong Possible" at 9·30 a.m. for work under the C.R.E. Repairing Roads. The Brigade was in DIVISIONAL RESERVE.	REF. MAP 51B FRANCE 1/40,000.
—do— and BIVOUAC AREA N.15.C.	2ND		The Battalion Paraded at 3·4 5 p.m. and moved by platoons to BIVOUAC AREA in N.15.C. where the arrived and settled by 5 p.m. The Right Transport were encamped with the remainder of the Brigade Transport at N.15.a.5·7. (SEE OPERATION ORDER No.64 Coy. No.2 attached) At 4. a.m. this Battalion moved forward by platoons to about 200 yards distance from one another and took up position in NEPEAL TRENCH where they were settled by 4·30 a.m. The Battalion remained here "STANDING BY" till in Reserve to the 41ST Brigade the whole day. About 8·30 a.m. the Brigade Transport Camp was heavily shelled. CASUALTIES among the Battn. Transport Personell WOUNDED 3. Other Ranks. Two horse were also Killed.	
—do— and NEPEAL Trench	3RD			
NEPEAL Trench	4TH		The Battalion still "STANDING BY" in Reserve to the 41ST Brigade. Orders were received about 12·40 p.m. that the 43rd & 42nd I. Brigade would take over the Divisional Front from the 41ST and 42ND July Brigades on the nights of 13TH May 1917. The Battalion were ordered to take up a position in SUPPORT to the 6TH 50TH K.O.Y.L.I. who had taken over the Front Trenches in the Right Sector. The Battalion moved forward by platoons at 5 minute intervals commencing with the first Platoon of "D" Coy. about 12. Midnight 4/5 th May 1917. (See 8.O. N°.65 Rifle BRIGADE Relief was completed by 3·30 a.m. 5/5/17 attached) The Battn. H.Q.s of this Battn. CASUALTIES Officers 1. Other Ranks Wounded till 2. relieved the 6TH Battn.	

May 1917. |

WAR DIARY or INTELLIGENCE SUMMARY

SHEET No. 2

6th (S). Bn. D.C.L.I.

Army Form C. 2118.

Place	Date	Hour	Summary of Events and Information	Remarks and references to Appendices
TRENCHES	5th		The Battalion was in trenches and situated as follows:- "D" Coy in EGRET Trench "C" Coy in DUCK Trench. A&B Coy being very much under strength were combined together under the O.C. "A" Coy. and known for the time being as "A" Coy. They had Two platoons in CURLEW Trench and Two platoons in BUZZARD Trench. Batn. HQrs were in ALBATROSS Trench at N.2.H.0.0.5. Casualties. One OR Wounded.	51/35W. 1/20000
	6th		In trenches as above. One Company employed on Hogges and improving fire and Communication trenches. EGRET, DUSK, CURLEW and SNIPE. Casualties. Two OR Killed.	
	7th		In trenches as above. Work as per the 6th. Casualties - Two OR Killed. Five OR Wounded - Relieved 6 & 10 KOYLI in front line. In trenches situated as follows:- Companies in JACKDAW 1815 and	
	8th		HERON Trenches - Batn. HQrs in STAG Trench at O.19.d.2.4. Relief complete by 2.30AM. Casualties. One OR Wounded. Work at night on JACKDAW, 1815, HERON and GANNET Trenches.	
	9th		In trenches as above. Companies employed on work on JACKDAW 1815, HERON and GANNET Trenches and primary concentration for Batn. HQ in HERON Trench. Casualties. Two OR's Wounded.	

P. J. Hannis
Lt Col
Comdg 6/DCLI

May 1917.

Army Form C. 2118.

SHEET No 3

WAR DIARY or INTELLIGENCE SUMMARY.

6th (S) Batt. D.C.L.I.

(Erase heading not required.)

Place	Date	Hour	Summary of Events and Information	Remarks and references to Appendices
TRENCHES	10th		In Trenches as above. Companies employed as work during the day on IBIS and HERON trenches. Relieved by 6th KOYLI and 6th KSLI in the line. The Battalion moved into support in trenches West of EGRET. Batt. HQ in ALBATROSS N.24.c.8.05. Casualties – One OR wounded. OO attached.	51. S.W. 1/20000
	11th		In trenches in support as above. Relief complete 5.30 p.m. Companies employed at night on deepening SHIKAR LANE from ALBATROSS to CURLEW, by 2 Coys by day on improving trench West of EGRET. Casualties from OP Relief twenty two ORs wounded.	
	12th		In trenches as above. Work same as for 11th. Casualties – Nil	
	13th		In trenches as above. Work as for the 11th. Casualties One OR wounded.	
	14th		In trenches as above. Relieved by the 8th DCLI, 61st Brigade. The Battalion proceeded to trenches on the COTEUR SWITCH about N.14.a. as Divisional Reserve. Casualties – One OR killed.	
SUPPORT AREA	15th		In trenches on COTEUR SWITCH. Relief complete 3.30 a.m. Battalion in the Run by 4.50 a.m. During the relief the enemy heavily shelled the COTEUR VALLEY. The Battalion moved at 3 p.m. to Divisional Rest Area at M.P.L., arriving there at 4.30 p.m. when the 43rd Brigade were bivouaced together. Casualties- Nil ORs Wounded.	
RESERVE CAMP				

May 1917

E.J. Denn... Lt Col
Comdg 6/D.C.L.I

Army Form C. 2118.

WAR DIARY
or
INTELLIGENCE SUMMARY. 6th (S) Batt'n D.C.L.I.

SHEET NO 4

(Erase heading not required.)

Instructions regarding War Diaries and Intelligence Summaries are contained in F.S. Regs., Part II. and the Staff Manual respectively. Title pages will be prepared in manuscript.

Place	Date	Hour	Summary of Events and Information	Remarks and references to Appendices
RESERVE CAMP	16th		The Battalion went in training at 19.10.d. The training consisted of:- Physical Training, Bayonet Fighting, Bombing and Lewis gun instruction, Musketry, Signalling, Drill &c	51 S.W. 1/20000
	17th		Training - as above	
	18th		Training - as above	
	19th		Training - as above	
	20th		Training - as above	
	21st		Training - as above	
	22nd		Training - as above	
	23rd		Training - as above	
	24th		Training - as above	
			Battalion Sports were held.	
SUPPORT AREA.	25th		Training during morning. Relieved 6 & 8 R.R.F.C. 41st Brigade over the Battalion marched via BEAUPRÉS - NEUVILLE-VITASSE Ronor tunnel relieved the 7 R.B. in the Support Area in N.20. Relief complete by 8.30 P.M. Batt'n H.Q. at N.20.a.15.50.	
	26th		In Support Area. Day time engaged in building Bivouacs and improvement of trenches, and working parties found at night 150 men - Clearing and deepening LINNET from THE NEST to EGRET	

May 1917

E. J. Lewis
Lt Col
Comdg 6/D.C.L.I.

WAR DIARY or INTELLIGENCE SUMMARY.

Army Form C. 2118.

SHEET No 5.   6th (S) BATT D.C.L.I.

(Erase heading not required.)

Place	Date	Hour	Summary of Events and Information	Remarks and references to Appendices
SUPPORT AREA.	27th		In Support Area. Work as for the 26th.	S| BW 1/20000
	28th		In Support Area. - Brigade Drill Competition in which the Battalion won the Championship at Arms. Were presented with a Silver Bugle. Working parties of 200 men at night. Orders sent as on 26th. - Parties were shelled in ALBATROSS - Cassula. 2nd Lieut E.C. MATHESON wounded. Two ORs killed and ten ORs wounded.	
	29th		In Support Area - Working parties as for 28th	
	30th		In Support Area — Greasing, Salvaging, and Bathing	
	31st		In Support Area — Salvaging, Cleaning Equipment and making new Bivouacs, and drawing Trenches after heavy Thunder Storm.	

May 31st 1917

L.J. Lewis Lt Col
Comdg 6/DCLI

SECRET.

6TH. (SERVICE) BATTALION DUKE OF CORNWALL'S LIGHT INFANTRY.

OPERATION ORDER No. 64.

Copy No. 2

1. ROUTINE. Reveille......2.0.a.m.   Breakfast.......2.45.a.m.

OFFICERS' TRENCH KITS, &c. Officers' Trench Kits and Other Ranks Packs to be on the ~~xxxxxxxxxxxxxxxxxxxx~~ Country Cart & G.S. Waggons respectively by 2.30 a.m.

In tomorrow's attack, the 43rd. Infantry Brigade will be in DIVISIONAL RESERVE.
The 41st. Infantry Brigade is attacking on the right and the 42nd. Infantry Brigade on the left.

The 6th. D.C.L.I. will be in reserve behind the 41st. Brigade.

Zero is at 3.45.a.m. tomorrow morning, 3rd.May. At Zero the Battalion will be Standing to Arms ready to move lined up in the trench alongside the Bank in the following order from right to left:-
   "D", "C", "B", "A", Headquarters.
Men to be fully equipped with :-

Riflemen:-   220 rounds S.A.A. on man.
Bombers:-   Throwers 6., Carriers 10.
Rifle Grenadiers:-   6 Rifle grenades per man.
Lewis Gunners:-   30 pans per gun.

TOOLS:-   All available wire cutters will be carried.
          Every man 3 sandbags, 50% with shovels,
                                25% with picks.
Waterbottles full - Haversacks on back.

After Zero no man will take off his equipment until ordered by the O.C.
Company Commanders are to keep their Companies in hand formed up and ready to move at a moment's notice, even though the Battalion may not be used during the whole-day.

After Zero the Battn. will move into NEPAL TRENCH, as soon as the 7th. K.R.R.C. move out from there.
From NEPAL TRENCH Battn. will move to the SUNKEN ROAD under the Western slopes of WANCOURT TOWER ridge, as soon as this has been vacated by the battn. in front.

6th. Somerset L.I. will be on the Battalion's left, and the 18th. Division on Battalion's right.

The 43rd. Trench Mortar Battery will move with the 6th. D.C.L.I.

The 2 G.S. waggons and the country cart will be parked in Battalion lines tonight.

No papers maps or letters likely to be of use to the enemy are to be taken into action.

A Forward Dump for S.A.A., Bombs, water, etc. is at N.23.d.

(1).

P.T.O.

E. Forsyth Capt-Adjt
6th Bttn. D.C.L.I.

Continued:-   - 2 -

Water Carts and all Petrol Tins to be filled tonight before 11 p.m.

Rations will be drawn the same as usual from Refilling Point.

Battn. H.Q. will move with Battn. into NEPAL TRENCH, and from there with the Battn. to Western slopes of WANCOURT TOWER ridge

ACKNOWLEDGE.

                      (Sd). E. C. Codyre,   Capt. &
                              Adjt., 6th. D. C. L. I.

Copy No.		Copy No.	
1.	C.O.	8.	Specialists.
2.	2nd. in Cmd.	9.	Transport Officer.
3.	Adjt.	10.	A/Quartermaster.
4.	O.C. "A" Coy.	11.	BRIGADE.
5.	O.C. "B" "	12.	R. S. M.
6.	" "C" "	13.	R. Q. M. S.
7.	" "D" "	14.	O. O. File.

SECRET.   6th. (S). Battalion Duke of Cornwall's L.I.

O P E R A T I O N   O R D E R   No. 65.

The 43rd. Inf: Bde. are taking over the Divisional Front from 41st. and 42nd. Inf: Bdes. to-night 4/5th. May, 1917.

FRONT TRENCHES.   6th. K.O.Y.L.I.   in right sector.
                   6th. S.L.I.   in left sector.

IN SUPPORT.   6th. D.C.L.I.   in right sector.
                   10th. D.L.I.   in left sector.

The 6th. D.C.L.I. will relieve the 7th. R.Bs., 41st.Inf: Bde in Support Right Sector.

Distribution of battalion:-

    "D" Company in EGRET Trench.
    "C" Company in DUCK   "
    "A" Company (2 platoons in CURLEW Trench.
               (2 platoons in BUZZARD   "
Batt: Hd.Qrs. in ALBATROSS Trench near N.24.c.0.5.

Battalion will leave NEPAL Trench in the following order:-
    Hd.Qrs., "D" "C" "A".

Coys. will move by platoons in file at 5 minutes interval.

2 Vickers guns are posted in DUCK Trench.
O.C. "C" Coy. should ascertain their positions.

WATER.   Coy.Commanders will arrange to carry up 30 petrol tins of water tonight per Coy - These will be dumped in ALBATROSS Trench outside Batt: Hd.Qrs., as they pass. Sergt.KING, & the Regtl.Police will be at new Hd.Qrs. to take tins over from Coys. and guard them.

O.C.Coys. are warned that it may not be possible to reach their trenches in daylight, so all necessaries in the way of water & rations should be taken with them tonight. As soon as Coys are settled in their trenches, fatigue parties are to be sent back to Hd.Qrs. to draw their water tins.

TOOLS.   All tools, bombs, Very lights, flares, Rifle Grenades, Technical Stores & S.A.A. in possession of Coys. to be taken up with them tonight.

The leading platoon of "D" Coy.to arrive at 41st.Bde. Hd.Qrs. N.22.d.5.7. at 12.30.a.m. 4/5th.May. Guides will meet each platoon of Battalion at this spot and guide them to ALBATROSS Trench N 24 c 0.5.
Guides for each platoon from the 7th.R.Bs. will meet them here, and guide platoons into their respective trenches.

Coy.Commanders will ascertain from the Coys. they relieve who are on their right and left flanks, and will immediately get in touch with these units.

Coy.Commanders are responsible for sending out patrols to ascertain the way to front line trenches, so that no delay will be caused, if the Battalion are called upon to reinforce the front line tonight.

All trench stores, bombs, rockets, etc. to be located & carefully checked before being signed for.

(1).   P. T. O.

continued :- - 2 -

WORK. Improvement of trenches will be commenced as soon as possible after arrival.

Men will keep on equipment at all times until further orders whilst in the support trenches.

Coys. will **STAND TO** for 1 hour before daylight, and 1 hour before dark.

Rifle inspection will invariably be held before men are dismissed from the morning STAND TO.

Completion of relief tonight to be reported to Hd.Qrs. by runner.

ACKNOWLEDGE.

May 4th. 1916.
(Sd). E. C. Cedyre, Capt.
& Adjt., 6th.D.C.L.I.

SECRET.

6th. (S). Battalion Duke of Cornwall's L.I.

OPERATION ORDER No.66.

The 43rd Bde. will take over from the 53rd. INFY. Bde. the front as far South as O.25.d.5.0.

Inter-Battn. Boundary as follows:-
Junction of JACKDAW Trench and KESTRELL LANE inclusive to the Northern Battn. Thence a line to O.26.a.15.75., that is, the lowest point where HERON crosses the valley to Cross Roads O.25.b.7.8. to road junction N 24 d.1.1. to N.23 d.7.4.

Divisional Southern boundary O.25.d.5.0. between the road and the Cable Trench to O.25.c.0.5. from Cable Trench, i.e. inclusive to the 18th.Division then South of STARLING Trench to N.30.a.2.0. thence South of Cross Roads N.29.a.8.6.

The 6th. K.O.Y.L.I. will take over the new front from 10th.Essex Regt., and the Southern portion of HERON, IBES and JACKDAW from 6th. D.C.L.I.

The 6th. S.L.I. will take over the sector held by the 10th.D.L.I. and the Northern portion of JACKDAW, IBES and HERON from 6th.D.C.L.I.

On relief, the 10th.D.L.I. will occupy all trenches west of PANTHER and EGRET and north of inter-Battalion boundary.

6th.D.C.L.I. will occupy all trenches west of EGRET inclusive between inter-battalion boundary and Divisional Southern boundary. Both Battn.Hd.Qrs.will be in ALBATROSS as before.

Trench Stores and any maps showing dispositions will be handed over by 10th. D.L.I. and 6th.D.C.L.I. to relieving units.

The Advanced Brigade Dump belonging to 53rd.Brigade at O.25.c.5.5. will be taken over by the 6th.K.O.Y.L.I., as a Battn.Dump.

O.C.6th.S.L.I. will detail the necessary parties to carry for the PIONEER TUNNELING COMPANY at S T A G, so that the work is continuous on night of relief.

Guides from Battn.Hd.Qrs.will meet Companies at the junction of KESTREL and EGRET at 11 p.m. tonight.

Companies will provide the following guides for 6th. K.O.Y.L.I.

"A" Coy.   3 Guides to report to
           O.C. Y Coy. 6th. K.O.Y.L.I. at Coy.Hd.Qrs.
           in DUCK at 9.30.p.m.

"A" abd "B" Company will have the whole Company digging out JACKDAW up to SPOR LANE to 5 FEET deep, from 9.30.p.m. till the trench is finished. The 6th.S.L.I. will have to occupy this piece of JACKDAW before daylight, so trench must be finished.

When Trench is finished "A" abd "B" Companies will proceed to DUCK Trench.

(1).   P. T. O.

continued:- - 2 -

After relief, "C" and "D" Companies will proceed and occupy EGRET from Railway, as far South as Trench exists.

"C" Company on the RIGHT.
"D"   "   "   " LEFT.

All Trench Stores such as Tools will be collected in Company's trenches and handed over to relieving unit. receipts being obtained for same, and forwarded to Battn. HdQrs.

All empty water tins to be brought out with Companies.

Water and Rations will be drawn by Companies from the old Water Dump in ALBATROSS, as soon as they are settled in their new trenches, empty water tins being returned to water dump at the same time.

"A" and "B" Companies Rations and Water will be carried up into DUCK by the N.C.O. and 16 men now on fatigue at STAG. These men will look after the rations until the Company arrives. They will then remain with the Company.

"C" Company's Rations and water will also be taken up to EGRET for them by the ten men now on fatigue at STAG. They will remain with the Company.

O.C. "C" Coy. will detail one Officer, 3 N.C.Os. and 40 men with picks and shovels to report to O.C. "A" Coy. at 9.15.p.m.tonight to assist him in digging out JACKDAW up to SPOOR. They will rejoin their Company in EGRET as soon as Trench is complete.

RELIEF COMPLETE TO BE SENT TO BATTN.HD.QRS IN ALBATROSS BY RUNNER.

All Companies will proceed to DUCK and EGRET via road to KESTREL, and then along KESTREL Trench.

"D" Coy.will detail EIGHT Guides to be at Junction of KESTREL & DUCK at 9.30.p.m. tonight.to guide 6th.S.L.I. to IBIS.

"C" Coy. will detail four guides to be at Junction of STAG and Railway at 9.30.p.m. to guide 6th.S.L.I. to BISON and down HERON as far as New Battn. Boundary.

                    (sd). E. C. Codyre, Capt. & Adjt.,
10/5/17.   D U N .

Vol 26

War Diary

6th D.C.L.I.

JUNE 1917

Volume 26

26N

Army Form C. 2118.

WAR DIARY
or
INTELLIGENCE SUMMARY. 6 (S) Bn. The D.C.L.I.
SHEET 7.

(Erase heading not required.)

Place	Date	Hour	Summary of Events and Information	Remarks and references to Appendices
Support Area	1st		In Support Area – Salvage, cleaning up of area and work on Reserves and Drain Trenches after heavy rainstorm	S.S.121/13 S.S.1.1.
	2nd		As for the 1st and range practice	
	3rd		As for the 2nd. Relieved the Oxfords Bucks (52 Brigade) in Reserve Line (and O.O. No.66 copy 14)	
Kortepijp	4th		Relief complete 12.45 a.m. Companies did not carry out any fire orders and general movement of troops. Filled one O.P. Wounded two O.R.'s. Work on posts	
	5th			
	6th		Relieved by 7 R.W.F. (and O.O. No.69 amended) and moved into the Support Line	
Westoutre	7th		Relief complete 12.30 a.m. Entrained 4.30 a.m. for moving to Lytton Line. Major R.A. Scott rejoined at P.B.	
			7. Major R.A. Scott C.O. 13. Scott	
			D.S.O. took over as Second in Command. Containers moved back and hand bombs and rounds	
June 30/17				R.G. Hewis Lt. Col.
				Comdg. 6 (S) D. L. I

WAR DIARY or INTELLIGENCE SUMMARY

Army Form C. 2118.

Place	Date	Hour	Summary of Events and Information	Remarks and references to Appendices
[illegible]	June 9th		A Coy provided working parties for dugouts MALLARD trench	5/1/3
	10th		Coys carrying on work as before	L.O. one
	11th		Work continuing as before 9th	
	12th		The Battalion were relieved by the 6th Yorkshires and proceeded to NEUVILLE VITASSE by Infantry Route (vide O.O. No 70 Coy H.) Relief complete 10.30 am	
NEUVILLE VITASSE	12th			
BEAU METZ	13th		The Batt. proceeded to BEAUMETZ via A.ONY - WAILLY - RIV-IERE (vide O.O. No 71 Coy 14) and attacked billets by 7.15 am	
			[illegible] at [illegible]	
LAHER LIERE	14th		The Batt. proceeded to LA HERLIERE via MONCHIET - BAC-au SUD - LARBRET (vide O.O. No 72 Coy 14). Battalion reached area The Batt. arrived billets by 6.35am No men fell out on the march	
BUS-LES-ARTOIS	15th		The Batt. proceeded to BUS-LES-ARTOIS - ALTHIE REST-coach (vide O.P. No 73 (Coy 14)) and rose arrived by 3.45 [illegible]. No men fell out	

June 30/17

D.J.Stewart
Lt. D.C.L.I.

Army Form C. 2118.

WAR DIARY
or
INTELLIGENCE SUMMARY. 6 (S) Batt. D.C.L.I. SHEET 3

(Erase heading not required.)

Instructions regarding War Diaries and Intelligence Summaries are contained in F. S. Regs., Part II. and the Staff Manual respectively. Title pages will be prepared in manuscript.

Place	Date	Hour	Summary of Events and Information	Remarks and references to Appendices
BUS.LES ARTOIS AUTHIE REST CAMP	June 14th		The Batt employed cleaning rifles + equipment. camp generally	N of Tilt M1 PER CAMP
	15th			
	16th		As for 16th	
	17th		The Batt employed with Musketry - Bayonet fighting - Physical	J23a
	18th		Drill - aim Drill - Range Practice and L.G. Dentition	
	19th		Musketry - J.D. and Range practice and L.G. work and Ent [?] area	R.13.M.
	20th		As for 18th. Draft of about 100 arrived Entraining area	P.C. 82
	21st		As for 18th and Bathed Order and Coy on parade	10.2.82
	22nd		Rather Marked out draft. 420 men fell out (wounded)	
	23rd		As for 18th June, all marked in	
	24th		Church Parade - COs general inspection + inter coy	
	25th		and etc.	
	26th		Training as for 18th	
	27th		Training	
	28th		Training	
	29th		Training	
	30th		Training	
	July 30/17		Training	

E.J. Henrie
Lt Col.
Comd 6th D.C.L.I.

SECRET.   D.U.N.
                       OPERATION ORDER No. 68.   Copy No. 14

1. RELIEF.   The 43rd. Brigade will relieve the 42nd. Brigade in the
                front line on the night of 3rd/4th. June, 1917.

                6th.D.C.L.I. will relieve the 5th. Oxford & Bucks in the
                right front line.

                Companies will arrive at the rendez-vous for guides
                N.22.d.5.6. in the following order:- A., B., C., D., H.Qrs.

2. MOVE.   Platoons will move at 100 yards interval.
                Leading Platoon of "A" Coy. to be at rendez-vous,
                N.22.d.5.6. at 9.30.p.m. on June 3rd.
                It should leave here at 8.45.p.m.
                Platoons will proceed to rendez-vous by the Infantry
                track they were shown this morning.

3. DISPOSITION. Position of Companies will be as follows:-

                "A" Company in .... JACKDAW TRENCH.
                "B"   "   " left Sector of BULLFINCH   "
                "C"   "   " right   " "   "   "
                "D"   "   " in support behind "C" Coy., in MALLARD.
                They will form the Carrying Party for all Company
                rations, water, R.E.Stores, etc.

                BATTN. HEADQUARTERS - N. 30 b 5.1.

   GUIDES.   Guides from 5th. Ox: & Bucks for platoons will be at N.22
                d.5.6. at 9.30 p.m.
                2 Guides for "C" Coy. - 2 guides for "D" Coy. -
                3 guides for "A" Coy. - 3 guides for "B" Coy.
                2 guides for Headquarters.

                O.C. "C" Company will get in touch with the Battalion
                on his right on completion of relief, belonging to 18th.
                Division, and O.C. "A" Coy. will get in touch with 10th.
                Durham L.I. on his left.

   S.A.A.,   All S.A.A., Grenades, Trench Stores, Trench Maps and
   GRENADES,   Aeroplane photographs will be taken over by relieving
   TRENCH   units, and a list of articles so taken over (in
   STORES,etc. duplicate) will be sent to Battalion Headquarters on
                completion of relief.

   SIGNALS,   The Code word for the 18th. Division is O L I V E .
     etc.
                The S.O.S. Signal at present in use is 2 Red Lights fired
                in quick succession, and repeated at intervals until our
                Artillery open.

   RELIEF   Completion of relief to be reported by wire, the figure
   COMPLETE.   101 being used, and the time.

                                        (Sd).   E. C. Codyre,   Capt. &
                2/6/17.   Adjutant, DUN.

                Copy No. 1. C.O.   Copy No. 8. Signalling Officer,
                  "   " 2. Adjt.,   "   " 9. A/Quartermaster,
                  "   " 3. 2/in/Cmd.   "   " 10. Transport Officer.
                  "   " 4. O.C. "A".   "   " 11. Brigade.
                  "   " 5. O.C. "B".   "   " 12. R. S. M.
                  "   " 6. O.C. "C".   "   " 13. O.O. File,
                  "   " 7. O.C. "D".   "   " 14. W.D. " .

Operation Orders No 69.

The 6th K.O.Y.L.I. will relieve the 6th D.C.L.I. in the right front tonight 6th/7th June. On completion of relief the 6th D.C.L.I. will move into the Support trenches vacated by 6th K.O.Y.L.I.

Disposition of Coys in Support line will be as follows.

"A" Coy in NEPAL Trench, and will be relieved by "Y" Coy. KOYLI —

"B" Coy 1 platoon in Duck.
2 platoons in EGRET LOOP.
Coy Hd Qrs in DUCK.
and will be relieved by "X" Coy KOYLI —

"C" Coy in THE NEST and will be relieved by "W" Coy. KOYLI —

"D" Coy in EGRET. Coy Hd Qrs in DUCK and will be relieved by "Z" Coy KOYLI —

Batt. Hd Qrs in THE NEST.

Coys will be relieved in the following order B — C — D — A, commencing at 10 pm — The relief for A Coy will come down KESTREL — A Coy will leave front line via KESTREL, and then proceed through WANCOURT along the WANCOURT road, + enter NEPAL trench at bottom end, past

HANCOURT Cemetery.
All the other Coys will use
FOSTER AVENUE. Owing to working
parties &c, it will probably be quicker
for platoons to walk on top
alongside FOSTER AVENUE when
coming out —
All platoons to keep 5 minutes distance
apart —
The following guides are required from
Coys Rendez-vous. Batt. Hd Qrs —
One Guide from each Coy for
relieving units Lewis gun teams, to
be at Batt Hd Qrs at 5.p.m. this afternoon —
Relief of Lewis gun teams to be
complete by 6.p.m. this evening —
ONE man per Lewis Gun detachment
will be left by ~~relieving~~ outgoing Coys
with the relieving detachments till
6.a.m. to-morrow morning — These men
will then ~~report to Batt HdQ~~ rejoin
their Coys.
THREE Platoon guides and ONE
Coy Hd Qr guide from "C" Coy and
"D" Coy respectively

Two platoon guides + 1 Coy H'd Q'r guides from B. Coy.

All DCLI guides to be at Batt H'd Q'rs at 9.15 p.m.

No guides are required from "A" Coy

The platoon of "X" Coy KOYLI in Duck will find its own way to B Coy left flank, coming down KESTREL.

No guides will be supplied by 6th KOYLI. Coys will make their own way out from trenches along FOSTER AVENUE. Runners from H'd Q'rs will meet each platoon as they pass Batt H'd Q'rs & guide them into Egret, Egret Loop and the NEST.

B. Coy will be guided to DUCK + Egret Loop as they pass Batt H'd Q'rs.

Relief complete to be sent to Batt H'd Q'rs by runner.

All empty water cans to be brought out by Coys, ~~and dumped at THE NEST~~ ~~ration dump through~~ As soon as they are settled in their trenches. Empty tins and water & ration parties will go to ration dump in ALBATROSS + get their water rations.

A Coy will take their water turn with them to Nepal Trench —

Their rations will be dumped at NEPAL I/c of their Coy QMS — A water cart also their water —

Lists of tools + trench stores handed over to relieving Corps to be sent to Batt Hd Qrs —

Also list of aeroplane photos + maps handed over —

OC B Coy will detail 1 platoon as permanent garrison of EGRET. This platoon will work in its own sector of trench + will on its own front, but will not be taken for any other working parties, and its water + rations will be carried up for it —

6th KOYLI will provide guides for above gun teams when they are relieved. 1 guide for each pair of guns per coy.

OPERATION ORDER   No 40.   4

The Right Front line and right Support-
line will be relieved on the night 11/12th June
6th A.C.L.I. being relieved by the 8th Suffolks
Regt.

The following guides are required from
Companies - rendez-vous for guides;
N 22. d. 5. 6. at 10.30 p.m. night of
11/12th June.

"B" Coy. 4 guides for "C" Coy 8th Suffolks
These guides will take each platoon
of "C" Coy Suffolks to BUZZARD Trench -
KESTREL LANE being the left
boundary - Route from rendez-vous
via KESTREL LANE.

Leading Platoon of "C" Coy SUFFOLKS
to be guided to the MANCOURT TOWER
end of BUZZARD, and so on.

"D" Coy.
4 guides for "A" Coy 8th Suffolks
Platoons of "A" Coy. Suffolks to be
guided into EGRET Trench from
rendez-vous up FOSTER AVENUE and
then along EGRET. Leading Platoon
of "A" Coy Suffolks to be guided to the far
end of EGRET up to KESTREL,
remaining 3 Platoons in sequence
behind them.

"D" Coy. 2 guides for "B" Coy Suffolks to guide 2 platoons of this Coy. from rendez-vous up FOSTER AVENUE to EGRET - leading platoons to go about 200 yards along EGRET and then into Trenches, the 2nd platoon to be in FOSTER AVENUE end of EGRET.

"B" Coy. 2 guides for 2 platoons "B" Coy Suffolks to guide them from rendez-vous up FOSTER AVENUE to EGRET LOOP

"C" Coy. 4 guides for "D" Coy Suffolks from rendez-vous up FOSTER AVENUE to the NEST.

Battn. Hd. Qr. 2 guides for Suffolks Batt. Hd. Qrs. from rendez-vous to the NEST.

Relieving Units will arrive by Platoons at the rendez-vous at 5 minutes interval between platoons in the order named i.e. "C" Coy - "A" Coy "B" Coy "D" Coy - Batt. Hd. Qr.

"A" Coy will not be relieved by any unit but will leave NEPAL TRENCH by Platoons at 200 yards interval starting at 10.30 p.m. night of 11/12th and proceed back to BEAURAINS Camp (same camp as before) via road junction N 21 b 10. q. – NEUVILLE VITASSE – BEAURAINS.

"B" "D" & "C" Coys on completion of relief will proceed by platoons at 200 yards interval, back to NEUVILLE VITASSE, along the same Infantry track they came by when Batt. last left NEUVILLE VITASSE trenches and then along NEUVILLE-VITASSE – BEAURAINS road to same camp at BEAURAINS as before.

Relief Complete to be reported by all Companies (except "A" Coy) BY RUNNER to Batten H.Q. at the NEST, as soon as Suffolks have taken over command of their Trenches. It is not intended that the relief complete report is delayed till the whole Company is out of the Trenches.

All 6th D.C.L.I. platoons will leave trenches alongside KESTREL and FOSTER AVENUE – along the top

3.

The inside of trench is for use of incoming units.

As many Stores, Mess Kit, etc. as possible to be sent back to Transport lines by ration and water limbers tonight.

On the night of the 11/12th Lewis Gun Limbers will be at road junction N.21.b.10.9, ie. 2 limbered wagons, also 1 limbered wagon for Mess Stores etc.

Lewis Gun teams will take their guns to this point and proceed with limber, also Officers Servants etc., with Kit. A Coy Lewis Gunners will wait to use these limbers. Limbers will be at N.21.b.10.9 at 12.30 midnight.

1 limber will be at Ration dump junction of FOSTER AVENUE and ALBATROSS at 10 pm. night of 11/12th to take back ALL WATER TINS.

ALL Water tins to be at Ration Dump by 10 pm.

All Aeroplane photographs Maps and information likely to be of use

4

together with Trench Stores to be handed over to incoming units, and receipted lists of same sent to Battn H.Q., BEAURAINS.

Company Commanders will render a certificate to Battn HQ by the Runner who reports relief complete stating that their trenches have been in a thoroughly clean and tidy state.

Company Officers will obtain an acknowledgment in writing from relieving Companies that this is so which will be attached to their certificate.

10/6/1917. [signature] Capt. Adjutant
6th Battn. D.C.L.I.

S.E.C.R.E.T.

6TH. (SERVICE) BATTALION DUKE OF CORNWALL'S L.I.

OPERATION ORDER No.71.

Copy No. 14

1. **MOVE.** The 43rd. Brigade Group will march to BEAUMETZ - MONCHIET tomorrow morning 13th. June, starting at 3.45.a.m.
   ROUTE. AGNY - WAILLEY - RIVIERE - BEAUMETZ.

   Intervals of 150 yards will be maintained between units on the march.

   Transport will move with Units

   6th. D.C.L.I. will march behind the 6th. Somersets.

   Starting Point - Railway M. 9. c. 5 1.

   The head of 6th. D.C.L.I. column will pass starting point at 4.7.a.m.

   6th. D.C.L.I. will be billited in MONCHIET.

2. **BILLETING PARTY.** Advance Billeting Party consisting of 2/Lt.Glencross, 4 Coy. Q.M.Sergts., and H.Q. A/Q.M.Sergt. will proceed to MONCHIET in advance this afternoon, leaving here at 3.p.m. They will report to Town Major at MONCHIET to be allotted billets, and meet the Battn. as they march in.

3. **DRESS.** Battle Kit - Packs will be carried by Motor Lorry.

   Order of March:- Headquarters, A., B., Band, C., D., Transport. Pack animals will be with Transport and not behind their Companies.

4. **OFFRS' VALISES, PACKS, STORES, &C.** All Packs to be stacked in the front of Camp, opposite the Cookers by 1.a.m.
   Officers' valises alongside the packs by 2.a.m.
   All office kit, Q.M.Stores. etc will be packed in G.S. wagons overnight.

   Lewis Gun limbers to be properly packed, guns in boxes and drums in tin boxes by 7 p.m. tonight.
   2 Lewis Gunners per Coy. will march with the Lewis Gun limbers, remainder of Lewis Gunners with their Coys.

   BATTALION WILL BE PARADED IN FRONT OF CAMP IN ORDER OF MARCH READY TO MOVE OFF AT 3.45.a.m. 13th. inst.

5. **MARCH DISCIPLINE.** The Brigadier General Commanding wishes the necessity of strict march discipline to be impressed on all ranks. Troops are to be warned that all men who fall out, and men who are placed in ambulances will have their names taken by their units, and also by the R.A.M.C. These names will be rendered each night to the Staff Captain after reaching billets.

P.T.O.

Continued:-   - 2 -

After arrival in the Rest area extra route marches for those men who have fallen out will take place under Brigade arrangements.

This order in addition to being read out with other orders today will be again read out by Platoon Commanders prior to the Battalion moving off tomorrow morning.

6. KIT, &C. Cleaning of.— O.C.Companies will see that all men of their Company clean their kit, equipment clothing steel helmets, etc. this afternoon.
The Commanding Officer expects the Battalion to be well turned out tomorrow morning for the march, and a credit to the good name of the Battalion.

7. TECHNICAL STORES. All Technical Stores will be handed in to the Q.M. Stores by 4.p.m. this afternoon.

Men are not to carry sandbags or grenade bags on the march, filled with odds and ends. The pack holds all that men require.

8. TENTS, &C. Tents bivouacs and camp are to be left scrupulously clean before unit leaves tomorrow.

The Q.M.Sergt and 6 men will remain behind to load packs, etc. on the lorry, and will travel on the lorry themselves.

9. COOKERS. Cookers will cook on the march, so as to have breakfasts ready for the men when they get in about 6.a.m.
An issue of hot tea will be made to the troops at 1.30.a.m. prior to starting on the march.

10. FOOT INSPECTION. On arrival at destination, Platoon Commanders will take the earliest opportunity of inspecting men's feet.

The Medical Officer will see ALL RANKS who have bad and blistered feet at 10.a.m.

                                (Sd). E. C. CODYRE,   Capt. &
12/6/17.   Adjutant, 6th.D.C.L.I.

Copy No. 1. C.O.   8.   2/Lt. T.S. Reay.
         2. 2nd.in Cmd.   9.   Transport Officer.
         3. Adjutant.   10.   A/Q.Mr.
         4. O.C. A.Coy.   11.   Brigade.
         5.   "   B. "   12.   A/ R.S.M.
         6.   "   C. "   13.   O.C.File.
         7.   "   D. "   14.   W.D. File.

SECRET.

6TH. (SERVICE) BATTALION DUKE OF CORNWALL'S L.I.

OPERATION ORDER No. 72.

Copy No...14...

1. MOVE. The 43rd. Brigade Group will move to the SAULTY area tomorrow 14th. instant, starting at 4.a.m.

   6th. D.C.L.I. will be billeted in LAHERLIERE.

   STARTING POINT - Q.27.b.1.6. Road Junction.
   Route, MONCHIET - BAC du SUD - LARBRET - LAHERLIERE.

   The usual halts will take place at ten minutes to every hour.

   6th. D.C.L.I. will be paraded on the side of road opposite "D" Company's huts ready to move off at 4.15.a.m., 14th. instant, in the following order :-
   Headquarters, "D" "A" Band, "B" "C".
   DRESS:- Battle Order.

   Transport will join on to rear of Battalion as they march past its lines.

   An interval of 100 yards will be maintained between units.

   6th. D.C.L.I. will join column behind the 89th. Field Coy., R.E., as the latter pass through MONCHIET.

2. OFFRS' VALISES PACKS, &c. All men's packs and Officers' valises will be stacked outside the Q.M.Stores by 3.a.m.

   Transport Officer will arrange that the 2 G.S.wagons Mess Cart, Cookers and Maltese Cart are with his Transport by 3.30.a.m., and clear of the road by that time.

3. STORES, &c. All Office Stores, Q.M.Stores, &c. will be packed on Transport overnight.

   The Motor Lorry will leave MONCHIET on its first journey by 3.40.a.m. If not clear of MONCHIET at that time it will have to wait till the Brigade Column has all passed.
   Company Commanders and 2/Lt.Reay will render certificates to Orderly Room on arrival at LAHERLIERE that the billets vacated by them in MONCHIET were left thoroughly clean.

   The Commanding Officer wishes to congratulate the Battn. on its good march discipline today, but regrets that one man of "B" Coy. fell out.

4. SUPPLIES. No.4 Coy. Train will deliver supplies to units on the 14th.

   An issue of tea will be made to the troops at 3.a.m. Cookers will cook on the road, and have men's breakfasts ready on arrival.

5. FOOT INSPECTION. M.O. will inspect sick and bad cases of sore feet at 10.a.m. on the 14th.

(1). P.T.O.

continued:- - 2 -

On the 15th. the Brigade will march to the BUS les ARTOIS - AUTHIE Rest area.

6th. D. C. L. I. will be billeted in BUS - les - ARTOIS.

2/Lt. GLENCROSS and his Advance Billeting Party will report to the Staff Captain at the TOWN MAJOR'S Office BUS - les - ARTOIS at 5.30.p.m. on the 14th. inst.

                    (Sd).   E. C. Codyre,   Captain & *Adjt*
13th. June, 1917.

6th D.C.L.I.

Distribution:- Same as O.O.71, dated 12/6/17.

S E C R E T.

6TH. (SERVICE) BATTALION DUKE OF CORNWALL'S L. I.
OPERATION ORDER No. 73.

Copy No. 14

1. MOVE. The 43rd. Brigade Group will move to the BUS-les-ARTOIS-AUTHIE Rest Area tomorrow, 15th. inst.

    6th. D.C.L.I. will be billeted in BUS-les-ARTOIS.

    Route:- LAHERLIERE to immediately west of L of LA in LA CAUCHIE (see Lens 11 edn.2) to GAUDIEMPRE to HENU to COUIN to BUS-les-ARTOIS.

    The usual halts will take place at ten minutes to every hour.

    6th. D.C.L.I. will be paraded on the side of road running past the Transport Lines. Head of Column to be on Road opposite the Q.M.Stores ready to move off at 4.45.a.m., in the following order:- H.Q., "C", "D", Band, "A", "B".
    DRESS:- Battle order.

    Transport will join on to rear of Battalion as they march past its lines.

    An interval of 500 yards will be maintained between units.

    6th.D.C.L.I. will join the column behind 6th.S.L.I.

2. OFFRS' VALISES. Officers' Valises will be stacked outside the Q.M.Stores by 4.a.m.

3. STORES,&c. All Office Stores, Q.M.Stores, &c. will be packed on Transport overnight.

4. SANITATION. Company Commanders and 2/Lieut.Reay will render certificates to Orderly Room on arrival at BUS-les-ARTOIS that the billets vacated by them in LAHERLIERE were left thoroughly clean.

    A Clearing up party of 1 O.R. per Coy, 1 H.Q., 1 Transport will report to the Qr.Mr. at the Q.M.Stores at 5.a.m. Billets and surroundings will be thoroughly cleaned ready for inspection by 45th. Sanitary Section by 6.30. a.m. tomorrow, 15th.inst.

    The Quartermaster will obtain a certificate as to the cleanliness of the billets and horse lines from the Town Major.

5. SUPPLIES. No.4 Coy.Train will deliver supplies to units on the 15th.

    An issue of tea will be made to the troops at 3.45.a.m. Cookers will cook on the road, and have men's breakfasts ready on arrival.

6. MEDICAL INSPECTION. M.O.will inspect sick & bad cases of sore feet at 10.a.m.

7. DISCIPLINE. The Brigadier General Commanding desires it to be made known to all ranks that when the Brigade is on the march and passes him he does not wish any compliments paid unless specially ordered.

    (Sd). E. C. Codyre, Capt. &
    14/6/17. Adjt., 6/D.C.L.I.

Vol 27

27^N

Confidential

War Diary

of

6th Duke of Cornwall's Light Infantry

From July 1st 1917   To July 31st 1917

Army Form C. 2118.

WAR DIARY
or
INTELLIGENCE SUMMARY.

SHEET ① 6TH (SERVICE) Battalion
Duke of Cornwalls L.I. for JULY 1917

(Erase heading not required.)

Place	Date JULY.17	Hour	Summary of Events and Information	Remarks and references to Appendices
BUS-LES-ARTOIS	1ST		TRAINING. The Batn. paraded at 5.30 am and moved off to No.1 Training Area at 6.45am where they carried out a SCHEME in conjunction with the 6th Batn. Somerset L.I.	
– " –	2ND		TRAINING. North of JUNIPER CAMP. Also Musketry on the 200 yard Range and 30 yards Range and J.D.	
– " –	3RD		TRAINING. As for the 2nd inst. also Open Order Drill.	
– " –	4TH		TRAINING.	
– " –	5TH		TRAINING. "A" and "B" Coys. FIELD FIRING. "C" and "D" Coys. Advance Guards Scheme.	
– " –	6TH		TRAINING.	
– " –	7TH		TRAINING. also Kit. Equipment and Boot Inspection for all ranks.	
– " –	8TH		TRAINING. "C" and "D" Coys. FIELD FIRING. "A" + "B" Coys. Physical Training, Musketry + Drill.	
– " –	9TH		TRAINING. The Batn. paraded at 5 + 6 am and moved off at 6am. for No.1 Training Area where they carried a TACTICAL EXERCISE "The Attack. Training Platoons for Offensive Action. Brigadier Genl. P.WOOD Assembled the Batn with the SILVER BUGLE which they won at the Brigade Competition held near TELEGRAPH HILL near BEAURAIN	
BUS L-ARTOIS incl GEZAIN- -COURT	10TH		The Battalion paraded at 9am. and marched to GEZAIN COURT (See O.O. No.74 attached).	
GEZAIN COURT	11TH		The Batn Remained at GEZAINCOURT till 11.40pm when they marched to DOULLENS (NORTH) where they entrained for BAILLEUL where they arrived at 8.30am on the 12th inst. (See O.O. N°75. attached).	

P.J. Nunn Lieut. Colonel
Commdg. 6th Bn D.C.L.I.

31-7-1917

Army Form C. 2118.

WAR DIARY
or
INTELLIGENCE SUMMARY.

6th (S) Bn. D.C.L.I.
for JULY. 1917.

SH 27 (2)

(Erase heading not required.)

Place	Date	Hour	Summary of Events and Information	Remarks and references to Appendices
	July 1917			
BAILLEUL	12th		The Battalion detrained about 8.30 a.m. and marched to CORUNNA CAMP. SHEET. 28.	
CORUNNA Camp	13th		M. 15. c. 5. 5. where they arrived and were settled by 11.45 a.m.	
CORUNNA Camp.			TRAINING. Physical Training was carried out from 9 to 9.45 a.m. The remainder of the day Coys were at the disposal of Company Commanders.	
CORUNNA Camp	14th		TRAINING.	Reference Map. SHEET 28 FRANCE S.W. EDITION 5.a.
"	15th		DEVINE SERVICE.	
"	16th		TRAINING. Physical Training and ROUTE MARCH	
"	17th		TRAINING. " " "	
"	18th		TRAINING. Physical Training and FIRING on the RANGE. at R.23.a.5.3.	
"	19th		TRAINING. " " and ROUTE MARCH.	
"	20th		TRAINING. " " and FIRING on the RANGE at R.23. a. 5. 3.	
"	21st		TRAINING. 7¼? 9 a.m. The Batn paraded at 8.45 am in Marching Order and moved off at 9 am. to take Part in the Brigade Concentration march	
"	22nd		DIVINE SERVICE.	
"	23rd		The Battalion Paraded (As STRONG AS POSSIBLE) at 6am. in BATTLE KIT and marched to the TRAINING AREA where they had Breakfast. After Breakfast the Battn was marched to a position on the high ground to watch the 10/D.L.I Carry out a Brigade Scheme working with CONTACT AEROPLANES, from 9 am to 11 am. From 11.30 to 12.45 pm the Coys were placed at the disposal of Coy Commanders for DRILL.	

1.8.17
E. Edwards Lieut Colonel
Commdg 6th (S)

Army Form C. 2118.

WAR DIARY
or
INTELLIGENCE SUMMARY.

SHEET (3) 6th (S) Bttn. D.C.L.I.

for July 1917.

(Erase heading not required.)

Place	Date July 1917.	Hour	Summary of Events and Information	Remarks and references to Appendices
CORUNNA CAMP.	24th.		PHYSICAL TRAINING from 7 to 7.45 a.m. "A" "B" and "C" Coys. Paraded in Full Marching Order at 5.30 p.m. and marched to a Camp at N.25.d.1.8 (Sheet 28) under the Command of MAJOR C.F. MILLER D.S.O. (2nd in Command of the Battn) for work under the A.D. SIGNALS, 9th CORPS. "D" Coy. Carried on TRAINING.	Reference Map: FRANCE (SHEET 28) S.W. BAILLEUL S.A.
"	25th.		"D" Coy. TRAINING. "A" "B" & "C" Coys. at Camp N.25.d.1.8.	
"	26th.		"A" Coy. and all the DETAILS of the Battalion Paraded at 10 a.m. As STRONG AS POSSIBLE in DRILL ORDER and were inspected with the remainder of the Brigade by THE ARMY COMMANDER GENERAL SIR HERBERT C-O PLUMER G.C.M.G. K.C.B. A.D.C.	
"	27th.		At 4 a.m. 25th inst. "D" Coy. marched to "B" Area BAILLEUL and carried out Training under company arrangements. "A" "B" & "C" Coys. under the Command of MAJOR C.F. MILLER D.S.O. returned from the Camp at N.25.d.1.8. and arrived at CORUNNA CAMP at 4.30 p.m.	
"	28th.		"D" Coy + Details of "A" "B" "C" Coy. Fired on the Rifle Range at NOOTS-BOOM. "A" "B" "C" Coys. Bathed at ST JANS CAPPEL.	
"	29th.		TRAINING. Under Company Commanders.	
"	30th.		TRAINING. As for 29th inst.	
"	31st.		Physical Training from 7 am to 7.45 am. The Battn. Paraded at 9 am in Marching Order and Went on a Route March till 12.30 p.m.	

1.8.1917. 2 Yellow Lieut Colonel
Commdg. 6th D.C.L.I.

SECRET. 6th. (SER.) BATTN. DUKE OF CORNWALL'S L.I.

OPERATION ORDER No.74.

Copy No. 14

1. MOVE.
Reveille........ 5.a.m.
Sick parade.... 5.15.a.m.
Breakfast...... 7.0.a.m.

The 14th. DIVISION are moving tomorrow, on being transferred to 2nd. Army. The move will be by rail.

The 43rd. Brigade will make a preliminary march to GEZAINCOURT on July 10th.
Entrainment will probably take place the following day.

The 6th. D.C.L.I. will parade at 9.a.m. on the Battn. parade ground. Head of Battalion to pass Starting Point junction of COUIN-BUS- and BUS AUTHIE Road at 9.26.a.m.
6th. D.C.L.I. will march in rear of 6th.Somerset L.I.

Transport will accompany units.

Intervals of 500 yards will be maintained between Battalions.

The usual halts will take place at ten minutes to the clock hours.

Order of March:- H.Qrs. C. A. Band, B. D.

DRESS:- Full Marching Order. Caps will be worn, and tin helmets carried on the back under the cross-straps of the valise.

Dinners will be ready for issue to the men on arrival at GEZAINCOURT.

2. SUPPLIES. No.4 Coy. Divisional Train will deliver supplies to units on arrival at GEZAINCOURT.

3. SICK. Any sick for evacuation will be collected by 42nd. Field Ambulance at 6.30.a.m. tomorrow.

4. ADVANCE PARTY. 2/Lieut: REAY and H.Q. and Coy.Q.M.Sgts. to proceed in advance, and meet the Staff Captain at Town Major's Office, GEZAINCOURT at 12 NOON tomorrow.

5. SANITATION. Company Commanders, Quartermaster and Transport Officer will render certificates to this office before leaving this camp that their lines are thoroughly clean.

6. OFFICERS' KITS, STORES, etc. Officers' Kits to be outside Quartermaster's Stores at 7.a.m.
Lewis Gun Carts, Q.M.Stores, Orderly Room Stores, etc. to be loaded by 9.p.m. tonight.
All Transport will be loaded and ready to move off by 8.a.m. tomorrow.
Extra sandbags and bomb buckets of men's surplus kit will not be carried.

(Sd). E. BYRNE, 2/Lieut:
A/Adjt., 6th. D.C.L.I.

9/7/17.

SECRET.   6TH. (SERVICE) BATTALION DUKE OF CORNWALL'S L.I.

OPERATION ORDER No. 75.

Copy No.......

1. MOVE. The 43rd. Brigade Group entrain for BAILLEUL (MAIN) at DOULLENS (North) on the 11th/12th. July.

6th. D.C.L.I. will leave DOULLENS on the morning of the 12th. by the 2.19.a.m. train (No.7) arriving BAILLEUL at 8.15.a.m. on the 12th.

Baggage (exclusive of baggage on transport vehicles) may be carried in the covered trucks, so long as the space required for personnel is not restricted.

6th. D.C.L.I. (less "B" Coy.) will parade outside Battalion Headquarters ready to march off at 11.40. p.m. tonight.   DRESS:-   Full Marching Order.
ORDER OF MARCH:-   "A" "C" "D", BAND.   All Details (except Transport) will march with their Companies.

Water Bottles to be filled.

2. BAGGAGE. Baggage will be loaded on the train in the transport vehicles.

3. ENTRAINING & DETRAINING OFFICER. The B.T.O. will be acting as Bde. Entraining Officer at DOULLENS (North) and the Assistant Staff Captain as Detraining Officer at BAILLEUL.

4. ENTRAINING. The entraining of all units must be completed half an hour before the time of departure of the train - when it will be moved from the loading siding.
Transport and Supply waggons will accompany their units.
Ropes for lashing vehicles to trucks will be provided by the Railway.
Transport Officer will arrange to draw breast ropes for all his horses from the B.T.O. on the loading siding, DOULLENS (North) at 10.p.m. tonight (4 hours before the train leaves).
Harness will be taken off and packed neatly in sets in the centre of each truck, so that it can be quickly put on when the destination is reached.

5. HORSES. All horses must be provided with head collars and head ropes for the journey.
Arrangements must be made to water all horses immediately before entrainment.

6. WATERCARTS. Water Carts must entrain F U L L.

7. BILLETING PARTY. A Billeting Party consisting of 2/Lt. BELL, 4 Coy. Q.M. Sgts., & L/Cpl. Jones for H.Qrs. will proceed by the first train with "B" Coy., and will parade with "B" Coy. at 3.15.p.m. this afternoon.

(1).   P. T. O.

- 2 -

7.	BILLETING PARTY, continued:-	On arrival at BAILLEUL, this Billeting Party will report to Capt. Douglas, Area Commandant, No.14 Area (at M.20.d.5.5.) MONT VIDAIGNE (1½ miles N.E. of St. JANS CAPPEL). Capt. Scott will probably meet the Billeting Party at the Station on arrival.
8.	LATRINES, &c......	If a Unit halts outside a Station and has to wait before entraining, existing latrines must be shown to the men, or, if none are available, latrines must be dug immediately. When the unit moves into the Station, the latrines that have been dug will be filled in, and all paper, rubbish, etc. buried in them. Pits for rubbish will be dug, if latrines exist.
9.	RAILHEAD.	Railhead on July 11th. is at ROSEL-on and after July 12th. it will be at HAEGEDOORNE.
10.	RATIONS.	All units will entrain with :- (1). Iron rations on the man. (2). Rations for 12th. on the man, or on the Cooker. (3). Rations for 13th. on the Supply Waggons.
11.	MARCHING OUT STATE.	Supply Waggons and Teams will be included on the Marching Out States of units by the Orderly Room Sgt. Supply Waggons and Teams will rejoin their Companies of the Train on July 12th., after delivering rations for consumption on the 13th.
12.	PICQUETS.	The Adjutant will post picquets for each end of the train to prevent men leaving the train. They will be posted in trucks near the end of each train.
13.	TRANSPORT, &c.	All horses, Transport waggons and personnel will be ready to move off from Transport Lines at 10.p.m. tonight, and will arrive at the Station 3 hours before the train leaves. The Train journey is about 6 hours. Animals should be fed before leaving Camp. No personnel or Stores are to be carried in the 2 Brake Vans attached to each train. A party of Traffic Control men will be attached to 6th. D.C.L.I. for the journey.
14.	SANITATION.	Os.C. Companies, Transport Officer and Quartermaster will render certificates to Adjutant at the Station that their billeting areas were left clean and tidy.
15.	DISCIPLINE.	Once the Battn. is entrained no N.C.Os or men will leave the train without permission from the O.C.Train.
16.	OFFICERS' VALISES, etc.	Officers valises to be at Q.M.Stores by 6.p.m. " Mess Stores " " " " " 9.p.m.

(Sd). E. Byrne, 2/Lieut:
A/Adjt. 6th.D.C.L.I.

11/7/17.

War Diary

6th D.C.L.I.

August 1917

Volume No 28

Army Form C. 2118.

WAR DIARY or INTELLIGENCE SUMMARY.

(Erase heading not required.)

SHEET (1) 6th (Service) Battn.
Duke of Cornwalls Light Infantry
for August 1917.

Place	Date August 1917	Hour	Summary of Events and Information	Remarks and references to Appendices
CORUNNA CAMP.	1st		The Battalion was encamped at CORUNNA CAMP M.15.c.S.6. SHEET 28 FRANCE. near WESTOUTRE. Work carried on TRAINING, under Company Commanders.	
— " —	2nd		As above TRAINING.	
— " —	3rd		As above TRAINING	
— " —	4th		The Battalion paraded at 9 a.m. in Full MARCHING ORDER and proceeded on a Route March till 1 p.m.	
— " —	5th		DIVINE SERVICE. All Officers attended a Lecture on the Pneumatic Compass and the use of same by Major C.F. MILLER D.S.O. the Second in Command of the Battalion	
CORUNNA CAMP and CAESTRE area	6th		The Battalion paraded at 10.45 a.m. and moved with the remainder of the H 3Rd/Brigade Group to CAESTRE area and was billeted in and around HAZEWINDE Sheet 27 FRANCE P.36.d.4.3. The Battalion arrived and was billeted by 3.30 p.m. (see Operation Order No. 76 of 5/8/17 attached.) TRAINING under Company Commanders. Bombing Lewis Gun Classes were held under 2/Lt. E. BYRNE and Sgt. MASON respectively	
HAZEWINDE	7th		As above for 7th inst.	
— " —	8th		As above for 8th inst. The Commdg. Officer, Asst. Col. Commdre. and the four Coy. Op. M.C. Sgts. proceeded to the Brigade Transport Camp and witnessed the Brigade Pioneer Company give a demonstration in country looks with the aid of the YUKON PACK.	
— " —	9th		TRAINING	

16/8/17

Commdg. 6th Battn D.C.L.I
Lieut. Colonel
E.J. Hewins

Army Form C. 2118.

WAR DIARY
or
INTELLIGENCE SUMMARY.

SHEET (2). 6th (Service) Batt. Duke of Cornwall's L.I.
for August 1917.

(Erase heading not required.)

SHEET 2 of FRANCE

Place	Date August 1917	Hour	Summary of Events and Information	Remarks and references to Appendices
HAZEWINDE	10TH		TRAINING. The Batt. Paraded at 9 am and proceeded on a Route March. Divs Full Marching Order. They returned to billets at 1·15 pm.	
"	11TH		TRAINING: Companies carried out training under the Coy Commdrs, also Classes in Bombing Lewis Gun and Rifles Grenades. The Specialists were training for a Brigade Test.	
"	12TH		Divine Service was held at 10 am after which the men cleaned their Equipment.	
"	13TH		TRAINING. The Batt. paraded at 9 am. As STRONG AS POSSIBLE in Full Marching Order and proceeded on a Route March from which they returned to billets about 1·30 pm.	
"	14TH		A large carrying party composed of 16 Officers and 500 Other Ranks under the command of Major C.F. MILLER D.S.O. Paraded at 12 Noon in Marching Order and proceeded to CASTRE Station where they embussed at 1 pm. and proceeded to the Infantry Barracks YPRES. On arrival they debussed and were met by an Officer and Guides of a Special R.E Company, who conducted the different parties to certain Dumps and supervised the carrying of Munitions from thence to the places they required same. Whilst performing this duty the parties were caught by a barrage put down by the Enemy somewhere in the vicinity of SANCTUARY WOOD. CASUALTIES:- KILLED 1. Other Ranks WOUNDED 10 Other Ranks. MISSING 1 Other Rank TOTAL 12. The Details, Specialists and Transport of the Batt. Paraded at 8·45 am and moved off at 9 am by WIPPEN HOUCK ARGA Wheel Kd. Arrived at 12·45 P.m. and were Quartered in PATRICIA CAMP.	
"	15TH			

L. 29 M. P. G. Shur. 27 FRANCES. Major MILLER and Carrying Party were absent there.

SHEET (3)

Army Form C. 2118.

WAR DIARY
INTELLIGENCE SUMMARY.

(Erase heading not required.)

6 B.N Duke of Corn's Light Infy
August 1917.

Place	Date August 1917	Hour	Summary of Events and Information	Remarks and references to Appendices
MIPPGN HOUCK	16th		Training. Coys at the disposal of Company Commanders.	
"	17th		Orders were received at 5 am for the Batt to proceed to OUDERDOM via RENINGHURST where it had to pass through at 8-15 a.m. On arrival at RENINGHURST instructions were received to proceed to CORNWALL CAMP G.30.a.6.3. where they arrived at 9.30 a.m. Whilst here further Orders were received for the Battalion to move at once to a Camp near DICKEBUSH H.33.a.6.4. where they arrived at 5 p.m and settled by 6 pm.	
CAMP DICKEBUSH	18th		The Camp was repitched and been cleaned up. The Batt was Standing By for Orders.	
"	19th		Divine Service was held. All Anti Gas Appliances were thoroughly inspected. The Commdg Officer and Company Commanders visited the front of the line the Batt was to take over on the 20th. All Officers and N.C.Os visited the MODEL TRENCHES in SANCTUARY Cnmt to give them an idea of the Ground they were going to fight on.	SHEET 28 FRANCE
"	20th		The Batt paraded at 9am in FIGHTING ORDER and practised "THE ATTACK" over some open ground where the different OBJECTIVES had been FLAGGED out. The Batt paraded again at 4pm and marched off at 4.15pm by Platoons at 200 yards distance for the Trenches to relieve the 7th Batt K.R.R.C. (Please see Operation Order No. 78. attached) The Relief was completed by 1 am 21st inst.	
IN TRENCHES	21st		The early morning was very misty up to about 7 am. The remainder of the day was fine and bright.	

E. J. Elliott
Lt Colonel
Commdg 6 D.C.L.I.

Army Form C. 2118.

WAR DIARY
or
INTELLIGENCE SUMMARY.

SHEET (+)

6TH Bttn Duke of Cornwalls
Light Infantry August 1917

SHEET 27 FRANCE

Place	Date	Hour	Summary of Events and Information	Remarks and references to Appendices
TRENCHES	1917 Aug. 21st		The enemy shelled our Trenches and back area along the Menin Road and SANCTUARY WOOD very heavily with all Calibre from 12 NOON and through the hours of darkness. He also sent over Gas Shells.	
"	22nd		Please see Copy of NARRATIVE attached.	
"	23rd		The Battalion was relieved by the 7th Battn K.R.R.C on the night of the 23rd inst	
"	24th		The Battalion on relief proceeded to Shelters at ZILLE BEKE BUND where they were quartered for the night.	
ZILLEBEKE BUND	25th		The Battalion paraded at 11am and moved off at 11.30am by Coys at 200 yards distance and proceeded to the CAFÉ BELGE where they embused about 12.30pm and were conveyed to DOMINION CAMP G.23.8.5.5. where they arrived at 2.30pm.	
DOMINION CAMP	26th		Coys were at the disposal of the Coy Commanders for the purpose of Re-organizing and Re-equipping.	
"	27th		TRAINING Coys at the disposal of the Coy Commders.	
"	28th		TRAINING - under Company Commanders	
"	29th		The Battalion paraded at 5pm and moved to LG ROUKLOSH. 1.4.25 area and was quartered in billets where they arrived and were settled by 10pm.	
LG ROUKLOSHI	30th		TRAINING under Company Commanders	
	31st		TRAINING	

31.9.1917
E. J. Henry ? Lieut Colonel
Commdg 6th D.C.L.I

SECRET.

6TH. (SERVICE) BATTALION DUKE OF CORNWALL'S LIGHT INFANTRY REGIMENT.

OPERATION ORDER No. 78.6

Copy No. 14

1. **MOVE.** The 43rd. Brigade Group move by March Route to CAESTRE area on 6th. August.

    6th.D.C.L.I. will march in rear of 6th. Somerset L.I.
    Strict March Discipline to be maintained.
    A distance of 500 yards will be maintained between units.
    Transport will accompany the Battalion.

    The Battalion will be formed up on the Road in fours facing SOUTH ready to march off at 10.45.a.m. tomorrow. Order of March:- "A" "B" Band "C" "D".
    Dress:- FULL MARCHING ORDER. Steel Helmets will be worn.

2. **TRANSPORT.** Transport will be drawn up on the road facing SOUTH by 10.45.a.m. tomorrow in rear of Battalion.

3. **BILLETS.** The Battalion will be billeted round HAZEWINDE, (P.30 & P.36).

    2/Lieut:GLENCROSS, Coy.Qr-Mr.Sergts., and L/Cpl.Jones will proceed in advance as billeting party. They will meet the Staff Captain at the Church FLETRE at 10.a.m. tomorrow, 6th.instant.

4. **OFFICERS' VALISES.** Officers' valises will be stacked outside Qr.-Mr. Stores ready for loading by 8.a.m. tomorrow.

5. **STORES, etc.** All Mess Stores, etc. loaded on Cookers by 9.a.m.

    Lewis Gun Limbers to be loaded by 8.p.m. tonight.

6. **HANDING OVER.** 2/Lt: Rowe will remain behind to hand over Camp to the Area Commandant.

5/8/17.

(sd). E. C. Godyre, Capt.,
Adjutant, 6th. D.C.L.I.

****

Copy No. 1. C.O.   Copy No. 8. 2/Lt.Glencross.
         2. 2/in/Cmd.   9. Transport Offr.
         3. Adjutant,   10. A/Quartermaster
         4. O.C. "A" Coy.   11. Brigade.
         5. "   "B" "   12. R. S. M.
         6. "   "C" "   13. O.O.File,
         7. "   "D" "   14. W.D.File.
                         15. M.O.

SECRET.

6th. (Ser:) BATTALION DUKE OF CORNWALL'S L. I.

OPERATION ORDER No.77.

Copy No. 6.

1. ROUTINE. Reveille........5.a.m.
Sick parade....5.15.a.m.
Breakfast......7.0.a.m.

2. MOVE. Transport, Signallers and Details of 6th,D.C.L.I. will parade ready to move off at 9.a.m. on the side of the Road, opposite "A" Company's billets.

DRESS:- Marching Order. Steel Helmets to be worn.

Officers' Chargers to be in pairs in rear of Transport with Pack Animals.

The four Cookers with Cooks, 1 water cart and the Country Cart will leave "A" Company's billet at 4.a.m. tomorrow morning under the charge of the Regimental Sergt-Major.

The Sergt.Cook will arrange to have breakfasts ready (for the four Companies on fatigue today) by 7.a.m. tomorrow, and Dinner ready by 1.p.m.

Signallers, Band and Details will have their Breakfasts cooked by the Transport Cook tomorrow.

3. SANITATION. "A" Company's billets and Transport Lines to be left thoroughly clean.

(Sd). E. C. Codyre, Capt.,
14.8.17. Adjutant, 6th. D.C.L.I.

Copies to :-

Commanding Officer,
Adjutant,
Transport Officer,
Quartermaster,
R.S.M.,
W.D.File,
O.O.FILE.

S E C R E T .

6TH. (SERVICE) BATTALION DUKE OF CORNWALL'S L.I.

O P E R A T I O N   O R D E R   No.78.

Copy No.

1. **RELIEF.** The 6th.D.C.L.I. will relieve the 7th.K.R.R.C. in front line, left sector of Brigade, tonight.

2. **MOVE.** The Battalion will parade ready to move off at 4.15.p.m. this afternoon. DRESS:- Full Fighting Kit. Periscopes, wire cutters, wiring gloves, rifle grenade cups, bomb carriers, etc. will be drawn by Companies and issued to men - care being taken that Company Commanders know the names of men who are responsible for them.

   Each man will carry 120 rounds S.A.A., and tomorrow's rations.

3. **DISTANCE between PLATOONS.** A distance of 200 yards will be maintained between each platoon - connecting files with front platoons to be put out.

4. **ROUTE.** DICKEBUSCH - Cross Roads H.29.c.3.9. - H.29 Central - Cross Roads H.29.b.8.5. - Cross Roads H.30 d.3.1.- across Canal at I 19.d.5.6. - Shrapnel Corner I.14.c.7.8. along MENIN Road to I.15.c.o.10 to I.15.c.9.3. where 1 guide per platoon from the 7th.K.R.R.C. will meet Coys.

5. **ENEMY AIRCRAFT.** If enemy aeroplanes are seen all troops will halt and NOT LOOK UP.

6. **ORDER OF MARCH.** Order of March:- Headquarters, "C" "D" "A" "B". Leading platoon of "C" Coy. to be at guide rendez-vous I.15.c.9.3. at 8.p.m.

7. **DISPOSITIONS** Companies will take over dispositions in front line same as 7th.K.R.R.C. hold - approximately "C" Coy. in left of sector and 3 platoons of "D" in right of sector, - remainder in the Tunnel.

8. **RECEIPTS.** Receipts in duplicate of all S.A.A., Bombs, Rifle Grenades Tools, Trench Stores, etc. to be taken and one copy sent to Headquarters.

9. **GAS ALERT.** GAS ALERT will be in force during the march and during the relief.

10. **BOMBS.** Bombs to be drawn and issued before NOON.

11. **PACKS.** Packs to be collected and stacked outside the Quartermaster's Stores by Companies, commencing with "C" Company at 1.45.p.m., "D" Company 2.p.m., "A" Company 2.15.p.m. "B" Company 2.30.p.m.

12. **LEWIS Guns & LIMBERS.** Lewis Guns in Carts will go with Coys. as far as the MENIN Road, I.14.a.6.8. and then be unloaded and sent back. One N.C.O. and one man per Lewis Gun Team to accompany the L.Gun limbers for the purpose of unloading same. They will rejoin their platoons as they pass.

13. **RELIEF COMPLETE.** Relief complete to be sent by Runner. Hd.Qrs. J.13.b.35.15. (Map 28.N.E.)

14. **OFFICERS' VALISES.** Officers' valises, kits, etc., to be sent to the Transport at once.

(Sd). E.C. Codyre, Capt.,
20/8/17.   Adjutant, 6th. D.C.L.I.

6TH. (SERVICE) BATTALION DUKE OF CORNWALL'S LIGHT INFANTRY.

OPERATION ORDER No.80

Copy No...13...

1. MOVE. 6th. D.C.L.I. will move to Le ROUKLOSHILLE area this afternoon by march route.

    The Battalion will parade ready to march off at 5.p.m. on the Square.

    DRESS:- Fighting Order. Steel Helmets will be worn.

    ORDER OF MARCH:- "A" "B" BAND, "C" "D" Companies.

2. ROUTE. RENINGHELST - WESTOUTRE - SCHAEXKEN.

3. DISTANCES East of RENINGHELST - POPERINGHE Road 200 yds. distance will be maintained between Companies and Transport.
    At the first halt Companies and Transport will be closed up to 10 yds. interval.

    Transport will join in 200 yds. in rear of "D" Coy., as it passes the Transport lines.

4. MARCH DISCIPLINE Strict March Discipline will be maintained during the march.

5. OFFICERS' CHARGERS. Officers' Chargers will march in rear of Companies.

6. TEA. Tea will be issued to Companies on reaching billets.

7. SANITATION Companies will be outside their huts by 4.30.p.m., and fatigue parties detailed to clean up inside and out.

8. PACKS. 1 man per Coy. will remain behind in charge of packs, and travel on the Motor Lorry.

(Sd). E. C. CODYRE, Captain,
Adjutant, 6th.D.C.L.I.

29th.Aug: 1917

Copies to:-
1. C.O.,
2. 2nd. in Command.
3. Adjutant,
4. O.C. "A" Company,
5. "   "B"   "
6. "   "C"   "
7. "   "D"   "
8. Transport Officer,
9. Quartermaster,
10. R.S.M.
11. Brigade.
12. O.O.File.
13. W.D.File.

NARRATIVE of the Operations on 22nd. and 24th. August.

The 6th. D.C.L.I. were allotted as their front from the Southern edge of GLENCORSE WOOD on the left to the Northern edge of INVERNESS COPSE on the right.

The orders for the Battalion were "C" and "D" Companies to form two waves and to occupy the final objective L shaped House to FITZCLARENCE FARM (exclusive) to "C" Company and FITZCLARENCE FARM (inclusive) to J.14.d.5560 to D.Coy.

"A" Company to form 3rd. wave and occupy the intermediate line between final objective and JARGON Trench. "B" Company to form 4th. wave and occupy JARGON Trench and provide the Carrying Party.

The Battalion to form up in this formation in rear of the Front Line trench (except the first wave which remained in the front line trench) by 6.a.m. on the 22nd. - provided there was a thick mist (as there had been the previous morning). In the event of there being no mist, Battalion was to be in Assembly position by 5.a.m. to enable the 10th.D.L.I. to occupy the tunnel before they could be observed.

The morning was clear, and companies were ready to start moving into assembly position at 4.a.m., but this was delayed owing to the carrying parties, composed of "B" Coy. sent out the previous night at 8.45.p.m. to fetch water and rations having lost their way in the dark. At 5.a.m. no water or rations had arrived, and practically the whole of "B" Company were away on this duty. Orders were given for companies to get into assembly positions at once, and after "C" and "D" and part of "A" were in position, the carrying parties of "B" Company arrived. But by this time it was getting light, the D.L.I. had arrived, and tunnel was not cleared. An enemy aeroplane appeared low over our line and observed the whole Battalion lining up in the open behind the ridge. A certain amount of machine gun fire from the enemy aeroplane and from enemy machine guns on our left opened fire,

- 2 -

caused some confusion, but the Battalion was in position by 5.30.a.m and men sent along singly with water to fill men's waterbottles as far as possible.

At Zero, the attack commenced, and, when only about 50 yards from our front line, the leading wave was held up by heavy machine gun fire from both flanks J.14.a.8.4 Gun pits - J.14.c. 55.98 - J.14.c. 55.75 and GLENCORSE WOOD and from the centre. The result being that touch with the barrage was completely lost, and the advance of the Battalion stopped. Enemy could be clearly seen reinforcing from the rear, and reinforcing the trench running N. & S. from J.14.c.6.6. to J.14.a.6.4. Our Vickers Guns and Lewis Guns inflicted heavy casualties among them. A Tank then came out of INVERNESS COPSE and went along the trench J.14.c.66. and then across to the strong point at about J.14.b.0.4. This Tank performed most valuable service, and the advance was continued and the trench J.14.c.6.6. to J.14.a.6.5. occupied. The strong point at J.14.c.55.98 being captured by a strong bombing party and 4 machine guns captured, and the strong point at J.14.c.55.75. being silenced by the tank, and the Garrison killed as they came out. This strong point was a concrete emplacement, capable of holding 50 men. 2 Machine guns were captured here, 1 Officer and about 20 killed.

Lieut: WHITBY and about 20 men advanced from this strong point to about J.14.c.8. 8. but were unable to get any farther, and remained out there and no communication could be got with them. Further advance was held up by heavy machine gun fire from the corner of GLENCORSE WOOD and from the direction of the ruined house N. of INVERNESS COPSE. I issued orders for the trench held by the Battalion to be consolidated and the C.Ts. JARGON DRIVE, JAP AVENUE and a C.T. running along the N.edge of INVERNESS COPSE to be blocked and held as sapheads, and to get in touch with the flank Battalions. I also sent out to Lieut:
WHITBY

WHITBY to withdraw from his isolated position and back to our general line, as, at that time, I was unaware the S.L.I. had a post in advance of my line, but was under the impression that WHITBY was quite isolated by himself. The Battalion was reinforced by 1 platoon from the D.L.I. that evening.

At about 1.a.m. on the 23rd. I received orders from O.C., D.L.I. that W. & X. Companies, K.O.Y.L.I. would reinforce my Battalion and the Platoon of D.L.I. was to rejoin its Battalion. One platoon of "W" Company was already in touch with my right in INVERNESS COPSE, and the remainder of "W" Company was sent to reinforce my right, and get in touch with the S.L.I. This was done, and I then found the S.L.I. had a post in advance of my line. "X" Coy. of K.O.Y.L.I. never joined me, as it could not be found.

Orders for the attack in conjunction with Tanks were then received and issued to Companies.

The Tank attack and a counter-attack by the enemy on our front were delivered simultaneously, and the enemy counter-attack was completely defeated by our rifle and machine gun fire, and by the Tank Machine gun fire.

This counter-attack was delivered from about J.14 central through INVERNESS COPSE. Enemy had fairly large numbers, but they were advancing slowly from shell hole to shell hole, and with little energy.

The Tank attack then broke down, as the leading Tank was knocked out by an anti-Tank gun firing from GLENCORSE WOOD direction, and the remaining 2 Tanks withdrew - one of these Tanks breaking its driving band as it got clear of INVERNESS COPSE, and the other going right back with the crews of the other tanks.

The day of 23rd. was spent improving position held. The enemy bombarded our new line and old line very heavily the whole of the night, inflicting heavy losses - a strong barrage

was

was also put down by the enemy in our rear.

About 4.30.a.m., the enemy counter-attacked, using flammenwerfer on my right flank, and on the centre of my line, and appear to have surprised the garrisons of the blocks in JARGON and JAP AVENUE by strong bombing attacks. The centre of my line was driven back, and the flanks then retired as well. A counter-attack was delivered on the right about 5.a.m., composed of all troops that could be collected on the right flank, and this was successful on the S. of the MENIN ROAD, but could not get across the open ground on the N. of MENIN ROAD. On my left flank, when I got across, I found only about 40 of my Battalion. They were reorganised and the only Officer I had left put in charge. I asked for a barrage to be put down on the trench I had lost to help me to get across the open ground and endeavour to retake this trench. I only received information that the barrage was arranged 10 minutes after it had started, and, on going up to get the counter-attack started I found the barrage was falling behind the enemy position. Also, in conjunction with the Commanding Officers of the 9th.R.B. and 8th.K.R.R., I decided that, with the few troops left, if the counter-attack was unsuccessful, the holding of the original line would be endangered.

The enemy were seen to be reinforcing on my left flank, and it was reported that they were attacking the Battalion on my left later in the morning, but I could not see any signs of this myself. The enemy made no further attempt to gain more ground.

Bombing blocks were then established up JARGON DRIVE and JAP AVENUE, and I had sides of JAP AVENUE garrisoned, in advance of our old line, where they could cover the left flank of the Battalion on my right.

The Battalion was relieved that night.

CASUALTIES during these operations
KILLED Officers 7 Other Ranks 55. WOUNDED Officers 8. Other Ranks 252.
MISSING Other Ranks 28.
Total Casualties 350

31st. August, 1917. .... Lieut-Colonel, Commanding 6th. D. C. L. I.

WAR DIARY.

September 1917.

6th Bn. Duke of Cornwall's Light Infantry.

Volume 29.

Army Form C. 2118.

6TH BN Duke of Cornwall's
Light Infantry for SEPTEMBER 1917

WAR DIARY
or
INTELLIGENCE SUMMARY

(Erase heading not required.)

SHEET (1)

Place	Date Sept 1917	Hour	Summary of Events and Information	Remarks and references to Appendices
LE ROUKLOSHILLE	1ST		TRAINING:- The Battalion Paraded at 9 a.m. in FULL Marching Order for Battalion Drill. The remainder of the morning from 10 a.m. to 12.30 p.m. Coys were training under their Company Commanders in Bayonet Fighting, Musketry and Box Respirator Drill.	SHEET 27 FRANCE
"	2ND		DIVINE SERVICE. Cleaning Equipment and clothing.	
"	3RD		TRAINING. As for the 1.9.17.	
" and	4TH		The Battalion Paraded in Billets by Companies ready to move off at 9.20 a.m. at 200 Yards interval for a Camp at B.20.a.9.7 Sheet 36 via METEREN – BAILLEUL – road Junction B.8.a.8.7. See Operation Order No. 81 Copy No. 13 of 3/9/17. attached. The Battalion arrives at the Camp mentioned at 2 p.m. and were settled in Quarters by 2.15 p.m.	
Camp at B.20.a.9.7				
Camp at B.20.a.9.7	5TH		TRAINING:- Physical Training. Bayonet Training. Arm Drill and Rifle Firing was carried out under Company Commanders.	SHEET 36 Belgium and France EDITION 6 40,000
" – "	6TH		TRAINING. Battalion Drill from 9 a.m. to 10 a.m. From 10 a.m. to 12.30 p.m. as for 5/9/17.	
" – "	7TH		TRAINING. as for the 5th met up to 11 a.m. The Battn was allotted "B" RIFLE RANGE (at T.19.c.6.8 Sheet 28.S.W. 5a 1/20,000) from 1 p.m. to 6 p.m. Companies proceeded to the Range during the afternoon and all ranks were put through the following practice. TEN Rounds RAPID FIVE Rounds SLOW.	
	8th		Training up to 12 midday as for the 5th inst. The Battalion paraded in Full Marching Order for inspection by the Corps & Divisional Officers at 11 am	

E.J. Sturgis
Commdg. 6th Bn D.C.L.I.

8.9.1917

Army Form C. 2118.

WAR DIARY
or
INTELLIGENCE SUMMARY.

6th Bn Duke of Cornwall's Light Infantry

Sheet (2)   For September 1917.

Place	Date Sept	Hour	Summary of Events and Information	Remarks and references to Appendices
CAMBEZSOO -9.7 Sh. 36 Near NIEPPE	8th 1917		TRAINING:- "C" and "D" Coys were combined to make One Strong Company. They Paraded at 9.a.m. in Battle Order and proceeded to B.7 a.9.6 from where they carried out a Brigade Tactical Scheme. Attacking the Farm at B.1. central. A & B Coys carried out Training on the ground around the Camp as for the 5th inst. from 9am to 10 a.m. and at 11 a.m Paraded in Full Marching Order for inspection by their Company Commanders. The Battalion were allotted 3" Rifle Range and Lewis Gun Range (at T.19.4.6.? Sh. 28 S.W. 1/20.000) from 9am to 5 p.m. All Companies used the Range throughout the day and fired the following Practices. 5 Rounds Slow. 15 Rounds Rapid. DIVINE SERVICE was voluntary.	SHEET 28. S.W. EDITION 3. 1/20.000 BELGIUM and FRANCE but SHEET 36. EDITION 6. 1/40.000 BELGIUM and FRANCE
"	9th		The Battalion Paraded As STRONG AS POSSIBLE at 8 a.m. (Also 2 Officers and 50 Other Ranks of "A" Coy) who proceed to WULVERGHEM, (a work on Trench Tramways under the T.T. Officer) in Battle Order and proceeded to the Brigade Training Area in Square S.18. T 13. 14 and 19. Sh. 28 S.W. where Company Schemes were carried out from 9am to 1 p.m.	
"	10th		Companies carried out Physical Training from 7 to 7.30 a.m. The PALMER BATHS on the NEUVE EGLISE Road were allotted to the Batt.n from 9am to 12 Noon. Each Company on return from the Baths carried out 2 an hours Arm Drill and 2 an hours Bayonet Fighting Companies Paraded again at 9 p.m. and carried out 2 an hours WIRING by NIGHT. All the Officers paraded under the 2nd in Command at 8.30 pm. to Practice finding their way in the dark by Compass - Very STARS	
"	11th		- ATTACK of the WOOD	

11-9-1917   E. J. Newell Lieut Colonel
Commdg. 6th Bn D.C.L.I.

WAR DIARY or INTELLIGENCE SUMMARY

Army Form C. 2118

6th (Sv) Btn Duke of Cornwall Light Infantry

September 1917

SHEET (3)

Place	Date	Hour	Summary of Events and Information	Remarks and references to Appendices
CAMP 104 B. 20.d.4. nr Nepl	1917 12th		The Battalion was allotted "A" RANGE from 9am to 5.7pm and was only used on this day by "A" "D" Coys who fired the following practices 5 Rnds SLOW and 15 ROUNDS RAPD. "B" and "C" Coys would have fired this Practice also were received from Bonpare at 12.30am w.hr. 11/10.5 to 6 WORKING PARTY of 4 Officers and 100. Oth Ranks to work under A.O.D. at FRONT DUMP (S.27 b) SHEET 28 NEAR BAILLEUL. This Party paraded at 6.30 am and assembled after disembarking at 8 am. TRAINING. NCO's carried out under Company Commanders on the Ground arm of the Camp	
"	13th		From 9am to 11.15 am. The Battalion Paraded at 1pm. Jeanne d'arc in FIGHTING ORDER and Gas Fitness. Inc marches past Co's individually. Ten minutes interval to B.T.A.O.S. Sheet 36. to assume R&S/C SECRET DEMONSTRATION and undergo a GAS TEST under the supervision of the Divisional Gas Experts. The Demonstration that lasted till 4.15pm when the Battalion marched back to Camp by Co	
"	14th		The Battalion was allotted B. Range from 9am to 1pm. All Bad and Indifferent Shots were practiced in GROUPING during this time. 4 Officers + 150 Other Ranks paraded at 6.15am and proceeded in different fatigues in the Corps Area detailed by the Brigade. The Commanding Officer and different committees recommended the sector of the line the Battalion would shortly have to take over. The Battalion paraded at 9am and marched to NEUVE EGLISE where it arrived and was billeted by 11.15am	
"	15/9/1917			

WAR DIARY
INTELLIGENCE SUMMARY

6th (S) Batt. D of Cornwall LI
Lyth Infantry
for Sept 1917

Army Form C. 2118.

SHEET (A)

Place	Date Sept 17	Hour	Summary of Events and Information	Remarks and references to Appendices
NEUVE EGLISE	16th		Training was carried out by Company Commanders in a field by the side of the NEUVE EGLISE - BAILLEUL Road under Company arrangements. Physical Drill, Arm Drill Rapid wiring & Bomb.	
"		17th	— do — A+D Coy firing in the Range B+C Coys Carried out a Scheme under the 2nd in Command.	
"		18th	A+D Coy furnished 4 Officers + 120 Other Ranks for a Working Party. B+C Training.	
"		19th	"B+C" Coys furnished 4 Officers + 120 Other Ranks for a Working Party. "A+D" Coys Training.	
"		20th	"B" Coy furnished a working party of 2 Officers and 50 Other Ranks "C" Coy went to relieve them at 2pm. "A+D" Coys paraded to carry out a Scheme under the 2nd in Command. About 9.30am orders were received from the Brigade that we had to relieve the 41st Brigade in the line that night. Training was at once cancelled and "B" Coy recalled from work, and preparations were made for the move for the relief. The Battalion paraded at 5.30pm and moved off by Platoon. (See O.O. No. 83 attached)	
MESSINES	21st		The relief was carried out without incident and completed by 9-45 p.m. The Battalion was in Support to the 10th Bn D.L.I. and furnished Carrying and Working Parties under Brigade arrangements. Casualties Killed Other Ranks ONE. Wounded Six.	
"		22nd	— do — Casualties Killed Other Ranks Nil. Wounded Nil.	
"		23rd	— do — Casualties Killed Other Ranks ONE Wounded ONE.	
"		24th	— do — Casualties Killed Other Ranks ONE Wounded ONE. The Battalion moved up to relieve the 10th Batt D.L.I. in the Front Line (See O.O. 84 attached) The relief was carried out without incident. Casualties Nil.	

24/9/17
E.J. Senior Lieut Colonel
Commdg. 6/D.C.L.I.

WAR DIARY or INTELLIGENCE SUMMARY

Army Form C. 2118.

SHEET (5)   6th (S) Bttn Duke of Cornwalls Light Infantry

For September 1917

Place	Date	Hour	Summary of Events and Information	Remarks and references to Appendices
FRONT LINE TRENCHES NEAR MESSINES	25th	Sept 1917	The Battalion was in the Front Line Trenches. Disposition's as follows. "A" Company was the Right Company. "B" Company was the "Centre" Company. "D" Company was the Left Company. "B" Company was in Support. "A" Compy was in touch with the 6/5 Bttn Somersets L.I. on the Right. "D" Coy was in touch with the Right Batt of the Right Brigade of the 30th Division on the Left. The 19/D.L.I. were in Support in Reserve. The night 24/25 was quiet except for an occasional Burst or two of Enemy Machine Gun fire. During daylight on the 25th the Enemy Artillery and Aeroplanes were fairly active. Casualties Nil.	
	26th		In the Line. During the hours of darkness on the night 25/26th The Enemy shelled the Battalion sector in rear of the Right Company and around the Battalion Head Quarters, with 5.9 and H.2. The Trench around Batln H.Qrs was badly blown in. About 10 am the Enemy Gunners shelled the area around Battn HdQrs. Blowing in another portion of the trench and wounding Two men. One Sentry Pte Schorfg. One Batln Runner Pte Wallace. Total Casualties Other Ranks 4.	
	27th		Two "D" Coy were wounded in the Frontline. Pte Shine & Pte Clarke. During the hours of darkness 26/29, The Enemy was active with his Artillery and Heavy Trench Mortar. The Artillery shelling all parts of the Battn Sector. During the day his Artillery and Aeroplanes were very active. Casualties Nil.	
	28		During the hours of darkness 27/28 The Enemy was not quite so active with his Artillery. We held Test on T.M.s on 1915 Pattern. During the day his Artillery registered on different parts of Batn Sector. Aeroplane Orders were received from ...	

Army Form. C. 2118.

WAR DIARY
or
INTELLIGENCE SUMMARY.

(Erase heading not required.)

6/2(S) Batt. Duke of Cornwall's Lt. Infantry

For September 1917

Instructions regarding War Diaries and Intelligence Summaries are contained in F.S. Regs., Part II. and the Staff Manual respectively. Title pages will be prepared in manuscript.

Place	Date	Hour	Summary of Events and Information	Remarks and references to Appendices
Front line near Messines	28th		During the night of the 28th inst. the Battalion were relieved by the 9th Batt. K.R.R. Corps. (Please see B.O. Nº 85 of 28-9-17 attached) The relief was carried out without incident and completed by 10.45 p.m. On relief the Battalion marched back by platoons to the Camp at Canteen Corner. Map References Sheet 28. T.26.O.5.1. and Sheet 36.B.2.a.7.8. Where it arrived and was settled by about 1.30 a.m. on 29th inst.	
Camp Canteen Corner	29th		Companies were at the disposal of Company Commanders for the purpose of allowing men to clean their Clothing and Equipment etc.	
— do —	30th		The Battalion furnished a Working Party of 4 Officers and 100 Other Ranks, to work under the Tunnel Tramway Officer. They paraded at 7.15 a.m. and returned about 4.45 p.m. The Remainder of the Battalion attended CHURCH PARADE.	

E. J. Shears
Lieut. Colonel
Commanding 6th Batt. D.C.L.I.

SECRET.

6th. (Serv.) Battalion, Duke of Cornwall's Lt. Inf.

OPERATION ORDER No.81.

Copy No........

Reveille:......5.30.a.m.
Sick parade....5.45.a.m.
Breakfasts.....6.30.a.m.

1. MOVE: The 6th.D.C.L.I. will move by march route tomorrow 4th. September to camp at 36.B.20.d.9.7. Route:- METEREN - BAILLEUL - road junction B.8.a.3.7.
6th.D.C.L.I. will march in rear of 6th.K.O.Y.L.I.

2. INTERVALS. Two hundred yards interval will be maintained between units, between companies and between rear Company and Transport.

3. PARADE. The Battalion will parade in their Company lines ready to march off at 9.20.a.m. Order of March:- "D." "C." BAND, "A." "B."
"D." Coy. will pass the Starting Point 27.X.3.c.1.5. at 9.30.a.m., and leave his Company billets at 9.25.a.m. Companies will march off independently 200yards distance accordingly. Transport will be on the road outside Aid Post billet at 9.25.a.m. ready to follow "B".Coy.

DRESS:- FULL MARCHING ORDER. STEEL HELMETS.

4. OFFICERS' VALISES, STORES, etc.
"B" Coy. Officers' Valises will be stacked in Transport Lines by 7.30.a.m.

"A" "C" & "D" Coys. valises will be stacked in "D" Coy's yard by 8.a.m.

Transport Officer will arrange to load Headquarters and "B" Company's valises at 7.30.a.m., and the G.S.Wagon will then go to "D" Coy's lines, load the valises of "D" and "C" Companies and wait in "D" Coy's yard till the transport passes.
Cookers will join Transport column as it passes their billets.

Lewis Gun carts, Orderly Room Stores, Q.M.Stores, etc. to be loaded by 8.p.m. tonight.

5. SANITATION. Companies billets will be cleaned and all refuse burnt and buried, latrines filled in, etc, by Companies by 9.a.m. Pioneers will not go round Companies billets and do this for them.

Company Commanders will personally see that their billets are left thoroughly clean.

(Sd). E.C.Codyre, Captain,
3/8/17.   Adjutant, 6th. D.C.L.I.

Copies to:- 1. C.O.   6. O.C. "C" Coy.   11. Brigade.
             2. 2nd.in Cmd.   7. "   "D" "   12. O.O.File.
             3. Adjutant.   8. Transport Off.   13. W.D.
             4. O.C. "A" Coy.   9. Quartermaster.
             5. "   "B" "   10. R.S.M.

S E C R E T.

6th. (SERVICE) BATTALION DUKE OF CORNWALL'S LIGHT INFANTRY.

OPERATION ORDER No. 82.

Copy No....... 15

1. **MOVE.** 6th. D.C.L.I. will move by march route tomorrow, 15th. instant to NEUVE EGLISE area, T.14.b.9.4., and take over from the 5th. K.S.L.I.

   Route:- BAILLEUL Road - NEUVE EGLISE Road.

2. **PARADE.** The Battalion will parade ready to move off from parade ground at 9.a.m. Order of March:- C.D. Band, A.B. Transport will follow "B" Coy. 500 yards between Battalions to be maintained. 6th. D.C.L.I. will march behind the 6th. K.O.Y.L.I..
   Dress:- Full Marching Order. Box Respirators will be worn in the ALERT position. Head of "C" Coy. to pass Starting Point Road Junction B.3.a.8.7. at 9.49.a.m.

3. **BILLETING PARTIES.** Billeting Parties, Lieut: and Qr.Mr.GUNN, Coy.Q.M.Sgts., and L/Cpl.F.G.Jones will be at T.14.b.9.4. by 7.30.a.m. tomorrow morning to take over from outgoing unit, 5th. K.S.L.I.

4. **SANITATION.** Tents, Huts, Cookhouses, Latrines, etc. to be thoroughly cleaned by Companies, Pioneers and Sanitary men by 9.a.m. tomorrow. All refuse round incinerator to be burned.

   Officers cookhouses to be pulled down, and the ground thoroughly cleaned. Quartermaster-Sergt.Mc.Vitie to remain behind and hand over to the representatives of 5th. K.S.L.I.

5. **BDE: H.Qrs.** Brigade Headquarters will be at WATERLOO Camp, S.12.c.8.2

6. **OFFICERS' VALISES, STORES, etc.** Officers' valises to be stacked on the side of the ERQUINGHEM Road by 7.30.a.m. tomorrow, ready for loading.

   Lewis Guns to be taken to Transport lines, and loaded in limbers tonight.

   G.S.Waggon for Qr.Mr's Stores to be outside Qr.Mr's Stores by 5.30.p.m.tonight.

   Orderly Room Stores, Pioneer's Stores to be loaded in Country Cart by 8.a.m. tomorrow.

14/9/17.

(Sd). E. C. Codyre, Capt., Adjutant, 6th. D.C.L.I.

Copy No.1 C.O.
2. 2nd.in Cmd.
3. Adjutant,
4. O.C. "A" Coy.
5. "   "B" "
6. O.C. "C" Coy.
7. "   "D" "
8. Sig: Officer,
9. Sniping "
10. Quartermaster.
11. Transport Officer,
12. R.S.M.
13. Brigade.
14. O.O.File,
15. W.D.

SECRET.

6th. (SERVICE) BATTALION DUKE OF CORNWALL'S LIGHT INFANTRY.

OPERATION ORDER No. 83.

W.D.

1. **RELIEF.**

    The 43rd. Brigade relieve the 41st. Brigade in the line tonight, 20/21st.

    The 10th.D.L.I. (less 1 Coy.) move into Support Line relieving the 8th.R.B. (less 1 Coy.) at 3.30.p.m.

    The 6th.D.C.L.I. move into the Support Line relieving the 10th.D.L.I. at 8.30.p.m. - the 10th.D.L.I. then moving up into front line.

    O.C. "D" Company will relieve 1 Coy. of 8th.R.B. on the East side of MESSINES RIDGE at about 8.30.p.m. Guides for "D" Coy. from 8th.R.B. will probably meet them at 41st.Brigade Headquarters at 7.30.p.m.

    "A" "B" and "C" Companies will find their own guides.

2. **MOVE.**

    The Battalion will parade ready to move off from Company billets at 5.30.p.m.   Order of March :-
    "D", "C", "B", "A".
    Companies will march by platoons at 200 yards interval.

    Lewis Gun limbers will accompany their Companies as far as WULVERGHEM, where they will be unloaded by Companies, and limbers will return to Transport Lines.

    "A" "B" and "C" Companies will take dicksees with them,- These can be carried on limbers - and will have tomorrow's rations on them. Stretcher Bearers will carry Stretchers and not rifles.

    Dress:-   BATTLE ORDER - Greatcoats will be taken up rolled over the shoulder. Haversack on the back.

3. **OFFICERS' VALISES, PACKS, STORES, etc.**

    Packs will be stacked in Q.M.Stores by 3.p.m. this afternoon.
    Officers' valises and Mess Stores will be stacked in Quartermaster's Stores by 3.p.m.

    Blankets will be rolled in bundles of ten and stacked in Q.M.Stores by 1.p.m.

    Names of all men issued with technical stores to be noted and men to thoroughly understand they are responsible for them.

4. **BATTN.H.Q.** Battalion Headquarters in Support will be at SWAYNES FARM.

5. **RELIEF COMPLETE.** Relief complete will be reported to Battalion Headquarters BY RUNNER.

6. **RECONNOITRING.** Company Commanders to reconnoitre the way to Left Battn. Headquarters in front line tonight. Each Coy. will detail one guide to go up with 10th.D.L.I. this afternoon, and report at Support Bn.H.Q. at 6.p.m.tonight.

20/9/17.
(Sd).   E.C.Codyre,   Captain,
Adjutant,   6th.D.C.L.I.

Copy.

6th. (Service) Battalion Duke of Cornwall's Light Infantry.

OPERATION ORDER No.84.

DUN will relieve BLACK in the FRONT LINE tonight.

The RELIEF will be carried out in the following order:-

"A" Coy. in the RIGHT Sector........ 3 Platoons.
"D" "   "   "   LEFT   " 4   "
"C" "   "   "   CENTRE   " 3   "
"B" "   in RESERVE, (less 1 Platoon to "D" Company).

Relief will commence at 8.p.m. The leading platoon of "A" Coy. will move off at 7.30.p.m. Platoons to keep 300 yards apart at ALL times.

Guides for Platoons and Company Headquarters will rendezvous at junction of FANNY Trench and Left Battn.Hd.Qr. Trench.

Nos.1 of Lewis Gun Teams of BLACK will remain in trenches till DAWN, and will be sent back to BLACK Hd.Qrs. in Support at 6.a.m. tomorrow.

Each Company will have 1 Lewis Gun team in Support at Coy.Hd.Qrs., except "D" Coy., who will have 1 platoon of "B" Coy. as well, in Support at his Coy.Hd.Qrs.

"A" Coy. will have 5 Lewis Guns in Front Line.
"C" ") "   "   3   "   "   "   "   "
) and one in support at Coy.Hd.Qrs.

"D" Coy. will have 4 Lewis Guns in Front Line and 1 in Support at Coy.Hd.Qrs.

"B" Coy. will attach ONE Lewis Gun Team to "A" Coy., and one Lewis Gun Team to "D" Coy.

Every man is to take up 4 sandbags tucked in his belt, with which to build up and revet the FIRESTEP and PARAPET tonight.

O.C. "D" Coy. will send out PATROLS every 1½ hours on his LEFT FLANK during the night, commencing immediately relief is complete.

Lists of Trench Stores and Receipts for same to be sent to Battn. Hd.Qrs.

All Coy.Hd.Qrs. and Coy. in reserve are warned to impress on ALL RANKS the necessity of avoiding all movement by day. Runners, especially, must keep under cover, and not expose themselves.

Wiring must be done by ALL Coys. in the line. This is most important, and should be carried on all night in reliefs.

"B" Coy. will carry up rations to each Coy.Hd.Qrs. nightly.

Relief Complete to be reported by RUNNER to Battn.Hd.Qrs. as soon as possible.

ACKNOWLEDGE.

Issued to Signals at 4.30.p.m.

(Sd). E.C.Codyre, Capt.
24/9/17.   Adjt., "D U N."

Copy.

6th. (Service) Battalion Duke of Cornwall's Light Infantry.

OPERATION ORDER No.85.

The following reliefs will be carried out tonight, - SCARLET relieving this Battalion :---

Reliefs in the following order:-

1. "A" Coy. DUN by "A" Coy. SCARLET.
2. "D" "   " " "D" "   "
3. "C" "   " " "B" "   "
4. "B" "   " " "C" "   "

Each Coy. (except "B" Coy.) will send 4 guides to SUPPORT Batt: H.Q. by 7.30.p.m.

"B" Coy. will send 4 guides to Junction of FANNY and Batt: H.Q.trench at 7.45.p.m.

Relieving unit has 3 platoons per Coy. remaining guide being for Coy.H.Q.

Relieving unit will send 1 N.C.O. per Coy. in advance to your Coy.H.Q. to take over Trench Stores, etc.

Receipts for R.E.Stores, S.A.A., Bombs, S.O.S. lights, etc., and all Trench Stores will be forwarded to Battn.Hd.Qrs. tomorrow morning by 8.a.m.

On Completion of relief, Companies will march back to CANTEEN CORNER opposite PALMER BATHS - intervals of 200 yds. being maintained between platoons throughout.

Limbers for Lewis Guns will meet Companies on road EAST of Bde:H.Q. 4 men per Coy. to march back with Lewis Gun limbers.

The Lewis Gun teams attached to Coys.from "B" Coy. will march back to camp with the Coys.they are attached to - the platoon from "B" Company attached to "D" Coy. will also march back to camp with "D" Coy.

On arrival in camp, these detachments will rejoin their Coy.

All water tins to be handed in to Battn.Hd.Qrs. by 8.p.m.

All gum boots to be carried out by Coys. A waggon will be with limbers to carry them back to camp. The deficiencies in Companies Gum boots will be noted by Qr.Mr., and Coys. will be issued with the same numbers of boots they hand in when they do their next tour in trenches, regardless of how bad the weather is.

All information re work in progress and to be done, information learnt by our patrols, etc. should be told to relieving Coy.Commanders.

When marching back, platoons will be kept closed up, and no straggling allowed.

Coy.Commanders will march in rear of their Companies, and platoon commanders in rear of their platoons.

Relief complete will be telephoned to Batt:H.Q., not sent by Runner. Code words, ORDERS NOTED being sent.

Sept.28th.

(Sd).E.J.Hewitt, Lt-Col.,
O.C., D U N.

WAR DIARY.

October 1917.

6th Bn. Duke of Cornwall's Light Infantry.

Volume 30.

Army Form C. 2118.

WAR DIARY
or
INTELLIGENCE SUMMARY.

6th Battn Duke of Cornwall's L.I.

(Erase heading not required.)

For OCTOBER 1917

SHEET 28. ¹⁄₄₀,₀₀₀
BELGIUM and FRANCE
EDITION 3.

Place	Date OCTOBER 1917	Hour	Summary of Events and Information	Remarks and references to Appendices
CANTEEN CORNER Camp T.26.c.5.0.	1st		The Battalion was quartered in Canteen Corner Camp. Map Ref. Sheet 28. T.26.C.5.0. and carried out Training under Company Commanders from 7.am to 12.30pm. The Battalion also furnished a Working Party of 4 Officers and 100 Other Ranks, which paraded at 7.15.am and proceeded to work on the French Tramway at T.20.a.4.5 Sheet 28.	
—do—	2nd		As for the 1st inst.	
—do—	3rd		—do—	
—do—	4th		—do—	
—do—	5th		—do—	
—do—	6th	2.30pm 6.15pm	The Battalion paraded at 2.30.p.m. and moved off by Companies at 100 yards distance to the WESTOUTRE area. On arrival at WESTOUTRE orders were received to proceed to a Camp at M.7.d.5.5. Sheet 28. Where we arrived and were settled by 6.15.p.m. (See Operation Order No. 86 of 5/10/17 attached)	
Camp at M.7.d.5.5.	7th		Companies were allotted accommodation in Huts, Tents and Bivouacs. Winter Clothing was issued and Companies placed at the disposal of the Company Commanders.	
—do—	8th	9am 10.30pm	The Battalion paraded at 9am in Full Marching Order. No stores as possible are sent for a ROUTE MARCH. Returned to Camp about 12.30.pm. Operation Orders were received at 10.30pm to move to CHIPPEWA WAR Camp at M.6.a.+7.N.W.+A.C.4.5.5. Sheet 28. the following day. (See C.O.'s N.S. 87, 48, 49 + 11.17 attached)	

Army Form C. 2118.

WAR DIARY
INTELLIGENCE SUMMARY
(Erase heading not required.)

S.H.S.B(2)   C3. B.Th. Duke of Cornwall's L.Ft. Infantry
For OCTOBER 1917

Place	Date 1917	Hour	Summary of Events and Information	Remarks and references to Appendices
Camp at M.7.C.5.5	9th		The Battalion paraded at 8.45 am and moved by Companies at 100 yards distance to CHIPPEWAR CAMP – M.6.a.4.7. via WESTOUTRE, LA CLYTTE where they arrived and were settled by 11. am.	FRANCE
CHIPPEWAR CAMP	10th		Companies were placed at the disposal of Company Commanders for TRAINING. Orders were received about 7.pm for the Battalion to move to the following area, to BEDFORD HOUSE SHEET 29. I. 26. C. 10.1. to relieve the 6th Battn K.O.Y.L.I who were under to move forward and relieve the 1st Battn D.C.L.I. on the FRONT LINE.	
— do —	11th		The Battalion paraded AS STRONG AS POSSIBLE at 8.30 am and moved off by Companies at 200 yards distance Commencing with "B" Coy. at 8.45 am. The Battalion arrived at BEDFORD HOUSE and was settled by 12 NOON. (See Operation Order No. attached)	
BEDFORD HOUSE	12th		The whole Battn was employed in making and improving the Bivouac accommodation with the exception of TWO OFFICERS and 100 Other Ranks who paraded at 7pm and were employed in carrying R.E. Material to the forward area.	
— do —	13th		do for the 13th inst except only 1 Officer & 50 Other Ranks were employed on R.E. Fatigues.	
— do —	14th		As above. The whole Battn were employed on Road making on the main Ypres to BEDFORD Ave.	
— do —	15th		The Battalion paraded at 1.30pm and moved off by Platoons at 200 yards distance to relieve the 1/5 Battn D.L.I. in Brigade Support in SANCTUARY WOOD. See Operation Order No. attached	

15/10/17   The 1/6 Battn D.C.L.I. Sheffield   one wounded and 200 arrived by 4.45 pm
B Company went forward with the main body to 5 pm and took up their position in Reserve trenches
in CAMBRIDGE COVERT. D. Coy. came up to Relieve the
(Signed) J.G. Lillingson
Commdy. 6 Bn D.C.L.I.

WAR DIARY or INTELLIGENCE SUMMARY

Army Form C. 2118.

Place	Date	Hour	Summary of Events and Information	Remarks and references to Appendices
SANCTUARY WOOD	16/9 1917		The Battalion who were in Brigade Support (to the 10th Bn. D.L.I.) moved to the Front Line Trenches) and new quarters in SANCTUARY WOOD in Dugouts and Shelters at R.1/D. at 5 p.m. During the night 16/17.5. the enemy shelled the portion of the Wood the Battalion was occupying with Gas Shells and High Explosive Shells. He also gave shellfire to troops as if about to attack. A "C" Coy moved up Rifle & LG 10/D.L.I. and one D Company, however the Wood at 5.30 p.m. in relief of an officer. Casualties Other Ranks 4 Killed, 7 Wounded. The whole 4th Bn Durhams at 5.30 a.m. and carried Trench Boards for the 11th Batt. Keep numbers Ryff who were making Tank Track A.	
SANCTUARY WOOD	17/9		As to the 165 men of the D.L.I. carried up rations to 10/D.L.I. & 11 & 12 D.L.I. "C" Company Paraded at 5.30 a.m. and carried Trench Boards. Casualties Officers Wounded 2. Other Ranks Killed 8) Wounded 39)	
SANCTUARY WOOD and Front Line Trenches S.1, 5 and ALL SLOPES at Ypres Sector Belgium	18/9		The Battalion less "B" Coy paraded in Sanctuary Wood at 5.15 p.m. and moved forwards by Platoons at 200 yards interval at 5.30 p.m. to relieve the 11/D.L.I. in the Front Line Trenches. Bloyer moved forward from Canadian Division at Dusk. The Relief was carried out without incident and completed by 8 to 9 p.m. Casualties in Sanctuary Wood on this day before Relief commenced Officers Killed 1, 2 Lieut. VOYINS, 2 Lieut. CHAPMAN MC 2 Lieut NUGS Other Ranks Killed 5. Wounded 8. During the night the enemy shelled the Batt. sector very heavily with Gas Shells and H.E. Shells in the Trenches in support places approaching the Front Line Stirling Castle Ridge Tor House	

M. Mullen, Major
Commanding 4 Batt.

Army Form C. 2118.

WAR DIARY
or
INTELLIGENCE SUMMARY.

(Erase heading not required.)

SHEET (1)   6th Batt. Duke of Cornwall's Light Infantry   for OCTOBER 1917

Instructions regarding War Diaries and Intelligence Summaries are contained in F. S. Regs. Part II. and the Staff Manual respectively. Title pages will be prepared in manuscript.

Place	Date	Hour	Summary of Events and Information	Remarks and references to Appendices
FRONT LINE TRENCHES U.15.b and T.16.a Sugar O.3 Rifleman's Trench	19th Oct 1917		The Battalion still in the Front Line Trenches. The enemy rather quiet during the day and straffed the area with his Minenwerfers when we were near PADDER WOOD CEMETERY. No movement except sniping took place during the day light, but at night he was very active on our front and placed with rifle fire various spots in rear of our Front Line. Rations were carried up & the Ration by the 6th Batt. SOMERSET L.I. CASUALTIES One (Other Ranks) WOUNDED 12.	
— do —	20th Oct	10 a.m.	Casualties One Rank KILLED 8 WOUNDED 13. Men improving the trenches considerably. Enemy fight type Aeroplane dropped bombs in vicinity of Front line and one was killed. Very heavy fighting on our Right where heavy losses	
— do —	21st	2 pm	Relief of the Battalion on the line by the 6th Batt. SOMERSET L.I. The relief was completed by 9 pm. The enemy shelling our front & support areas unusually. Quiet up till 10.30 p.m. The Battalion on completion of relief moved by Platoons to RIDGEWOOD CAMP where very heavy shrapnel in huts, tents and shelter. The arrival at this camp was effected at 12.30 am 23 inst 3.5 Shell 33 Men	
RIDGEWOOD CAMP	22nd		The Battalion received orders to move as a Company formed at H 36 c 3.5 which was the C.R.E. 10th Corps. The Battalion proceeded to RENINGHELST and the Hrfra party at H.36 was moved up in Peloton at H.12.30pm and moved up in Peloton at 100 yards distance arriving at the new camp at 1.30pm. Here they will quartered in BIVOUACS	

W. Thorpe Lt
acting for O.C.

Army Form C. 2118.

SHEET (5)

WAR DIARY
or
INTELLIGENCE SUMMARY.

6th Bn. Duke of Wellingtons

(Erase heading not required.)

Place	Date	Hour	Summary of Events and Information	Remarks and references to Appendices
BIVOUACS Lat 36.6.3.5 Sheet 28	1917 Oct 24th	4.30	The Battalion was paraded in Bivouacs at H.36.C.3.5. The parade at 4-30 a.m. under the command of Major C.F. MILNER D.S.O. 2nd in command by platoons at 100 yards distance to BIRR CROSS ROADS where they were to work under the instruction of the OFFICER i/c 37th DIVISIONAL Royal Engineer carrying out of timber to make up the track SANCTUARY WOOD known as PLUMER' DRIVE SOUTH	
do-	24th 25th		As to the 2.30 a.m. parade. No work was done this day, but the Royal Engineers. The whole Battalion are employed in cleaning Kit. Clothing arms & equipment. They are marched to the BATHS at RIDGEWOOD where they obtained a bath.	
do-	26th		The Battalion paraded at 8.30 a.m. and moved off by Coys to BIRR CROSS ROADS forming to heart "B" Coy to march to Sqn. CHADWICK 118 Sub. Pkt up Kingstone Rd. in carrying state of timber to form on the MENIN ROAD. "A" "C" and "D" Coy to be met by a Guide from the 118 Coy R.E. a.t. 9.30 a.m. and carry out of timber as R.E. MENIN Road & a laying or the new track to make up KNOWN OF R.E.'s GUIDE PLUMER DRIVE SOUTH. This carrying work to be undertaken by each Company. At 4.45 the 16th Draughts, all four Companies arrived every able to march to take 6th Coy Royal Engineers. Three men wounded by name. Only the drainage and part of the shuud compleated. Night too dark not to be carried on too broken Sunday about 6.30 pm got the compleated Casualties: O.Rs. Wounded 2. ...	40/000

WAR DIARY or INTELLIGENCE SUMMARY

Army Form C. 2118.

SHEET (6)

6th Bn. Duke of Cornwall's Light Infantry for OCTOBER 1917

Place	Date	Hour	Summary of Events and Information	Remarks and references to Appendices
Bivouacs at J.30.c.3.3. Sheet 28	28th Oct 1917	3.30 a.m	The Battalion paraded at 3.30 a.m. and moved off by Coys to BIRR Cross Roads. Jocks were made to get off at TR.83. Carrying parties of timbers for PLUMERS DRIVE SOUTH. The enemy shelled the camp occupied by the Battalion about 11.30 a.m. on the line with a Long Range Gun. No Casualties. No Casualties were caused. The Adv. Parties went forward to take over on old French line (B.27) and learnt the afternoon the Reserves which were in the huts of these were moved to safer places as the trench "D" Company moved at 2.15 a.m. not much was seen new huts at J.15.a.3.3. All Ranks were given permission to go to the Cross Roads KRUISSTRAAT-HOEK, to see the 1st Battn D.C.L.I. Pass (half point J.30.d.3.1.Sh.28.) in this way to the forward area.	Relief up Shelley 28 Beginning Part of France
-do-	29th		The Battalion paraded at 4.45 a.m. and pulled in Lorries at the cross roads H.30.d.3.1 at 5 a.m. from where they were conveyed to HELL FIRE CORNER arriving at BIRR Cross Roads by 6 a.m. and marched to Coys. took the [?] of NUMBER 2 in the LINE on the TIES and PLUMERS DRIVE SOUTH.	
-do-	30th		Coys first on the duty were detailed and the Battalion was standing by ready to the trenches. for the 4.30pm BOMBERS - [?] and relieved No 10 trenches.	
31/10/17			BERTHEN via BOESINGHE, YPRES, DUNLOP Street moved from J.15.d.3. L.S.RIDGE	

BERTHEN (Nord, France)

Commanding 6th Bn DCLI

WAR DIARY
INTELLIGENCE SUMMARY

SHEET (7)

6th Batt. Duke of Cornwalls Light Infantry

FOR OCTOBER 1917

Army Form C. 2118.

Place	Date	Hour	Summary of Events and Information	Remarks and references to Appendices
No 10 Area BERTHEN	1917 Oct. 30th	Continued	The Battalion arrived at No. 10 Area near BERTHEN and were quartered in Billets, by 5 p.m. Battalion H.Qrs were at R.33.b.5.6. Sut.27	Reference to SHEET 27
do.	31st		Companies were placed at the disposal of Company Commanders for the purpose of checking, and cleaning Clothing, Kit and Equipment.	31st Inf.

31/10/1917.

C.J. Miller Major
Commanding 6th Batt D.C.L.I

6TH. (SERVICE) BATTALION DUKE OF CORNWALL'S LIGHT INFANTRY.

OPERATION ORDER No. 86.

Copy No...... 15.

1. **MOVE.** The Battalion will march tomorrow in the direction of WESTOUTRE. Dress:- FULL MARCHING ORDER.

   Time will be notified later, but Battalion must be ready to move off early tomorrow morning.

2. **LEWIS GUNS.** Lewis Guns will be packed in limbers tonight.

3. **OFFICERS KIT.** Officers' Surplus Kit will be packed tonight and probably have to be stored tonight in NEUVE EGLISE. No Lorry has been allotted, so Officers' kits must be cut down to 40.lbs., and if over weight will be left behind.

4. **BLANKETS.** Orders re men's blankets will be issued later.

5. **S.A.A.,etc.** Quartermaster will have S.A.A. and Grenade Limbers loaded tonight, - also the tool cart loaded tonight.

6. **STORES, etc.** Band boxes and cases will be loaded in country cart tonight - also Orderly Room Stores and Quartermaster's Stores loaded in G.S.waggon or country cart tonight - also Pioneers, Shoemakers and Tailors Stores.

(Sd). E.C.Codyre, Captain,
5/10/17. Adjutant, 6th.D.C.L.I.

Copy No. 1. C.O.   8. Transport Officer,
        2. 2nd in Cmd.   9. Quartermaster,
        3. Adjutant,   10. Signalling Officer,
        4. O.C. "A" Coy. 11. Intelligence Officer
        5.   " "B" "   12. Brigade.
        6.   " "C" "   13. R.S.M.
        7.   " "D" "   14. O.O.File.
                          15. W.D.

S E C R E T.

6th. (SERVICE) BATTALION DUKE OF CORNWALL'S LIGHT INFANTRY.

O P E R A T I O N   O R D E R   No. 87.

REFERENCE Sheet 28 1/40,000.   Copy No...1....

1. **MOVE.**   The 43rd. Brigade Group will move on the 9th. instant to No.5 area N.W. of LA CLYTTE.

2. **ROUTINE.**   Reveille will be at 6.a.m.
   Sick Parade at 6.15.a.m.

   Officers Kits, and Men's blankets (rolled in bundles of ten) will be stacked in the Qr.Mr's. Stores shelter opposite the Battalion Quarter Guard by 7.a.m.

   Breakfasts will be at 7.30.a.m.

   The Transport Officer will detail one G.S.waggon to report to the O.C. "B" Company in the 6th. Somerset L.I. lines near RENINGHELST at 6.30.a.m. to fetch their Officers' kits and blankets to the present Camp.

   Company Cookers with Officers Mess Kits loaded on same will be ready to move at 8.15.a.m.

3. **TRANSPORT.**   The Transport will be ready to move by 8.30.a.m. but will remain drawn up on the Parade Ground and NOT on the Road.

   Transport will march with the Battalion.

4. **PARADE.**   The Battalion will parade on the Square at 8.45.a.m., and move to CHIPPEWAR - M.6.a.4.7. at 9.a.m. To pass the Starting Point WESTOUTRE CHURCH at 9.22.a.m. Head of "B" Company to be at the Bridge at M.9.c.4.5. by 9.20.a.m.

   Order of March:- "C" "D" BAND, "A" "B".Company.

   DRESS:- FULL MARCHING ORDER.

5. **DISTANCE.**   100 yards distance will be maintained between Companies and between the rear Company and Transport.

6. **BILLETING PARTY.**   2/Lt:GLENCROSS, the 4 Coy.Q.M.Sgts. and L/C.Jones will parade at 7.30.a.m., and leave on bicycles at 7.45.a.m., to meet the Staff Captain in the new camp at 9.30.a.m.

7. **SANITATION.**   All Officers Quarters, Tents and the ground surrounding will be cleaned up and ready for inspection by 8.15.a.m.

                                    (Sd). E. C. Codyre,   Captain,
8-10-17.   Adjutant, 6th. D.C.L.I.

Copies to:-   1.   O.C. "A" Coy.
                 2.   "   "B" "
                 3.   "   "C" "
                 4.   "   "D" "
                 5.   Transport Officer.
                 6.   R.S.M.
                 7.   O.O.File.   8.W.D.

Copy.

6TH. (SERVICE) BATTALION DUKE OF CORNWALL'S LIGHT INFANTRY.

O P E R A T I O N   O R D E R   No. 88.a.

The relief tonight will be carried out in the order issued to Coys. last night - i.e. 1 Coy. Somersets, C. D. A and B.

Companies will be ready to move off at 5.15.p.m.this evening. In the event of it being a clear evening, the leading Company will not leave till 5.30.p.m.

"C" Coy. will move off behind the S.L.I. Coy, keeping 100 yds. distance until it is too dark to see them, when connecting files will be sent out, and "C" Coy.will close up on to the S.L.I. Coy.

"D" and "A" Coy. will move off, "D" Coy. 100 yds. distance between "C" Coy. & "A" Coy. 100 yds. distance from "D" Coy. until it is too dark to see. "A" Coy. will then send out connecting files to "D" Coy., and close up on "D" Coy.

1 Guide from the D.L.I. will be guiding D.Coy., therefore D. Coy. can keep 100 yards distance from C.Coy., the whole way up.

Each platoon in each Coy. is to have a guide at the head of it who knows the way up to Front Batt: H.Q. in case Coys. or platoons get separated.

On arrival at Front Batt: H.Q., 1 guide per platoon, and 1 guide for Coy. H.Q. will be provided from D.L.I.

Every N.C.O. and man to carry 220 rounds S.A.A., and rations and water for the 19th. taken up with Coys.

D.L.I. are emptying their Lewis Gun Drums before leaving this S.A.A., and all other S.A.A., bombs, S.O.S.grenades, Very Lights, Trench Stores, etc. to be taken over and receipted lists obtained. Receipts to be sent to Batt: H.Q. morning of the 19th.

Relief complete will be sent to Batt: H.Q. by runner, the words "COMPLIED WITH" being sent, and the time.

On arrival in trenches, Os.C. C. and D.Coys. will send out patrols to get in touch with Battalions on their left and right respectively throughout the night, reports being sent in the morning stating how many times they met.

Coys.flanks must be carefully watched and patrolled.

All movement in the front line, between Coy. H.Q. and the front line, and between Coy.H.Q. and Batt.H.Q. is to be avoided during daylight. This especially applies to Coy.H.Q., where all ranks are to keep under cover from view all day.

Unless very urgent, messages will not be sent from Coys. to BattN H.Q., except during dusk, night time or early dawn.

All ranks must thoroughly understand any attack or enemy patrols, etc. must be driven off by rifle fire - bombs and rifle grenades are not to be relied on.

Enemy aeroplanes to be fired on with Lewis Guns, whenever they give good targets and are low down. Otherwise all ranks will keep still and avoid movement - also refrain from looking up. This must be impressed on all ranks.

Every opportunity will be employed by men to rub their feet at least once a day and during the evening.

continued:- - 2 -

Putties to be worn loose, or sandbags to be worn and boots laced up loosely.

The S.L.I. will carry up rations and water, Coys. will have their empty water tins collected at suitable places every night ready to hand over to the S.L.I. carrying parties to take back to ration dump on Corderouy Road.

Company Commanders will ensure they have a plentiful supply of S.A.A., S.O.S. grenades and Very Lights - reporting to Battalion Headquarters at once if they are short.

Smoke is to be avoided in Front and Support lines.

18-10-17.

(Sd). E.C. Codyre, Capt.,
Adjutant, 6th. D.C. L.I.

SECRET.

8th. (SERVICE) BATTALION DUKE OF CORNWALL'S LIGHT INFANTRY.

OPERATION ORDER No. 89.

Copy No........

1. MOVE.   The Battalion will move to Camp at H.36.b.3.3. – about 1½ miles.

   Battalion will be ready to move at 1.30.p.m. today.

   Order of March:- "A" "D" Band, "C" "B" Company. Companies at 100 yards interval.

   Dress:- FULL MARCHING ORDER and STEEL HELMETS.

2. TRANSPORT. Transport will remain in present lines, but will accompany Battalion to New Camp, and then return – leaving Cookers, Water Carts, Lewis Gun Limbers, M.O. and Mess Carts with the Battalion.

   Transport Officer will arrange for the G.S.waggons and Country Cart to move men's blankets, Officers' valises, etc. during the day.

3. OFFICERS' VALISES, etc. Officers' valises, men's blankets and packs of casualties to be stacked by 11.45.a.m. at a point off the duckboards between the Orderly Room and the Cemetery.

(Sd).   E. C. Codyre, Captain,
22/10/17.   Adjutant, 8th. D.C.L.I.

Copy No. 1.   H.Q.
        2.   O.C. "A" Coy.,
        3.   "   "B" "
        4.   "   "C" "
        5.   "   "D" "
        6.   Transport Officer
        7.   R.S.M.
        8.   O.C.File.
        9.   W. D.

SECRET.

6th. (Service) Battalion Duke of Cornwall's Light Infantry.

OPERATION ORDER No. 90.

Copy No.......

1. **RELIEF.** The following inter-Brigade relief will take place tomorrow, 30th. instant :-

    The 6th. K.O.Y.L.I. will relieve the 6th. D.C.L.I.

    On completion of relief the Battalion will proceed to No. 10 area near BERTHEN, and take over billets vacated by 6th. K.O.Y.L.I.

    Battalion Headquarters will be at R.33.b.5.6.

    The relief will be carried out as follows:-

    Details, Sick, etc. will have breakfast at 7.a.m.
    The Carrying Parties will have Breakfasts under Company arrangements on their return to the present Camp from work.

2. **TRANSPORT.** Coy. Cookers, and all Transport (less 2 G.S. waggons and Officers' Mess Cart) will be ready to move under the Transport Officer at 8.30.a.m.

3. **CARRYING PARTIES.** The whole of the Carrying Parties are being conveyed to the next billets by lorries, and will be standing by ready to move to KRUISTRAATHOEK Cross Roads, where they will pick up lorries about 12 NOON.
    Dress:- Full Marching Order, with one blanket strapped underneath the Supporting Straps of each man's pack.
    Dinners will be ready for this party as soon as possible after arrival at next billets

4. **DETAILS.** The remaining Details, Sick, etc. will have dinners at 12 noon, and parade in their Coy. lines ready to march off at 2.p.m. Dress:- Full Marching Order.

5. **OFFICERS' KITS, BLANKETS, etc.** All Officers' Kits and surplus blankets (other than the 1 per man to be carried by the party proceeding by lorries) and the blankets of Details will be rolled in bundles of 10, and stacked outside the Q.M. Stores by 10.a.m.
    One of the G.S. waggons remaining with the Details to be at "D" Company's Camp by 9.30.a.m. for the purpose of conveying Officers' Kits and blankets of that Coy. to the Q.M. Stores.

6. **BILLETING PARTY.** The Qr.Mr. and Coy.Q.M.Sgts. will meet the Staff Capt. at Brigade H.Q. (27. R.34.c.4.0.) by 11.a.m.

7. **SANITATION, &c.** 1 Officer & 1 N.C.O. per Coy. will be left in Camp to hand over to the relieving unit, and will ensure that the Coy. lines and ground surrounding are left in a thoroughly clean condition.
    Os.C.Coys. & Transport Officer will render a certificate to Battn. H.Q. by 7.30.p.m. tomorrow that this has been done.

8. **FIRE PRECAUTIONS** On arrival at the new billets, Os.C.Coys. will ensure that all precautions are taken as regards,
    (a) prevention against fires,
    (b) that every billet where either men, horses or stores are housed has a copy of fire orders put up and that the same are read out to ALL RANKS,
    (c) that there is a bucket of water and a bucket of dry earth kept handy.
    Certificate to be rendered as above.

(Sd). E.C. Codyre, Captain,
Adjutant, 6th. D.C.L.I.

29-10-17.

WAR   DIARY.

6th Bn Duke of Cornwalls Light Infantry.

November 1917.

Volume 31.

WAR DIARY

Army Form C. 2118.

S.D.R.I. 6th Bttn.
Duke of Cornwall's Light Infantry
for NOVEMBER 1917

Place	Date Nov 1917	Hour	Summary of Events and Information	Remarks and references to Appendices
Billets	1st		The Battalion was quartered in Billets in No. 10 Area near Berthen with Battalion Head Quarters at R.33.6.5.6. Sheet 27. The Rifle Range at R.20.d.80.70 was allotted to the Battalion and reallotted to Coys so that one hour each during whole time the carried out a Coy pamp practice. The time before and after firing was spent in Arms and Company Drills	
do	2nd		The Battalion was paraded at 8 & 6 a.m. and detailed off under specialist Officers and Instructors for Training in the following. 9.70.10 am Physical Training Remainder of the morning Lewis Gun, Rifle Grenade Firing, Musketry.	
do	3rd		At 9.0 the 2nd inst. locality so that the Commanding Officer and Company Commanders spent the morning with the Brigadier General Commanding in explaining his Schemes of Defence to him on the Ground. Copies of the General Scheme were being issued to Coms on the 15th inst. The Battalion paraded at 8.45 a.m. to study as above and dispersed at 11.0 a.m	
do	4th		Route March. O.C. Coys marched their Coys to the position they intended to take up in accordance with the Scheme's they explained to the B.G.C. on the 3rd inst. Captains B. & S. of the Royal Welsh Fusiliers lectured to all Officers & NCO.s on Trench Dispositions from 2.30 pm to 4 pm.	
do	5th		The Battalion who allotted the Rifle Range at R 20 d 86.70 from 9 am to 1 pm. Coys Captains for Company Practice. From 2 pm to 4 pm was spent in Rifle Grenade Firing, Lewis Gun Firing & Throwing Live Bombs.	

A 5831 Wt.W4973/M687 750,000 8/16 D.D. & L. Ltd. Forms/C.2118/13

Army Form C. 2118.

WAR DIARY
or
INTELLIGENCE SUMMARY.

SHEET (2)

Army Form heading: Duke of Cornwall's Light Infantry
For November 1917

(Erase heading not required.)

Reference Map Sheet 27
Belgium and France
Scale 2 : 40/000

Place	Date 1917	Hour	Summary of Events and Information	Remarks and references to Appendices
Billets N? of BERGHEM	Nov 6th		TRAINING under Company Commanders in Physical Training from 9 am to 9.45 am. The Battalion paraded in the field near B/Hop Billets at 10 am to Stand to Possible and was inspected by the Commanding Officer. On the completion of the inspection the Battn. was exercised in Battalion Drill "CEREMONIAL".	
— do —	7th		TRAINING. Coys were allotted the Rifle Range at R.20.d.30.70 in the forenoon. During which time the remainder of the Coys were getting the Refuse Practice 1.5.1.5 Rounds in Musketry. On return from the Range training in Lewis Gun & Vickers Rifle Grenades was carried out. Training was carried out under Company Commanders. New Lewis Gun Teams were formed under Lt G.D Seymour and Rifle Grenade Teams under Lieut S. J Rance for training.	
— do —	8th		As for 7th	
— do —	9th 10th		As for 8th inst. Officers & Coy Sergt Major & Company attended a Memorial Service at BERTHEN CHURCH which was held in memory of the British and French Soldiers who fell in the 9.11.14 in action during the German front at the village.	
— do —	11th		Divine Service. The Battalion paraded at 11am in Full Marching Order for inspection by the Commanding Officer. The New Lewis Gun Teams fired on the Range at R.20 d.70.70 under the supervision of Lt Seymour.	
— do —	12th		Training and fitting Equipment under Company arrangements. Cleaning up and preparing for the move to the new area on the 13th. The Transport paraded at 8.30 am and moved off at 9 am & head under the command of Lt. G.A BLYTH to the new Training Area near BOISDINGHEM.	
— do —	13th		The Battalion paraded by Companies at 9.30 am and moved off at 10 AM by march route to the Railway Station at CAESTRE. SEE Operation Order No. 91 attached.	

E. J. Hewith
Commdt 6th Bn. D.C.L.I.
Lieut Colonel

13/11/17

SHEET (3)

Army Form C. 2118.

6th Battn.

WAR DIARY
or
INTELLIGENCE SUMMARY.

Regt. of Cornwalls Light Infantry.

For NOVEMBER 1917.

(Erase heading not required.)

REFERENCE MAP
SHEET 27/A S.E.
FRANCE

Place	Date	Hour	Summary of Events and Information	Remarks and references to Appendices
ACQUIN.	"13TH" CONTINUED).		The Battalion arrived at the Railway Station CAESTRE by 11.44 a.m. and were entrained by 11.50 a.m. moving off at 12 noon for WIZERNES where they arrived at 3.45 p.m. and detrained. The Battalion was at once formed up and again moved off at 4 p.m. by march route to ACQUIN where they arrived and were settled in billets by 7.30 p.m.	
-do-	14TH		"X" RIFLE RANGE at V.24.a. SHEET. 27 A.S.E. was on this date allotted to the Battalion. "B" and "C" Coys. Paraded at 8 a.m. and fired from 9 a.m to 12 NOON. "D" and "A" Coys. Paraded at 12 NOON and fired from 1 p.m to 6 p.m. The whole Battalion (Trench Strength) was exercised in Musketry and the following Practices were fired. "GROUPING" 5 Rds at 100 yards. APPLICATION 5 Rds 200 yds.	
-do-	15TH		"X" RIFLE RANGE was allotted to the Battn. as for the 14th inst., and the following Practices were fired. SNAP SHOOTING. 5 Rds. at 100 Yds. at SILHOUTTE Targets. 10 Rds Rapid in 45 Seconds. Bayonets Fixed.	
-do-	16TH		"X" Range allotted and the following Practices were fired:- Snap Shooting at 200 Yards. 5 Rds. Application at 300 Yards.	
-do-	17TH		"X" Range allotted and the following Practices was fired:- Application 400 Yards. 5 Rounds.	
-do-	18TH		From 9 a.m. to 11 a.m. Training under Company Commanders was carried out in the following subjects. Physical Training, Bayonet Training, Musketry. "Y" RIFLE RANGE at V.24.t. was allotted to the Battalion from 4 p.m. on this date, for the purpose of firing PRACTICES Nos. 13 and 14. of the 14TH DIVISION CLASSIFICATION TABLE. Coys Paraded at 12 NOON and Commenced firing at 1 p.m. from 2ND LT. C.D. SEYMOUR and ONE Non-Com. Offr. Cry were given instruction in ANTI-AIRCRAFT SHOOTING by the 25TH Squadron R.F.C. at BOISDINGHEM.	

18 - 11 - 1917
E J Hern
Lieut Colonel
Commdg. 6th Bn. D.C.L.I.

SHEET (4)   6th Battalion
Duke of Cornwalls
Light Infantry

Army Form C. 2118.

WAR DIARY or INTELLIGENCE SUMMARY.

FOR NOVEMBER 1917

REFERENCE MAP
SHEET 27/ 1 S.E.
FRANCE 1/40,000

Place	Date Nov. 1917	Hour	Summary of Events and Information	Remarks and references to Appendices
ACQUIN	19th		"Y" RIFLE RANGE at V.24. & SHEET 27 A.S.E. was again allotted to the Battalion. PRACTICES. 15 and 16. of the 14th Divisional Classification Table were carried out (3rd Application and 15 Rounds Rapid in ONE MINUTE RANGE 300 Yards)	
-do-	20th		"Y" Range was allotted to the Battalion for this date and all Coys commenced firing PRACTICE 17. Div'nl Classification Table at 9 a.m. On the completion of Practice 17, N° 18. was completed 5th Application and 5 Rounds Rapid at 400 Yards. "B","C" and "D" Coys when moved to 200 Yards and completed Practice N° 19. Snap Shooting at Silhouette Targets. "A" Coy. did not fire Practice 19, on this date.	
-do-	21st		"Y" Range was again allotted to the Battalion. "A" Coy. fired Practice N° 19. and then marched to the Training Ground where they rejoined the other THREE Coys of the Battalion who were Training under their Coy. Commanders, in the following. Coy. Drill, Saluting without Arms, Description and Recognition of Targets, Officers + N.C.O.s giving Fire Orders etc. Artillery Formation, Box Respirator Drill. The CASUALS of the Battalion who did not fire with their Coys were fired a Preliminary Shoot at 200 - 300 - and 400 Yards, On the Completion of the Preliminary Shoot they fired Practices N° 13 - 14.- 15" and 16 of the 14th Div'nl Classification Table	
-do-	22nd		The Battalion & and Transport paraded on the football field IN MASS at 9. 30 a.m. DRESS. FULL MARCHING ORDER wearing Caps, for inspection at 10 A.M. by the Brigade Commander. Brigadier General. T.R. TEMPEST D.S.O. Scots Guards. On the Completion of the inspection about 12.30pm. Coys marched back to their billets	

22-11-1917 E J Nevill Lieut Colonel
Commandg 6 Bn D.C.L.I.

Army Form C. 2118.

WAR DIARY
or
INTELLIGENCE SUMMARY.

SHEET (5)

6th Bn.
Duke of Cornwalls
Light Infantry.
For NOVEMBER 1917.

REFERENCE MAP
SHEET 27
A / SE 40,000

Place	Date Novr. 1917	Hour	Summary of Events and Information	Remarks and references to Appendices
ACQUIN	23rd		"Y" Range was allotted to the Battalion and the Events completed their Musketry firing Practice. 17 - 18 - and 19. 14th Divl Classification Table. All the newly trained Lewis Gunners paraded under 2/Lt C.D. SEYMOUR on the Range at 9.a.m. and fired a L.G. Practice firing at Falling Plates at 400 Yards Range. On the completion of this they were put through Revolver Practice at 30 yds Range. Training was carried by Coys under their Coy Commdrs. One N.C.O + 6 Men per Company were training under 2/Lt A.L. POTTER and SERGT G.F. DOWSETT. Firing Live Rifle Grenades and Throwing Live Mills Hand Grenades on the Bombing Ground.	
- do -	24th		Devine Service, Scrubbing + Cleaning Equipment, Clothing etc. All Coy Commdrs Platoon Commdrs, + Platoon Sgts, met the Commanding Officer + Adjt. at 10.30 a.m. at Point Q.27.a.8.8. on the FIELD FIRING AREA and had the Field Firing Scheme explained to them on the ground the Battalion was to be exercises over the following day.	
- do -	25th		The Battalion carried out a FIELD FIRING SCHEME by Companies on the Ground around Q.27.a.8.8. The Adjutant Capt. E.C. COSYNS M.C and THE QUARTERMASTER Lieut. F. GUNN proceeded to CALAIS by Motor Bus with the other Adjt + Q.M.s of the Division to visit the ORDNANCE WORKSHOPS there	
- do -	26th		The Battalion paraded to carry to proceed at 9 a.m. ready to the Training Area near V.16.a.6.1. where they were to carry out an "ATTACK" practice in conjunction with the 6th D.L.S.L.I. This was however cancelled about 9.15. a.m. owing to inclement weather.	

26/11/17.
E.J. Harris Lt Colonel
Commdg 6th D.C.L.I

WAR DIARY or INTELLIGENCE SUMMARY

Army Form C. 2118.

6th (S) Battalion. Duke of Cornwalls Light Infantry FOR NOVEMBER 1917.

SHEET (6)

Place	Date	Hour	Summary of Events and Information	Remarks and references to Appendices
AQUIN	Nov 1917 27th		Training was carried out by Companies under their Company Commanders. On this date the results of the Battalion Musketry in the 14th Divisional Eleven-a-side Course Test was published and the following are the results:- The Best Shooting Coy. is "C" Company with 87.18 points next "D" Coy with 84.60 points, "B" Coy with 83.93 points, "A" Coy with 80.36 points. The best Shot in the Battalion is Pte No. 28644 L/Cpl COOK A. S. of "A" Coy. Total possible score 180 points. Score of L/Cpl COOK A.S. 148 POINTS.	Reference Map Sheet 27/B SE 1/40,000.
-do-	28th		Training was carried out by Companies under their Comp. Commanders.	
-do-	29th		Training under Coy arrangements from 9am to 10.30am. At 11am the Battalion Paraded on the Ground behind "X" Rifle Range and were exercised in ARTILLERY FORMATIONS by the Commanding Officer Lt Colonel S.T. HEWITT D.S.O. On this date the whole of the Officers and N.C.Os of the Battalion assembled in the Village School-room at 6pm. and were given a LECTURE by Lieut Colonel A.G. BAYLEY. D.S.O. O.C. 7th BUCKS.L.I. G.S.O. I of the 14th Light Division. Subject of Lecture "The PASSCHENDAELE Sector."	
-do-	30th		Training under Coy Commanders from 9am to 10.30am. Exercises in ARTILLERY FORMATIONS under the Commanding Officer from 11am to 12.45pm. So for the 29th inst.	

30/11/1917.

E.J. Hewitt
Lieut Colonel
Commdg 6th Bn D.C.L.I.

S E C R E T.

8TH. (SERVICE) BATTALION DUKE OF CORNWALL'S LIGHT INFANTRY.

OPERATION ORDER No.91.

Copy No...... 16 - W.D.

1. MOVE. The Battalion will move to the BOISDINGHEM area on the 13th.instant, and will be billeted in the village of ACQUIN.
8th.D.C.L.I., less loading parties, billeting parties and transport will march to CAESTRE, where they will entrain at 10.30.a.m. on the 13th instant. Bicycles will accompany the Battalion.
The Battalion will detrain at WIZERNES, and march to ACQUIN.

2. TRANSPORT. The following transport will leave their present lines tomorrow, 12th.inst., and move by road to new area. Starting Point Le ROUKLOSHILLE (X.1.a.7.9.) at 9.a.m. on 12th.
Order of March:-   8th.K.O.Y.L.I., 6th.Som: L.I., 43rd. M.G.Coy., 10th.D.L.I., 8th.D.C.L.I.
Lieut: G.A.BLYTH will be in command of this transport under the orders of the Bde:Transport Officer:----

```
9 Limbered Wagons....... 18 mules.   18 men.
1 Water Cart............  2 horses    2 men.
1 Country Cart..........  2 horses.   2 men.
7 Pack animals..........  7 horses.   7 men.
```

Lewis Gun limbers, S.A.A. & Grenade limbers will be packed today. Band Instrument Covers and Music, and Band's rifles to be loaded in Country Cart.
Signalling equipment and tools will be loaded in limbers today.
Transport personnel going by road will take their blankets, packs, enough dicksees and rations for the men and horses up to and including the 13th. instant.
Men's water bottles to be filled - water cart empty.

The following Transport under Lieut: S.G.ROWE will proceed by train and will leave BAILLEUL WEST Station at 9.p.m. on the 13th.inst. by No.12 train.

```
4 Cookers.       8 horses.   4 men.    4 cooks.
1 Water cart.    2 horses.   1 man     1 water man.
1 Mess Cart      1 horse.    1 man.
1 Maltese Cart   1 horse.    1 man.
2 Supply wagons. 4 horses.   2 men (A.S.C.)
2 Baggage    "   4 horses.   2 men (A.S.C.)
10 Riding Horses.            8 men.
5 Sick animals.              5 men.
```
Sgt.DAY will also accompany this part of the Transport.

The transport going by train will reach BAILLEUL WEST Station at 8.p.m., and will halt outside the Station Yard until permission from R.T.O. has been obtained to bring the Transport in. Lieut:ROWE will report to R.T.O. on arrival, and hand him a complete Marching Out State, showing all animals, waggons and personnel to be entrained.

Officers' valises - men's blankets - 2 dicksees per Coy., and one per Hd.Qrs. - Officers' Mess Boxes - will NOT be loaded on Baggage wagons, but all other Stores, Orderly Room Stores, Qr.Mr.Stores, etc. will be loaded in the two G.S.wagons by 7.30.a.m., 13th.instant. Officers' Mess Stores (less Mess Boxes) on Cookers as usual. Ropes for lashing vehicles to trucks will be supplied by the Railway, but Transport will supply their own breast ropes for horses in trucks. Drag ropes and picketing ropes will be used. Lieut:BLYTH will see that Sgt:DAY has enough for the Train Transport party.

(P.T.O.

Continued:- 2 -

Rations for the Transport animals and transport personnel going by train will be carried up to and including the 13th.
Water Cart must be filled and loaded on train full.
All other wagons and carts will be entrained loaded.
Harness will be taken off and packed neatly in sets in the centre of each truck, so that it can be quickly put on when the destination is reached.
All horses must be provided with head collars and head ropes for the journey.
All horses are to be watered immediately before entrainment.
The Senior Officer in each Train will be in command of the train and be responsible for the discipline during the journey.

3. **OFFICERS' VALISES, RATIONS, etc. etc.**
Officers' valises, one blanket per man, Mess boxes and two dicksees per Coy. and one per H.Q., with tea and sugar rations for Coys. inside them will leave present billets at 9.a.m. on 13th.inst. by lorry. Q.M.S.McVittie, 4 cooks and 5 O.R.from Q.M.Stores will proceed with the lorry to BAILLEUL WEST, and will unload lorry, the kits, blankets, etc. to travel in the No.11 train starting at 3.p.m., 13th.inst. Q.M.Sgt.McVittie and his party will accompany the kits and see none are lost. On arrival at WIZERNES this party will unload the kits from train into a lorry which will meet them, and a guide will meet them to show the way to billets.

4. **BRIGADE UNLOADING PARTY.**
2/Lt:A.GREEN and 50.O.R. from "D" Coy. will parade at Brigade Headquarters at 12 NOON on 13th. and march to BAILLEUL Station. They will form part of the Brigade unloading party and will entrain at BAILLEUL WEST leaving at 3.p.m. in No.11 Train. Dress:- Full Marching Order rations for the 13th.on the man and waterbottles filled. They will not carry any blankets with them. All the blankets of this party will go by lorry and be taken to billets by lorry with rest of kit.

5. **QUARTER-MASTER.**
Lieut: & Qr. Mr. F.GUNN will report to Bde.Hd.Qrs. at 8.a.m. on the 13th. and proceed to Area Commandant, BOISDINGHEM by Motor Ambulance to be allotted billets.

6. **ADVANCE BILLETING PARTY.**
Coy.Q.M.-Sgts. and L/Cpl.F.JONES and 1 N.C.O. R.E.Coy. will report to Capt.SOMERVILLE at CAESTRE Station at 7.30.a.m. 13th.inst., and will proceed by No.9 train, as Advance Billeting Party. They will carry 1 blanket each & Full Marching Order - also rations for 13th.

(Sd.) E. C. Codyre, Captain,
11th.Novr., 1917. Adjutant, 6th.D.C.L.I.

==*=*=*=*

Distribution:- Copy No. 1. C.O. 10. 2/Lt: S.G.Rowe.
2. 2nd.in Cmd. 11. " A.Green.
3. Adjutant, 12. 89.Coy.R.E.
4. O.C. "A" Coy. 13. R.S.M.
5. " "B" " 14. Brigade.
6. " "C" " 15. O.O.File.
7. " "D" " 16. W.D.
8. Transport Officer
9. Quartermaster.

S E C R E T.

AMENDMENTS to OPERATION ORDER No.91.

1. MOVE. The Battn. will move to the BOISDINGHEM area on the 13th.inst., and will be billeted in the village of ACQUIN.
6th.D.C.L.I., less loading parties, billeting parties and transport will march to CAESTRE, where they will entrain at 12.30.p.m. on the 13th.inst.

The Battn. will detrain at WIZERNES, and march to ACQUIN.

2. TRANSPORT ....
Officers' valises, men's blankets, 2 dicksees per Coy., and one per Hd.Qrs., Officers' Mess Boxes will NOT be loaded on Baggage wagons, but all other Stores, etc., etc., will be loaded in the two G.S. wagons by 8.30.a.m. 13th.instant.....................

4. BRIGADE UNLOADING PARTY. 2/Lt: A.GREEN and 50.O.R. from "D" Coy. will parade at Bde: Hd.Qrs. at 12 NOON., etc. etc., etc........

Dress:- Full Marching Order. Rations for the 13th. on the man and waterbottles filled.
They will not carry any blankets with them.

6. ADVANCE BILLETING PARTY. - Coy.Q.M.-Sgts. A/Cpl.F.JONES, and 1 N.C.O. R.E.Coy. will report to Capt: SOMERVILLE at CAESTRE Station at 9.30.a.m. 13th. inst., and will proceed by No. 9 train, as Advance Billeting Party. They will take bicycles, and carry one blanket each and Full Marching Order - also rations for 13th.
Remainder of bicycles to accompany Battalion.

12th.Nov., 1917. (Sd.) E.C.Codyre, Captain,
Adjutant, 6th.D.C.L.I.

WAR DIARY.

6th D.C.L.I.

December 1917.

Volume 32.

Army Form C. 2118.

SHEET (1)   6th (Q) Battn
WAR DIARY
or
INTELLIGENCE SUMMARY.

Duke of Cornwalls Lgt. Infy.
For December 1917.

Place	Date	Hour	Summary of Events and Information	Remarks and references to Appendices
ACQUIN	Dec. 1st 1917		The Battalion was quartered in the village of ACQUIN N.16.c.6.6 in Billets. Companies were placed at the disposal of Company Commanders for the purpose of packing up and getting ready for the move to the FORWARD AREA.	Sheet 27 A.S.B.
-do-	2nd	11 am	The Battalion attended DIVINE SERVICE. All Officers and N.C.Os proceeded to the village of BOISDINGHEM, where they watched a Demonstration by the 43rd Brigade Pioneer Compy. of how a Shell Hole could be converted into a Defensive Post and how a Shell for Two men Could be made in same. The greater part of the Battalions Transport moved off at 8.45 am by march route for the Forward Area. See (Operation Order No. 92 (Transport) of 1/12/17 attached.)	
-do-	3rd		The Battalion paraded at 2.30 am and moved off at 2.45 am. by march route for WIZERNES where they entrained at 6 am. This Train moved off at 6.15 am for ST JEAN where they detrained about 10.30 am and WE'S marched to JUNCTION CAMP C 27.a.10.B. Sheet 28. arriving about 11.15 am and were quartered in Huts and Tents. See Operation Orders No. 92 Copy No. 11 of 2/12/17.	Sheet 22 BELGIUM
JUNCTION CAMP	4th		Coys were placed at the disposal of Company Commanders for the purpose of improving the camp, and overhauling all S.A.A., BOMBS, Equipment, Trenches Stores and Gas Respirators.	
-do-	5th		All Company Commanders reconnoitered the Route from the Camp to the Support Battn. As for the 4th. Also three Officers per Company and one Guide from each Platoon reconnoitered the route to the Support Batn. Heights. Stretchers Passchendaele Sector.	

5/12/19.17.

Hall the Battn. Runners also reconnoitered the route.

E.J. Stevens
Comndg. 6/D.C.L.I.

Army Form C. 2118.

SHEET (2). 6th (S) Battalion
Duke of Cornwall's L.I.

WAR DIARY
or
INTELLIGENCE SUMMARY.
(Erase heading not required.)

FOR DECEMBER 1917.

Place	Date DECR. 1917	Hour	Summary of Events and Information	Remarks and references to Appendices
JUNCTION CAMP.	6TH		Companies were at the disposal of Company Commanders, for instruction and training in improving and making Shell Holes into Defensive posts. The Medical Officer Capt. FERGUSSON R.A.M.C. lectured to all Officers on The Care of Feet, How to inspect Feet, Precautions to be taken in the prevention of Trench Feet. All Ranks of H.Q Bn. bathed and Whale Oiled their Feet.	
— do —	7TH		Coys at the disposal of Cmpy Commdr. Parades same as for the 6.Decr. C' &D' Coy bathed and Whale Oiled their Feet. Stores were drawn and overhauled for going into the Line on the 8th. The Commdg Officer held a Conference of Company Commanders at 6.30pm re the move to the Line and Dispositions.	
— do —	8TH		The morning and afternoon was spent in preparing for the move to the Line. The Battalion less "A" Coy. Paraded at 7.15pm and moved off by Platoons at 7.30 pm to relieve the 7/5 Battalion RIFLE BRIGADE in the FRONT LINE System of Shell Holes at MEETCHEELE, Passchendale Sector. Please see Operation Order No.9.3. of 8/12/17 attached. The Relief was carried out without incident and completed at 4. A.M. The 9th inst. DISPOSITIONS. Frontline "B" Coy. Left. "D" Coy. Right. SUPPORT. "B" Coy. near MEETCHEELE in MEETCHEELE — MOSSELMARKT. No.5 and No.6 TRACKS, also in MOSSELMARK — MEETCHEELE ROAD.	
IN THE LINE	9TH		From 12 MIDNIGHT to about 3.30 am. He shelled throughout the day from about 9 am till DUSK CASUALTIES. Other Ranks. Killed ONE WOUNDED EIGHT. At Dusk. "A" Coy under the command of LIEUT C.T. LUCAS. moved up to the front line in rear of the 10/D.C.L.I and took over the position on the left of "C" Coy. relieving a Company of the 1st Batt. DORSETSHIRE REGT. 32ND DIVISION.	
9–12–17			The Relief was carried out without incident and completed by 12 MIDNIGHT. E.J. Nevins LIEUT. Colonel, Commdg. 6/D.C.L.I

Army Form C. 2118.

WAR DIARY
or
INTELLIGENCE SUMMARY.
(Erase heading not required.)

Sheet (3)   6 & (S) Battn. Duke of Cornwall L.I.

For DECEMBER 1917.

Place	Date	Hour	Summary of Events and Information	Remarks and references to Appendices
IN THE LINE	1917. Dec. 10th		The Enemy was quiet throughout the night. He shelled the area in rear of the Battalion sector throughout the day. CASUALTIES WOUNDED. TWELVE Other Ranks.	
—do—	11th		Intermittent shelling of VINDICTIVE Cross Roads N° 5 and 6 Tracks and the ground around Potts Hedge at MOSTCHELE throughout the night, and during the day. CASUALTIES. WOUNDED. OFFICERS 2. CAPTAIN J.S. OATES, and 2/LT. D.C. BROWN. Other Ranks 4. Two Germans surrendered and were made prisoners.	
—do—	12th		Intermittent shelling throughout the day of the area in rear of the Battalion Sector. CASUALTIES N.I.L. Information was received that CAPTAIN J.S. OATES had DIED of WOUNDS on the 11/12/17. The night was fairly quiet except for the usual intermittent shelling. This Battalion was relieved on this night 12/13th by the 5th Battalion OXFORD and BUCKINGHAMSHIRE L.I. The relief was carried out without incident and completed by 5.30 am on the 13/12/17.	
JUNCTION + CALAFORNIA CAMPS.	13th		The Battalion on relief returned to the following Camps. "A" & "D" Coys. CALAFORNIA Camp. "B" & "C" Coys and Battn. H/Qrs. JUNCTION CAMP. Where they arrived by Platoons and went to Billets by 7 & 9 am to Hospital & The day was spent in Resting and Cleaning up Clothing & Equipment &c.	
—do—	14th		The Battalion furnished a WORKING PARTY of 5 OFFICERS + 150 Other Ranks at 6 a.m. for Work under the direction of the 395th Coy. R.E. for Carrying Heavy Trench Boards to make a Track to the Firing Line. "B" & "C" Coys were allotted and proceeded.	
—do—	15th		The day was spent in overhauling stores and Equipment &c.	
15/12/17			to the Divisional Baths at CANAL BANK Sheet 28.1.1.d.9.9. from 9 am to 12 noon.	

Comdg. 6/D.C.L.I.

Army Form C. 2118.

WAR DIARY
or
INTELLIGENCE SUMMARY.

SHEET (4)

6/3 Battn
Dukes of Corn. L.I.
For DECEMBER 1917.

(Erase heading not required.)

Place	Date	Hour	Summary of Events and Information	Remarks and references to Appendices
IN THE LINE.	1917 Dec. 15th	CONTINUED.	The Battalion paraded for the line at 6.45pm and moved off at 7pm to relieve the 5/6 Battalion OXFORD & BUCKS L.I. The Enemy shelled the MESSEMARK - MEETCHELE Road and Nr. 5/6 Tracks during the march up to the lines causing the following casualties in "A" Co. Wounded 6 other ranks. The Relief was completed without further incident and was completed by 11.20pm. The Enemy's Artillery was quiet during the remaining hours of darkness. Disposition as per previous.	
-do.-	16th		The day was rather quiet and the Enemy shelling very little. At Night he shelled the back area of the Battalion sector and tracks. Also VINDICTIVE Cross Roads.	
-do.-	17th		The Enemy shelled Intermittently throughout the day, paying attention to the back tracks and the ground around Battn HQrs and the Support Company. Intermittent shelling throughout the night.	
-do.-	18th		Intermittent shelling of the MESSEMARK - MEETCHELE Road, VINDICTIVE Cross Roads, Nr. 5&6 Tracks and the front around Battn HQrs & MEETCHELE. Also throughout the night. The Enemy shelled the MEETCHELE Road from 5.30 a.m. 7am very heavily. The remainder of the day was quiet. The Battalion was relieved on that night by the 5th Battn OXFORD & BUCKS L.I. The Relief was carried out without incident and was completed by 12. MIDNIGHT. On Relief the Battalion rendezvous'd at the light Railway Siding, near CALAFORNIA Camp where they entrained on the LIGHT RAILWAY for RED ROSE CAMP, where they arrived and were settled in. 6.30 a.m. on the 29/12/17	

19/12/17

[signature]
Sur C.L.
Commdg 6/DCLI

SHEET (5)

Army Form C. 2118.

WAR DIARY or INTELLIGENCE SUMMARY.

5th Batt. Duke of Cornwall L.I.

For DECEMBER 1917.

(Erase heading not required.)

Place	Date Decr. 1917	Hour	Summary of Events and Information	Remarks and references to Appendices
RED ROSE CAMP.	20th		The Battalion was quartered in Huts in RED ROSE CAMP SHEET 28. H.1.d.8.9. near VLAMERTINGHE. The day was spent in cleaning up and refitting the men with Clothing and Equipment. "A" + "C" Coys were allowed the Baths at VLAMERTINGHE from 9am to 11am.	CHEET 28. BELGIUM
– do –	21st		Companies were placed at the disposal of Company Commanders for the purpose of overhauling Clothing, Equipment, and Technical Stores. Into Bcx Appleonar 88.	
– do –	22nd		The Battalion paraded at 9am. to Strong no Points and moved off at 9.15am for a Route March under the Commanding Officer and returned to Camp about 12.30pm.	
– do –	23rd		The Battalion Paraded at 2.45am. under Captn F.C.COBYEE MC for Work in the Forward Area. Six Motor Lorries were waiting at VLAMERTINGHE CrossRoads at 3.AM. These were used to convey the Battalion as far as SPREE FARM Dump near WIELTJE. Here the Batt. was met by Guides of the 89th Cy. R.E.S. who guided them different parties to their Work. On completion of their Work the Parties returned to OXFORD ROAD WIELTJE where they again entered the Lorries about 9.15am and were conveyed back to Camp where they arrived about 11am.	
– do –	24th		The Battalion paraded at 9am. and Church and Training until 12–30 pm. in the following subjects Under Coys. Commanders Physical Drill, Running, Drill, Company Drill, Arm Drill, Musketry.	
– do –	25th		Christmas Day. The Battalion attended Divine Service at 10.a.m. From 11am to 12.30pm Companies were with the disposal of Company Commanders for the purpose of Fitting Equipment. The Field Transport paraded at 8-30am and moved off to go to the rest area. Q. John Lieut Colonel Comm 5th D.C.L.I.

WAR DIARY

SHEET (6) 6th Battalion Duke of Cornwall L.I.

Army Form C. 2118.

INTELLIGENCE SUMMARY.

For DECEMBER 1917

Place	Date Decr. 1917	Hour	Summary of Events and Information	Remarks and references to Appendices
RED ROSE CAMP.	26th		The Battalion Paraded at 12.15 p.m. to STROP to ROCULT and moved off by Platoons at 12.30 p.m. for BRANDHOEK Railway Siding, where they entrained at 1.10 p.m. for WIZERNES near ST. OMER. The Train arrived at WIZERNES about 4.30 p.m. Here the Battalion detrained and marched to BOISINGHEM where they arrived and were settled in Billets by 10 p.m. Hot Tea was provided and issued to the men (See Operation order No. 95 attached).	
BOISINGHEM.	27th		Companies were at the disposal of Company Commanders.	
— do —	28th		Training was carried out from 9 a.m. to 12.30 p.m. under Company Commanders.	
— do —	29th		— do —. All Coy. Commanders attended a Lecture by Brig. General R. TEMPEST. D.S.O. "Training a Company. Points on."	
— do —	30th		R. TEMPEST. D.S.O. in the Saddle at 3.30 p.m. SUBJECT. Training a Company. Points on.	
— do —	30th		Training was carried out from 9 a.m. to 12.30 p.m. under Company Commanders. All Officers attended a Lecture by Brig. General R. TEMPEST. D.S.O. at 4.30 p.m. Subject. "How to Command."	
— do —	31st		This day was observed as a HOLIDAY and the W.Os. N.C.Os and Men had their Christmas Dinner at 2.30 p.m.	

31/12/1917

Lieut. Colonel
Commdg. 6th Bn. D.C.L.I.

Vol 33

33N.

War Diary
of
6th D.C.L.I.

January 1918.

Volume 33

Army Form C. 2118.

WAR DIARY
or
INTELLIGENCE SUMMARY.
(Erase heading not required.)

Instructions regarding War Diaries and Intelligence Summaries are contained in F.S. Regs., Part II. and the Staff Manual respectively. Title pages will be prepared in manuscript.

Place	Date	Hour	Summary of Events and Information	Remarks and references to Appendices
	1918			
BOISDINGHEM	Jan. 1.		The Battalion paraded as strong as possible at 9.45 a.m. and moved off at 10 a.m. for a Route March under the Commanding Officer and returned to Camp about 12.30 p.m.	
do.	Jan. 2.		The Battalion paraded at 9.45 a.m. and marched to STOMER Railway Siding where they entrained at 12.30 p.m. for EDGE HILL. The train reached EDGE HILL at 11 p.m. Here the battalion detrained. Hot cocoa and biscuits were provided and issued to the men. The Battalion marched to BRAY-SUR-SOMME where they arrived and were settled in billets by 6 a.m. on 3rd Jan.	
BRAY-SUR-SOMME	Jan. 3.		Companies were at disposal of Company Commanders	Amiens Sheet 62 D
do	Jan. 4		do	
do	Jan. 5		All Gas & Box Respirators were tested and all ranks put through gas by the Brigade Gas Officer. All ranks that had not been inoculated within six months of this date were inoculated by the M.O. for the rest of the day. Companies were at the disposal of Company Commanders.	
do	Jan. 6		Church Parade at 10 a.m.	
do	Jan. 7		The Commanding Officer inspected the Battalion by Companies. Companies also did one hour's musketry drill and one hour's Bayonet fighting.	
do	Jan. 8		The Battalion paraded as strong as possible at 8.45 a.m. and moved off at 9 a.m. for a Route March under the Commanding Officer and returned to Camp at 1 p.m. The Armourer Sergeant inspected rifles at 2 p.m.	
do	Jan. 9		The Battalion paraded at 9 a.m. and carried out company training under Company Commanders until 12.45 p.m. — P.T. and Bayonet fighting — Arm Drill — Box Respirator Drill — Cleaning in Lewis Gun and Bombing	
do	Jan. 10			

P.J. Lewis Lt Col
Comdg 6th B.C.L.I.

Army Form C. 2118.

WAR DIARY
or
INTELLIGENCE SUMMARY.
(Erase heading not required.)

Instructions regarding War Diaries and Intelligence Summaries are contained in F. S. Regs., Part II. and the Staff Manual respectively. Title pages will be prepared in manuscript.

Place	Date	Hour	Summary of Events and Information	Remarks and references to Appendices
Bray sur Somme	Jan 11 1918		Three Companies has been training this morning the remainder of the time was spent in PT, Arms Drill, Bayonet fighting, wiring - Lewis Gun and Rifle Grenade Classes	See D
do	Jan 12		The Battalion paraded by Companies from 9am to 1pm to training in wiring, musketry, Range firing Classes for instruction in Lewis Gun and Rifle grenades	
do	Jan 13		The Battalion paraded for Divine Service at 9.45 am	
do	Jan 14		The Battalion paraded by Companies from 9am to 1pm for training in wiring, Bayonet fighting, musketry and firing on the range - Firing Lewis Guns and Browning Grenades by the classes under instruction	
do	Jan 15		The Battalion was inspected by the B.G.C. at 10 a.m.	
do	Jan 16		The Battalion carried out training by Companies from 9am to 12.30 pm - firing on Range, musketry, wiring Attack formation - Extended order drill - from 5.30 to 7pm patrolling.	
do	Jan 17		The Battalion carried out training as on the 16th inst	
do	Jan 18		The Battalion paraded by Companies and marched to open ground K22 b - (sheet 62D) leaving Bray at 9am. Artillery formation and Battalion in attack was practised under the Commanding Officer. The Battalion returned to billets at 1.30 pm	
do	Jan 19		The Battalion paraded by Companies from 9am to 1pm and carried out training - firing Lewis Rifle Grenades, musketry, firing Lewis Guns, Box Respirator Drill. From 5.30 to 7pm Patrolling.	
do	Jan 20		Voluntary Church parade for Divine Service at 9.45 am	
do	Jan 21	2.30pm	Lectures by Commanding Officer to all Companies - Companies at disposal of Company Commanders for the remainder of morning. Lecture to all officers and NCOs on Gas by 2L GF Taylor (Staff)	

E. Hewitt Lt Col
Colg 6th B.C.L.I.

Army Form C. 2118.

WAR DIARY
or
INTELLIGENCE SUMMARY.
(Erase heading not required.)

Instructions regarding War Diaries and Intelligence Summaries are contained in F. S. Regs., Part II. and the Staff Manual respectively. Title pages will be prepared in manuscript.

Place	Date	Hour	Summary of Events and Information	Remarks and references to Appendices
BRAY SUR SOMME	1918 Jan 22		The Battalion paraded at 12.15 am and marched under the commanding officer to WIENCOURT L'EQUIPPE arriving there at 4.30 pm.	
WIENCOURT L'EQUIPPE	Jan 23		The Battalion paraded at 7.45 am and marched under the commanding officer to CARREPUITS arriving there and billeted by 4.15 pm. (Sheet 66 D M 24)	Sheet 66 D
CARREPUITS	Jan 24		The Battalion paraded at 10.30 am and marched under the Commanding Officer to QUESMY arriving there after gas. Got into billets at 5.30.	St QUENTIN 18.
QUESMY	Jan 25		The Battalion paraded at 12.30 pm and marched under the commanding officer to REMIGNY arriving in huts there at 7.45 pm (Sheet 66 C SW N.13)	St QUENTIN 18.
REMIGNY	Jan 26		French officers were turned out and the Battalion marched off at 5.30 pm relieving the 307th French in the line at Relay complete at 11 pm. Situation all quiet. Casualties nil.	Sheet 66 C NW & 66 C SW
In the line	Jan 27		All quiet. Casualties Nil. Work on trenches and construction of fire steps.	
In the line	Jan 28		Hostile Artillery shelled the Boyau de CUESNON and the front line trench on either side of it about fifteen yards of trench was obliterated also a gap of about forty six yards cut in the wire at this point; this took place about midday. Two hostile aeroplanes flew low over our line. Enemy machine gun action during the night-firing from ALIENCOURT. Casualties - ONE self inflicted	do
In the line	Jan 29		Hostile artillery inactive. Occasional bursts of hostile machine gun fire during the night. Casualties One (accidental) nil.	
In the line	Jan 30		Hostile artillery slightly more active mainly shelling artillery areas and areas well behind the front line about 2 pm junction of BOYAU de CUESNON and Trench de RENNES was again shelled by S.Q. Boyau de CUESNON slightly damaged. Enemy aeroplanes fairly active but all flying high. Standing Patrol near CHATEAU (J26.c.9.5) saw nothing. Casualties Nil.	do
In the line	Jan 31		Hostile artillery inactive - a very noisy day - Aeroplane inactive - bursts of hostile machine gun fire during the evening - Casualties Nil.	

signed E.J. Stevens Lt Col
Comdg 1/5 K.L.R.

SECRET.

6TH. (SERVICE) BATTALION DUKE OF CORNWALL'S LIGHT INFANTRY.

OPERATION ORDER No.98.

Copy No. 13.

1. MOVE.
The Battalion will march to ST.OMER Station on the 2nd January, and entrain there for EDGE HILL, on transference from 4th.Army to 5th.Army.
The Train journey is about 6 hours.

6th.D.C.L.I. Train No.10 leaves St.OMER at 2.p.m. on Jan., 2nd.

The battalion will move off about 9.33.a.m. on the 2nd.January from BOISDINGHEM - arriving ST.OMER at 12.30 p.m.
Dress:- Full Marching order - caps will be worn, & helmets carried under the valise straps.
Unexpired portion of rations for Jan.2nd. (less tea and sugar) will be carried on the man Waterbottles filled. Rations for the 3rd.January on the Cookers or Supply wagons.

2. TRANSPORT.
All transport will accompany units in the train, including G.S. baggage and Supply wagons.
All transport, pack ponies and chargers will leave BOISDINGHEM about 8.a.m.on the 2nd.January, and march to St.OMER Station, arriving there at 11.a.m.

Arrangements must be made to water all horses before entraining. Cpl.Green will proceed in advance of transport on the morning of the 2nd.Jan., and find out the nearest place to the Station horses can be watered at, and meet the Transport as it comes in to St.OMER.

Ropes for lashing vehicles to trucks will be supplied by the Railway.

Breast ropes for horses in trucks will be supplied by Units. Picketing ropes or drag ropes should be used.

All horses must be provided with head ropes and head collars for the journey.

Harness will be taken off and stacked neatly in sets in the centre of each truck, so that it can be quickly put on when the destination is reached.

Rugs will be put on all horses and animals as soon as they are unharnessed, and will be kept on during the journey.

Water carts must entrain full Also G.S.wagons and Supply wagons.

Supply wagons will rejoin their Companies after delivering rations for the day after arrival.

3. ADVANCE PARTY
An Advance Party consisting of Lieut:R.J.O.Adams, M.C. Company Quartermaster-Sgts. and Regtl.Sgt.-Major will proceed with the 42nd.Brigade by No.6 train, leaving ST.OMER at 2.a.m. on the 2nd.January.
They should leave BOISDINGHEM at 10.p.m. on the 1st. Jan. reporting to Capt.Ruffer, the entraining officer, at 1.a.m. on Jan. 2nd. Rations for the 2nd.Jan. to be carried with them.
This party will arrange to meet their units, and guide them to their respective destinations as they arrive at EDGE HILL.

(1.) P.T.O.

continued:-   - 2 -

4. LOADING PARTY.
"C" Company are detailed as Loading Party.
They will proceed in advance of Battalion, leaving BOISDINGHEM about 7.a.m., and report to Captain Ruffer at 10.a.m. on the 2nd.Jan.
They will proceed by the same train as the Battn. and unload the train at EDGE HILL on arrival.

5. TRAINS, Composition.
All Trains consist of:-

    1 Coach for 30 Officers
    30 covered trucks each to hold   40 men
                                       or 6 H.D.Horses
                                         8 L.D.Mules.
    17 flat trucks each to hold   4 axled

Baggage will be loaded in the covered trucks, but space for personnel must not be restricted.

Two brake vans accompany each train. No personnel or stores are to be loaded in either of these brake vans.

6. MARCHING OUT STATE.
A complete marching-out state showing the numbers of men, horses, G.S.wagons, limbered wagons and two wheeled carts and bicycles will be sent down with the transport of each unit, and given to the R.T.O. before entrainment begins.

7. ENTRAINMENT.
Entrainment of all units must be completed ½ an hour before the train is due to start.

8. LORRIES.
Two Lorries for carrying blankets and kits to the Station will be at Quartermaster's Stores at 9.a.m. on the 2nd.January.

                          (Sd.) F.G.Haylett, 2/Lieut:
1-1-18.   A/Adjt., 6th.D.C.L.I.

Copies to:-   No.1. Commanding Officer.
                  2. A/Adjutant.
                  3. O.C. "A" Company.
                  4.   " "B"   "
                  5.   " "C"   "
                  6.   " "D"   "
                  7. Quartermaster.
                  8. Transport Sgt.
                  9. R.S.M.
                10. Lt: R.J.O.Adams, M.C.
                11. R.Q.M.Sgt.
                12. Cpl.Green (Transport)
                13. W.D.
                14. O.C.File.

No 247.

BATTALION ORDERS
by
LIEUT-COL: R. J. HEWITT, D.S.O.,
COMMANDING 6th (SERVICE) BATTALION, D.C.L.I.
-:-

Thursday, 24th January, 1918.

PART 1.
-:-:-:-:-:-

1. ROUTINE. Reveille 7.30.am. Breakfasts 8.30.am. Sick Parade 9.30.am.

2. PARADES. The Battalion will parade ready to move off at 12.pm.
Dinners will be on the road about 2.30.pm. Cooks will make the same arrangements as before, and have Teas ready for the Men on arrival in billets.
The Battalion will be billeted in REMIGNY.
Route:- BEHANCOURT - OUGNY - FLAVY -le-MARTEL - MONTESCOURT - REMIGNY -

The Advance Billeting Party under Lieut. & Qr, Mr, Gunn, the same as to-day. They will leave QUESMY at 6.30.am. and report to TOWN MAJOR, R E M I G N Y.

Each Company will send 1 Officer & N.C.O. to report to Brigade Road Quarters at GUISCARD at 1.15.pm. tomorrow.
"C" Company will send 1 Man who can talk French, in addition to their Officer, and an N.C.O. A Lorry will take them to the line -.
Above party will reconnoitre the line to be taken over by their Companies, and remain in the line till their Companies arrive. They will meet their incoming Coys: on the night of the 26th/27th, with the French Guides, and assist in the relief.
They will take the unexpired portion of tomorrow's Rations, and Rations for the 25th with them.
N.C.O's will take their Jerkins, Waterproof Sheets, and 3 pairs of socks with them. Their Packs will be handed to Quartermaster's Stores before leaving.
Officers will take as much trench Kit as they can carry - remainder will be brought by their Companies as soon as more is learnt about the line. French Guides will meet this party at 5.30. pm. on the Western Outskirts of LY.FONTAINE -.
The Commanding Officer will see all Officers and Platoon Commanders at Battalion H.Q. at 10.30.am. Trench Maps, 33c,N.W. & S.W. to be brought.
Billets to be left thoroughly clean by Companies before leaving to-morrow.

Attention is called to Battalion Order that Estaminets can be used from 12. to 2.pm. & 6 to 9.pm. ONLY. No drink of any description can be carried away from Estaminets under any circumstances. Any disobedience of this order, will be severely dealt with -
Company Commanders will impress on their Men that they are now in an Area which has never been occupied by English troops before, and that the Commanding Officer
(orders

C
A
B
D

Heads of Columns
at Cross Roads
N of Village

Battalion Orders (continued)   27th Jan. '18.

orders all ranks to ensure that the inhabitants have no cause to complain of the behaviour of British Army Troops, so far as the D. C. L. I. are concerned anyhow.

(Signed)   F. G. MAYCOTT, 2/Lieut.
            A/Adjutant, 6th D.C.L.I.

(2).

OPERATION ORDERS.

Saturday 26th Jany. 1918.

The Battalion will be ready to move off at 5.30.pm. this evening.   DRESS:- Full Marching Order - Boxes S.A.A. as ordered.
Order of March:- "A", "C", "B", "D", Head Quarters -
Platoons will keep 100 yards distance apart.
Guides, 1 per Platoon, and 2 for Battalion Head Quarters, will rendezvous at R E I G N Y (Poste de Police) opposite Aid Post at 5.30.pm.
Also 1 Guide for the Cooks cart, which will follow 100 yards in rear of Head Quarters - about 8.pm.
Lewis Guns, Drums, Trench Stores, Grenades, Rations for the 27th inst., (less meat, tea & sugar which will be carried by Company Cooks with dicksees) will be taken on the Man.
Teas will be at 4.pm. to-day.
2 Hd, Qtr. Runners will accompany each Company into the line to locate Company Hd, Qtrs. - Company Commanders will arrange for Coy: Runners to locate Battalion Head Quarters on arrival.
'Relief Complete' will be sent by Runner to Battn. Hd, Qtrs: -
Lists of all Maps, Photographs, Trench Stores, T.S.Stores etc. taken over will be sent to Battn. Head Quarters, signed & receipted by both English and French Company Commanders.
Company Commanders will get in touch with the troops on their left and right as soon as they have taken over.
A report to be sent to Battalion Head Quarters by Runner, stating when and with whom they are in touch with.
Battalion Head Quarters will be at I.25. a. 5.8. -   3.4.
20 Picks and 30 Shovels will be taken up by each Company.
O.C. "D" Company on completion of relief will draw 10 Boxes S.A.A. from La GUINGUETTE, and bring them to Battalion Head Quarters before daylight 27th instant.
The French S.O.S. - a rocket bursting into white spangles will be used until Noon February 1st 1918.
Company Commanders will make rough Sketches of their dispositions, as soon as they can, and send them to Battalion H.Q.
O.C. "B" Company will take over the Observation Post at I.31 c 3.5. - These men to keep themselves hidden by day.
The 10th D.L.I. will be on our left, and the 279th Regiment on our right.
If the Communication Trenches are available for use, Mens' Breakfasts can be drawn in daylight - if not, they must be drawn before daylight.

(Signed) F. G. Maylett, 2/Lieut:,
A/Adjutant, 6th D.C.L.I.

WAR DIARY
INTELLIGENCE SUMMARY
(Erase heading not required.)

Army Form C. 2118.

6 MDCLI

Place	Date	Hour	Summary of Events and Information	Remarks and references to Appendices
	1918			
In the field	Feb. 1		All quiet – artillery and aircraft active. The Bn. was relieved by the 15th K.R.R. which completed at 9 p.m.	Shut 66 S.W.
			On completion of relief two companies marched by platoons to REMIGNY and were billeted there – one remaining two companies and Bn. H.Qrs. to LY FONTAINE	
LY FONTAINE	2		The Bn. less two companies marched by platoon to JUSSY taking over Camp on STATS-VINS from the 7th R.B. Two companies remained at REMIGNY doing working parties in the line.	Shut 66 S.W.
JUSSY	3		The Bn. less two companies at Depôt of Company Commander – Two companies working parties in the line	do
JUSSY	4		The Bn. less two companies – rests intervals 10 am to 1 pm	do
JUSSY	5		Training. Two Companies rejoined Bn. at Camp on STATS-VINS from REMIGNY	do
JUSSY	6		Officers, NCOs and men proceed to 1/5th M.D.C.L.I. left the Battn.	do
JUSSY	7		Remainder of Battalion Training	do
JUSSY	8		Officers NCOs & men posted to 10th M.D.C.L.I. left the Battn.	"
JUSSY	9		Officers NCOs & men posted to 4th M.D.C.L.I. (including the Regtl Band complete) left the Battn.	do
			The Hon'ble Lieut Colonel Regt Sgt Major proceeded to CASTRES for work at Divisional Headquarters	do
			Remainder of Battn. Training	do

[signature]

Army Form C. 2118.

WAR DIARY
INTELLIGENCE SUMMARY. 6th D.C.L.I.

(Erase heading not required.)

Instructions regarding War Diaries and Intelligence Summaries are contained in F. S. Regs., Part II. and the Staff Manual respectively. Title pages will be prepared in manuscript.

Place	Date	Hour	Summary of Events and Information	Remarks and references to Appendices
JUSSY	Feb 10.		Working parties on Regt. Hd. Qrs. proceeded to CASTRES for work at Divisional H.Q. on Schemes.	
			Remainder of Battn. training.	
JUSSY	Feb 11.		As for yesterday. 10th February.	
JUSSY	12		Remainder of Battn. (Details after draining to 1/5th & 7th D.C.L.I. Battalions)	
			proceeded by March Route to III Corps Reinforcement Camp. CRISSOLLES	
CRISSOLLES	13		Surplus personnel cleaning up billets. Billet and rifle inspections.	
	14		Surplus personnel Training. Billet and rifle inspections	
	15		do. do.	
	16		do. do.	
	17		do. Billet and rifle inspections.	
	18		do. do. Training.	
	19		do. do.	
	20		Surplus personnel posted to 16th Entrenching Battn. under command of Lt.Col. Littledale	
			late 6th K.O.Y.L.I.	

www.ingramcontent.com/pod-product-compliance
Lightning Source LLC
Chambersburg PA
CBHW080917230426
43668CB00014B/2145